The Rt Hon Sir Keith Joseph Bt MP
Secretary of State for Industry
Ashdown House
123 Victoria Street
London   SW1E 6RB

16 November 1979

Our Committee of Inquiry into the Engineering Profession was appointed by your predecessor in the previous Administration, the Rt Hon Eric Varley MP, with the following terms of reference:—

To review for manufacturing industry and in the light of national economic needs:—

(i) the requirements of British industry for professional and technician engineers, the extent to which these needs are being met, and the use made of engineers by industry;

(ii) the role of the engineering institutions in relation to the education and qualification of engineers at professional and technician level;

(iii) the advantages and disadvantages of statutory registration and licensing of engineers in the UK;

(iv) the arrangements in other major industrial countries, particularly in the EEC, for handling these problems, having regard to relevant comparative studies;

and to make recommendations.

An announcement of these terms of reference and the appointment of the Committee's chairman was made to the House of Commons by Mr Varley on 5 July 1977. Mr Varley further announced the membership of the Committee in answer to a Written Parliamentary Question on 14 December 1977.

Upon the present Administration taking office we were pleased to receive your encouragement to continue and complete our work.

We now have the honour to submit our report.

SIR MONTAGUE FINNISTON (*Chairman*)

MISS C AVENT

W E BUCKLEY

T J CRISPIN

H DARNELL

J H DAWES

DR J F DICKENSON

PROF J H HORLOCK

HOWIE OF TROON

DR B C LINDLEY

W McCALL

SIR JAMES MENTER

MAJOR GENERAL H MACDONALD-SMITH

H R G NELSON

DR J A POWELL

MRS E M SADLER

PROF D H WEIR

MRS J B WILSON

Engineering Our Future

Report of the
Committee of Inquiry
into the Engineering Profession

Chairman
Sir Montague Finniston, FRS

*Presented to Parliament by the Secretary of State for Industry
by Command of Her Majesty
January 1980*

LONDON
HER MAJESTY'S STATIONERY OFFICE
£5·00 net

Cmnd 7794

Note: The estimated cost of producing this Report is £401,130. This includes £26,130 for printing and publishing. The remaining £375,000 covers staff costs, which includes a proportion for accommodation and supporting services, travel and subsistence expenditure, consultants' fees and the cost of surveys, which amounted to approximately £41,000.

Members of the Committee

Sir Montague Finniston
FRS, FRSE, BSc, PhD, FRSA, FIM, FInstP, FIChemE, FBIM
Lately Chairman, Sears Engineering Ltd

Miss Catherine Avent OBE, MA
Careers Guidance Inspector, Inner London Education Authority

William E Buckley BSc(Eng), MEd, C Eng, FIMechE, MBIM
Director of North Cheshire College

Thomas J Crispin
National Secretary, Power and Engineering Trades Group, Transport and
General Workers Union.

Herbert Darnell OBE, MEng, CEng, MIEE
Director, Special Duties, British Steel Corporation

James H Dawes TEng, FIPlantE
Lately Divisional Controller, Rolls-Royce Ltd

Dr Frank Dickenson BSc(Eng), PhD, CEng, FIMechE
Director of the North Staffordshire Polytechnic

Professor John H Horlock FRS, FEng, MA, PhD, ScD, FIMechE, FRAeS
Vice-Chancellor and Professor of Engineering, University of Salford

Lord Howie of Troon BSc, CEng, MICE
General Manager of 'New Civil Engineer' and other Thomas Telford Ltd
magazines

Dr Bryan C Lindley BSc(Eng), PhD, FIMechE, FIEE, FInstP
Director of Research, Dunlop Ltd, previously Managing Director of
ERA Technology Ltd

William McCall
General Secretary of the Institution of Professional Civil Servants

Sir James Menter FRS, MA, PhD, ScD, FInstP, FRSA
Principal of Queen Mary College, University of London

Major-General Hugh Macdonald-Smith CB, BSc, CEng, FIMechE, FIEE
Secretary to Council, Telecommunications Engineering and Manufacturing
Association, previously Director of Electrical and Mechanical Engineering,
Ministry of Defence

Henry R G Nelson MA, CEng, MIEE
Director and General Manager, RHP Automotive Bearings Division

Dr John A Powell MA, DPhil, CEng, FIEE, FRSE, SMIEEE, FBIM, FRSA
Lately Vice-Chairman EMI Ltd

Mrs Elizabeth M Sadler MA, CEng, MICE
Consultant Civil Engineer with the Ove Arup Partnership

Professor David Weir MA, DipPSA, MBIM
Dean of the Scottish Business School, Glasgow. Professor of Organisational
Behaviour, University of Glasgow

Mrs Jean B Wilson BSc
Adviser on Mathematics to the Tayside Region

Secretariat

M V Boxall — *Secretary*
C A Barclay
C H Richards (from May 1978)
R T M Neill (from May 1979)
I Bracken (from April 1978)
Mrs E Rowena
Miss E J Cookman
(from October 1978)
S H M Londesborough
(until May 1978)
Mrs C M Sonke (until May 1979)

Assessors

J I James MBE, Department of
Industry
J Wiltshire, Manpower Services
Commission
J G Lavender, HMI Department of
Education & Science
Dr K I Murray, Department of Health
and Social Security
G S Mutch, HMI Scottish Education
Dept

Research Unit

Miss S V Cunliffe — Statistician
V Edkins — Consultant
E R L Lewis — Manpower and Training Adviser

Contents

Index of Organisations

Glossary of abbreviations

ACARD	Advisory Council on Applied Research and Development
ACEC	Advisory Council on Energy Conservation
BAAS	British Association for the Advancement of Science
BIM	British Institute of Management
BSI	British Standards Institution
CAD	Computer-aided design
CAT	College of Advanced Technology
CBI	Confederation of British Industry
CEI	Council of Engineering Institutions
CEng	Chartered Engineer
CEPC	Committee of the Engineering Professors' Conference
CIEP	Committee of Inquiry into the Engineering Profession
CNAA	Council for National Academic Awards
CSEU	Confederation of Shipbuilding and Engineering Unions
DES	Department of Education and Science
ECPD	Engineers' Council for Professional Development
EDCs	Economic Development Councils
EEA	Electronic Engineering Association
EEF	Engineering Employers' Federation
EEMTEB	Electrical and Electronic Manufacturing Training and Education Board
EEC	European Economic Community
EITB	Engineering Industry Training Board
EOC	Equal Opportunities Commission
ERB	Engineers' Registration Board
FEng	Fellow of Engineering
FH	Fachhochschule
GATT	General Agreement on Tariffs and Trade
HNC	Higher National Certificate
HND	Higher National Diploma
ICE	Institution of Civil Engineers
IEE	Institution of Electrical Engineers
I Mech E	Institution of Mechanical Engineers
MSC	Manpower Services Commission
NCEE	National Council of Engineering Examiners
NEDC	National Economic Development Council
NEDO	National Economic Development Office
NIESR	National Institute of Economic and Social Research
OECD	Organisation for Economic Co-operation and Development
ONC	Ordinary National Certificate
OND	Ordinary National Diploma
OTIU	Overseas Technical Information Unit (Department of Industry)
PE	Professional Engineer
PSI	Policy Studies Institute
SATRO	Science and Technology Regional Organisation
SED	Scottish Education Department
SEFI	European Society for Engineering Education

SETS	Scottish Electrical Training Scheme
SITC	Standard International Trade Classification
SRC	Science Research Council
TEC	Technician Education Council
Tech (CEI)	Technician
TEng (CEI)	Technician Engineer
TH	Technische Hochschule
TU	Technical University
UGC	Universities Grants Committee
UKAPE	United Kingdom Association of Professional Engineers
VDI	Verein Deutscher Ingenieure
WES	Women's Engineering Society

Chairman's Preface

Terms of reference and procedure

In July 1977 I was invited by the then Secretary of State for Industry to chair an Inquiry into the engineering profession, with terms of reference announced to Parliament on 5 July 1977 as:

'To review for manufacturing industry, and in the light of national economic needs—

(i) the requirements of British industry for professional and technician engineers, the extent to which these needs are being met, and the use made of engineers by industry;

(ii) the role of the engineering institutions in relation to the education and qualifications of engineers at professional and technician level;

(iii) the advantages and disadvantages of statutory registration and licensing of engineers in the UK; and

(iv) the arrangements in other major industrial countries, particularly in the EEC, for handling these problems, having regard to relevant comparative studies;

and to make recommendations'.

The membership of the Committee was not announced until 14 December 1977, and the Committee had its first meeting shortly before that Christmas. In the following 23 months to the completion of this report, the Committee met 30 times in plenary sessions. In addition a total of well over 100 meetings were held of Working Groups, formed from members of the Committee to consider specific areas within the remit of the Inquiry. Nearly all of these plenary and Working Group meetings lasted all day, and a number were held over two days. In addition to the evidence cited below, we considered over 120 plenary papers and 60 Working Group papers as well as many drafts of this report.

Evidence

We received over 700 written submissions of evidence, about half of them in response to specific invitations from our Secretariat (see Appendix A) and the rest unsolicited. Of this total nearly 500 submissions were from individuals and over 200 from organisations and institutions with interests in the area of the Inquiry; the views presented to us varied from short notes to articles of book length. A full list of those who submitted written evidence is given in Appendix B to this report. Some 50 of these written submissions were followed up by meetings with their authors, also identified in Appendix B.

We benefited from the opportunity to hear the views of individual engineers at first hand at 16 open meetings organised on our behalf during the first half of 1978 by the Council of Engineering Institutions (CEI). Over 6,000 people attended these meetings which were held around the whole country. The information, opinions and impressions we gained from them were most helpful. A summary note of these prepared by the CEI is reproduced in Appendix C.

1

We made particular efforts to obtain evidence from the employers of engineers. We visited a carefully selected sample of 46 companies in the public and private sectors, each at least twice, for long and detailed discussions with their senior managements. A number of these submitted written views to us. The companies visited are identified in Appendix B. A summary of what we found and what they told us is contained in Appendix D. We were able to set our findings and impressions from these detailed discussions in the context of more general evidence from the Confederation of British Industry, the Engineering Employers' Federation and a number of trade associations.

Our remit required us to take account of arrangements in other major industrial countries, particularly in the EEC and to this end teams from the Committee visited Denmark, France, Germany and Sweden as well as Canada, Japan and the United States. The itineraries for these visits and summary of our main findings are given in Appendix E. In addition, representatives of the Committee went to Brussels (to talk with senior officials of the European Commission), the Netherlands (to review in detail the content of engineering courses), Italy (to the 1978 Conference of the European Society for Engineering Education), and a return visit to the USA (to participate in an accreditation exercise by the Engineers' Council for Professional Development).

We conducted several original surveys in pursuit of extra information relevant to our review. A major survey of individual engineers in two sample groups was undertaken on our behalf by the Policy Studies Institute. These groups related to members of engineering institutions and to those who expected to graduate in 1973 and 1976 in engineering and science. We also surveyed an ad hoc sample of 500 people who qualified as engineers but subsequently moved into other employment. The results of the PSI Surveys are to be published by HMSO. In addition, we surveyed a sample of UK schools of engineering and their staffs to ascertain the extent of their links with industry and the industrial experience of engineering teachers. We also had inserted into the regular Random Omnibus Survey conducted by National Opinion Polls some questions aimed at eliciting the perceptions and opinions of the general public towards engineers. These two latter surveys are described and summarised in Appendices F and G.

By any standards, we have been able to draw upon a remarkable volume of evidence in both depth and breadth, much of it original. We must express our deep and sincere thanks to all who made the effort (often considerable) to help us. In particular we would mention the Council of Engineering Institutions for organising the regional meetings: the Institution of Electrical Engineers for presenting experts on registration in other countries; the Engineers' Council for Professional Development in New York, the Comite d'Etudes sur les Formations des Ingenieures in Paris, the Verein Deutscher Ingenieure in Dusseldorf, the Royal Swedish Academy of Engineering Science, and the Technische Hogeschool, Eindhoven, for their assistance during and after our visits to their respective countries; and the staff of the British Embassies, High Commissions and Consulates-General in the countries visited, whose detailed knowledge and experience of the countries in which they were serving were invaluable. To these and to the many other organisations and individuals too numerous to list, we are most grateful.

2

On most issues to which we addressed ourselves, we found a wide diversity of evidence and even more of opinion, so that support could be marshalled for a variety of conclusions. Our conclusions are based upon our own judgment of the issues, the evidence to us and the pertinent facts, and we absolve all those who gave evidence to us from any responsibility for our conclusions.

Interpretation of remit

Our terms of reference identified a number of specific questions related to the role and contribution of engineers and engineering in promoting the efficiency and competitiveness of the country's manufacturing performance. Readers looking for linguistically precise definitions of manufacturing, engineering and engineers will be disappointed. We dropped the pursuit of such definitions early in our deliberations, not least because the alternatives proposed all created circular arguments which begged basic assumptions. Notwithstanding this lack of formal definitions, readers should have no difficulty in understanding our usages and meanings before they have read far into our report.

We have laid particular emphasis on the requirement that we conduct our review 'for manufacturing industry and in the light of national economic needs' since the answers to the particular questions posed in our remit would, unless placed in this wider context, be of limited help in addressing the fundamental challenges facing British industry. While we have therefore considered many issues of direct concern to engineers, the paramount consideration and test of our conclusions has been: 'Will this benefit manufacturing industry and further national economic needs?'. This led us to relate the particular issues before us to the general concept of the *engineering dimension—that is the effectiveness of manufacturing organisations in translating engineering expertise into the production and marketing of competitive products through efficient production processes.*

While the contribution of engineers to the engineering dimension is obviously central, and thus of critical moment for the future of British industry, attention to the numbers, qualities or organisation of engineers alone will not resolve the country's present economic situation. What is required is greater national acceptance, as is to be found in our more successful industrial competitors, of the importance to employment and prosperity of successful market-oriented, engineering-based manufacturing industries, and the mobilisation to this common purpose of supporting attitudes and policies among the whole range of functions and disciplines—engineering and non-engineering alike—which together determine the performance of manufacturing industry.

We are aware that the emphasis upon engineering within manufacturing industry specified in our remit has led some representatives of those engineers employed in other sectors of the economy to question whether our report will have any relevance for them. We hope that *all* engineers and *all* employers of engineers will read this report. It is relevant and applicable in the context of national economic needs across all areas of engineering activity.

Ours is the latest in a long pedigree of official inquiries covering different aspects of the same remit. All of these reports made many practical recommendations for changes, yet none has succeeded in initiating significant improve-

3

ments in the engineering performance of industry. Many of the recommendations of these earlier reports—Feilden[1], Swann[2], Dainton[3], and even as far back as Balfour[4] and Lyon Playfair[5]—are valid still, even after the many years since their issue, and one speculates with a sense of regret what improvement in our present economic situation might have been achieved if more effective action had been taken on implementing the recommendations of these earlier reports at the time.

It would be ill reward for the time and and effort put in by the many thousands who have contributed to this Inquiry to have this report pigeonholed to no purpose. *Our most important single recommendation* linked to very many other proposals in various sections of the report *is that the Government should establish a new statutory organisation—a national Engineering Authority—with powers granted it by Parliament to advance the engineering dimension in national economic life and particularly in manufacturing.* The case for such an Authority is a recognition of the need for an organisation accountable for ensuring action, both on this report and in the light of changing technological and market circumstances. Unless urgent actions are taken, continued relative and possibly absolute industrial decline is inevitable with unpredictable but certainly undesirable social consequences. We have made a number of recommendations towards such actions. They will require new initiatives from individuals and organisations. In some cases these recommendations are specific and can be implemented forthwith; elsewhere we have identified objectives and have specified first steps towards achieving them or have illustrated the kinds of measures which are necessary by referring to leading exemplars in this country and abroad; in a few instances, where the issues involved are highly complex, we have made indicative recommendations while suggesting that more detailed study is required. Some may think our recommendations do not go far enough; others will consider they go too far. If changes come only as fast and as far as we propose here, then there will be sufficient improvement in performance and in attitudes to begin arresting the long decline.

I welcome the freedom which this preface affords me to thank all my colleagues on the Committee for their unstinting efforts over the past two years.

---

[1] Engineering Design; Report of a Committee appointed by the Council for Scientific and Industrial Research to consider the present standing of mechanical engineering design—Chairman Dr G B R Feilden, HMSO 1963.

[2] The Flow into Employment of Scientists, Engineers and Technologists; Report of the Working Group on Manpower for Scientific Growth—Chairman Professor M Swann, Cmnd 3760, HMSO 1968.

[3] Enquiry into the Flow of Candidates in Science and Technology into Higher Education—Chairman Dr F S Dainton, Cmnd 3541, HMSO 1968.

[4] Committee on Industry and Trade. Final Report. Cmnd 3282 Vol ii HMSO 1929.

[5] On Technical Education—Lyon, Baron Playfair, Edinburgh 1852.

They are deserving of the highest praise and thanks from the public, whom they have served for the time and trouble which the Inquiry has demanded of them in travel, reading, research, debate, and drafting, all undertaken in addition to their normal work. The Committee was supported by an enthusiastic, devoted and hard-working secretariat led by Mr M V Boxall, to whom I and my colleagues offer our most grateful thanks.

Monty Finniston
(Chairman)   16 November 1979

CHAPTER I

Engineering, Manufacturing and National Economic Needs

(a) Manufacturing and national prosperity

'The relative industrial decline of this country is now widely seen as a matter of grave concern. If allowed to continue it would seem only too likely to lead to growing impoverishment and unemployment in years to come.'[1]

'For many years Britain's performance as a manufacturing and trading nation has been in relative decline with her major competitors. Many reasons can be identified as to why this is so, but a central cause of our decline must be our failure to unlock the full contribution of those working in manufacturing industry—or to attract into manufacturing those with a contribution to make.'[2]

1.1 These statements, the former from the Bank of England and the latter from the TUC, illustrate the deep concern of widely diverse organisations at the condition into which the British economy has declined, and the widespread but less universal recognition that reversing this decline is possible only through the regeneration of Britain as an advanced manufacturing nation.

Manufacturing in the UK economy

1.2 The importance of manufacturing to Britain's prosperity, and hence to the welfare and living standards of her people, cannot be overstressed. Manufacturing industries, including process industries like steel and chemicals as well as industries making capital and consumer products, generate 30 per cent of the nation's wealth and employ 32 per cent of the British working population (Table 1.1).

Furthermore, almost every sector of the economy has close links with manufacturing either through the provision of raw materials, the distribution and sale of goods, or by supplying finance or other services which add value to manufactured products. One study has suggested that half of those employed in non-manufacturing sectors depend for their jobs on these links with manufacturing industry.[3] Since these other sectors are also important customers for manufacturing industry, the dependence is mutual.

1.3 The manufacturing sector also occupies a key role in the international trading performance of the economy. Britain exports over one-third of her gross domestic product, a higher proportion than any other large industrial

---

[1] Bank of England: Quarterly Bulletin, September 1979

[2] Trades Union Congress—evidence to CIEP

[3] J Gershuny: After Industrial Society?, Macmillan 1978

nation;[1] 66 per cent of these exports come from manufacturing industry (Table 1.1) and the remainder from natural wealth (including North Sea oil) and traded services.[2]

Table 1.1. Manufacturing in the British economy

Year	Contributions to Gross Domestic Product by manufacturing industry*	Proportion of total numbers in employment in manufacturing industry†	Proportion of exports of goods and services contributed by manufacturing‡
	%	%	%
1963	33	37	69
1968	32	36	68
1973	29	35	67
1978	30	32	66

Sources: * National Income and Expenditure (before providing for depreciation and stock appreciation)
† *Department of Employment Gazette*
‡ Department of Industry

1.4 As in almost every other industrial nation, the proportion of the labour force working in manufacturing industry has fallen over recent years (Table 1.1). Some economists have postulated from this trend that Britain is moving into a 'post industrial' stage of development in which traded and public services will become the main source of future growth in employment.[3][4] This shift into services has important implications for the pattern of employment and income distribution within the UK economy but it in no way diminishes the importance of maintaining a strong manufacturing capability. This is because:

(a) manufacturing exports in 1978 amounted to £30bn, but exports of traded services to only £12bn; a 1 per cent fall in export earnings from manufacturing thus requires a 2·5 per cent offsetting rise in earnings from traded services to maintain the balance of payments. Although tourism, the financial and insurance institutions of the City of London and the traded services sector generally have long provided a surplus on their balance of payments, they have only limited capability to fund a large deficit from trade in manufactured products.

(b) The value of an industrial sector to national wealth creation need not correlate with its importance as an employer, since it is in the

[1] Department of Trade: Memorandum to NEDC, NEDC (78) 57

[2] Department of Trade: Export Performance—no room for complacency 'Trade and Industry' 1/9/78

[3] Moore, Rhodes et al: A Return to Full Employment?, Cambridge Economic Policy Review, 3/78

[4] 'Traded services' excludes such areas as government administration, education and public welfare provisions which, while important as employers and also vital to national wealth-creating abilities, do not themselves add significantly to wealth creation or overseas earnings.

nature of manufacturing that increased output and/or improved efficiency often rest upon the introduction of more capital-intensive, and hence less labour-using, processes; for example, in 1978 the chemicals sector provided 10 per cent of total manufacturing output and 15 per cent of manufacturing exports, but employed only 6 per cent of the manufacturing workforce.

(c) Personal incomes will inevitably be spent in part on manufactured goods, whichever sector provides those incomes. Indeed, as incomes rise, the discretionary element of consumer spending (after taxes, rents and rates, heating and lighting, essential foodstuffs and clothing) tends to rise first on purchases of manufactures, some of them substituting for spending on services (eg motor cars for public transport, washing machines for laundries, television or hi-fi equipment for 'live' entertainment).[1]

(d) To the extent that extra spending also goes on services, then the demand for manufactured goods is indirectly stimulated through the service sector, growth in which depends to a greater or lesser extent upon the availability of manufactured products required in the provision of such services; these products range from major capital investments, often in technologically sophisticated ones such as computers or aircraft, to more prosaic but no less essential items like furniture.

1.5 Notwithstanding the growing importance of the services sector as an employer and generator of prosperity, the long-term growth of the economy depends upon the value of domestic output of manufactured goods continuing to rise to meet a substantial share of domestic demand, both to meet those demands and to earn sufficient currency from sales abroad to pay for the imports of raw materials, food, fuel, manufactured products and services. Since Britain is firmly established as virtually an open market within the European Economic Community and within the General Agreement on Tariffs and Trade so the distinction between home and export sales has blurred. British producers must therefore be competitive in international terms since their products are in direct competition with the best on offer in the world in both overseas and home markets.

Indicators of manufacturing performance

1.6 Viewed in the perspective of its own past record, the performance of British manufacturing industry in meeting this requirement has not been without merit.

As Table 1.2 (page 10) shows, the value of manufacturing output rose 43 per cent in real terms between 1963 and 1973 (since when it has declined), with exports as a proportion of that output rising from 16 per cent to 25 per cent between 1963 and 1978 and thereby contributing greatly to the growth in national income. These gains were achieved notwithstanding a fall in the total workforce employed in manufacturing and with an improvement of over 50 per cent in productivity in the period.

---

[1] J Gershuny: After Industrial Society?, Macmillan 1978

Table 1.2. UK manufacturing performance

Year	Index of Production[a]	Index of Numbers Employed[b]	Index of Output per Head[c]	Ratio of Exports to Total Sales[d]
	(1975=100)	(1975=100)	(1975=100)	(%)
1963	76	111	69	16
1968	94	110	86	17
1973	108	104	104	20
1978	104	97	106	25

Sources: a–c—Monthly Digest of Statistics; d—Department of Industry Economic Trends

1.7 But although British manufacturers have achieved commendable gains, they have not done as well overall as their major overseas competitors. Manufacturing industry in Britain has been markedly less productive and less profitable than in other industrial countries.[1] Moreover the pattern of UK exports has been moving on trends increasingly divergent from those obtaining overseas. In the decade to 1977 exports of manufactures from all the major industrial countries together rose by 9 per cent each year, while British exports of manufactures rose by only 5 per cent per annum.[2]

As Table 1.3 shows, the UK share of 'world trade' in manufactures fell from 15 per cent in 1963 to under 9 per cent in 1973 (since when it has remained around this level), while—excepting the indigenously wealthy USA—all the other individual nations cited have held or even expanded their world market shares.[3]

1.8 Market shares have declined for almost every UK industrial sector: between 1964 and 1976 the world market shares of British cars fell from 11 per cent to 5 per cent, of ships from 8 per cent to 4 per cent, of steelmaking from $6\frac{1}{2}$ per cent to 3 per cent, of chemicals from $13\frac{1}{2}$ per cent to $9\frac{1}{2}$ per cent, of non-electrical machinery from 16 per cent to 10 per cent, and of electrical machinery from 13 per cent to $7\frac{1}{2}$ per cent. Some previously thriving UK industries, like motor-cycles and cutlery, have all but disappeared.[3]

[1] (a) F Blackaby (ed). De-Industrialisation, Economic Policy Papers 2, Heinemann/NIESR, 1979
(b) C Saunders: Engineering in Britain, West Germany and France—some statistical comparisons, Sussex Papers No 3 1978
(c) M Panic (ed): UK and West German Manufacturing Industry, 1954–72 NEDO Monograph 5, 1978
(d) Department of Industry: Britain's Pattern of Specialisation, mimeo, 1978
(e) Barclays Bank/BOTB: Report on Export Development in France, Germany and the UK, 1979

[2] Department of Industry: Trade and Industry 1/8/78, p 500

[3] British Overseas Trade Board: Annual Report, 1978 published 1979

Table 1.3. Shares of world trade* in manufactures†—per cent

Year	UK	W Germany	France	Italy	USA	Japan
1963	15	20	9	6	21	8
1968	11	20	8	7	20	11
1973	9	22	10	7	16	13
1977	9	21	10	8	16	15

Source: Monthly Review of External Trade Statistics.

> * 'World Trade' is defined as the exports of twelve major manufacturing countries.
>
> † 'Manufactures' is a narrower group of goods than the products of manufacturing industry referred to elsewhere, mainly because it excludes manufactured food and fuel.

1.9 While the proportion of UK manufacturing output going to exports has been increasing (see Table 1.2, col. 4), this increase has gone hand-in-hand with growing import penetration of home markets, often in the same product categories. Both trends are common to other industrial countries (except Japan), but they have been more pronounced in Britain. Imported manufactures now take over 24 per cent of the total UK market, and in certain sectors foreign producers supply two-thirds or more of the home market.[1,2] In recent years, whenever UK domestic spending has risen, imports of manufactures have risen disproportionately more, reflecting a combination of UK producers' inability to raise output sufficiently to meet increased demand and UK customers' increased preference for foreign products. Efforts by successive Governments to encourage domestic industry by stimulating consumer demand have often proved more beneficial for overseas than for British manufacturers, and once lost to foreign manufacturers, markets have proved very difficult to regain.

1.10 The implications of the growing disparity between British and European growth rates in manufacturing output and national prosperity have been graphically stated by the Bank of England:

'The consequences of failing to arrest this country's industrial decline are likely to become more pressing and obvious as time goes on. Now condemned to very slow growth, we might later even have to accept, if present trends continue, decline in real living standards.'[3]

If this inadequate national trading performance in manufactures seems remote from individual welfare and prosperity, Table 1.4 illustrates how British income levels have failed to grow at the rates achieved in other EEC countries.

Since 1966, when Britain was among the richest European nations, it has slipped to become one of the poorest.

[1] Department of Trade: Memorandum to NEDC, NEDC (78) 57

[2] Department of Trade: UK Imports, mimeo, 1978

[3] Bank of England: Quarterly Bulletin, March 1979

Table 1.4. Per capita GDP: EEC countries

[UK = 100]

Country	1966	1977
UK	100	100
W Germany	109	129
France	99	124
Italy	69	77
Netherlands	97	117
Belgium	93	119
Denmark	115	129

Source: Statistical Office of the European Communities, 1978; indices of GDP/head at market prices shown at purchasing power parities

1.11 Until the 1960s Britain continued to be one of the most prosperous countries in the world, thriving on her strengths as a trading nation and her position at the centre of the Sterling Area. From our meetings and discussions around the country during this Inquiry, it is clear to us that notwithstanding repeated warnings over many years *very many people in this country do not fully appreciate that those days are past; that Britain is now poorer than many of the countries she formerly outperformed; and that both the roots of that relative decline and the seeds of future recovery lie with the performance of her manfacturing industries.*

The need for growth

1.12 The decline of British manufacturing competitiveness relative to her major competitors has progressed insidiously over many years and *radical and fundamental improvements in UK manufacturing performance are required if the rising levels of private and public consumption to which the British people have become accustomed (and expect to continue) are not to fall further behind those in other industrial countries. There is no prospect that the contributions from natural resources (including North Sea oil and gas or coal) or growth in other sectors of the economy can generate wealth on the scale which can be earned by manufacturing industry;* for example the contribution of North Sea oil to GDP in 1978 was £2·3bn, equivalent to 8 per cent of the contribution made by manufacturing to total national value-added.

1.13 Growth in the economy as a whole and in manufacturing industries in particular, must be restored if Britain is to become a high-earning economy on a par with its main competitors, and one in which sufficient jobs are available for the young people entering the workforce for the first time and for the workers displaced by improved productivity in existing activities. That growth must come not only from existing activities but also from new enterprises emerging to replace traditional industries which have rationalised, declined or disappeared. In 1975 Britain produced only 5·6 per cent of total OECD output although her population was 7·5 per cent of the total within

12

OECD (which includes a number of much less industrially-developed economies than Britain). For Britain to raise her per capita industrial output to a level commensurate with her share of OECD population, which would still be much lower than that achieved in Germany, France or Japan, would require a rate of growth in industrial output 3 per cent higher than the rate for all OECD countries together, sustained for 10 years. By comparison, industrial output in Britain has risen by little more than 6 per cent overall, or well under 1 per cent p.a., in the nine years since 1970, and current forecasts predict no improvement.

(b) Britain as an advanced industrial nation

The structure of UK industry

1.14 A number of studies[1] have compared the characteristics of British manufacturing industry with those of competing industrial countries, to see whether differences emerge which might explain Britain's relative weaknesses. Characteristics considered include the relative sizes of British and overseas enterprises, the extent to which output is concentrated in a few leading companies, the categories of products in which different countries specialise, the sizes and types of export markets sought, the relative capital-intensiveness of British companies compared with their overseas competitors, and so on. A consensus emerges from these studies that, in respect of these measures, although the UK displays some differences, they are not so large individually or collectively to provide an explanation of why Britain has been less efficient and hence less successful than its competitors and other reasons must be sought.

Table 1.5. International comparisons of profitability 1955–77

Net rate of return* : Manufacturing

	Canada	United States	Japan	West Germany	United Kingdom
Averages for years†	%	%	%	%	%
1963–67	18·5	31·7	26·7	18·7	13·6
1968–71	15·5	21·6	28·4	19·0	10·7
1971–75	17·0	17·4	15·7	12·5	5·6
Years:					
1975	14·5	14·5	13·9	11·0	2·1
1976	13·3	18·1	na	13·5	2·5
1977	12·5	19·0	na	13·3	3·9

* Defined as net operating surplus as percentage net capital stock of fixed assets (excluding land).

† Each of these groups of years covers a cycle in UK rates of return. Figures for other countries for the same years may cover more or less than a complete cycle, and in this sense provide only a broad comparison with UK.

na – not available

Source: Department of Industry, 1979.

[1] Op cit

Productivity and profitability

1.15 Change and growth in industry depends on the level of effective investment in new plant for manufacturing new products or for making current products better; this in turn depends in large measure on the availability of finance through profits earned from existing plant and products. As Table 1.5 illustrates (page 13) although the profitability of manufacturing industries has been steadily declining in each of the major industrial nations over the past 25 years the fall has been very much more pronounced in Britain than in other countries.

The declining profitability of manufacturing industry reduces the availability of internal funds for the development of better products and for more efficient manufacturing systems and deters external investment in manufacturing. Real levels of investment in industry (in terms of the amount spent per employee) have fallen behind comparable levels in other countries, further weakening UK competitiveness.[1]

1.16 Furthermore the benefits accruing from such investment as has been made have all too frequently been attenuated by slow construction, with consequential high costs and delay in commissioning, and by the manifestation of poor industrial relations, manning levels markedly higher than those employed on comparable plant in other countries, and low output rates interrupted by industrial disputes.

1.17 Table 1.6 illustrates how far UK levels of manufacturing productivity have fallen behind those in competing nations over the last decade.

Table 1.6. Relative indices of manufacturing* productivity 1970–77

Level of productivity† UK=100

	1970	1973	1975	1977
UK	100	100	100	100
Belgium	156	146	160	na
France	177	185	197	205
West Germany	153	146	151	165
Italy	138	117	111	120‡
Netherlands	178	173	182	na
Japan	215	238	233	263
US	340	336	338	360

* The definition of manufacturing used here varies slightly—but not significantly—from that used in other tables.

† Value Added per employee, measured at $ purchasing power parity rates of exchange in 1970.

‡ 1976.

na—not available.

Source: After NIESR Review February 1979.

[1] (a) D Jones: 'Output, Employment and Labour Productivity in Europe Since 1955', National Institute Review, 1978

    (b) J Barnett/HM Treasury: 'The Nuts and Bolts of the Economy', The Sunday Times, 25/6/78

In 1970 the UK level of productivity was 65 per cent of that in West Germany and only 47 per cent of that in Japan but by 1977 the comparison showed a further deterioration to 61 per cent of the German level and 38 per cent of the Japanese.[1]

1.18 The wide spread between the levels of productivity achieved in the best UK firms and the worst in particular industries emphasises the considerable scope which exists for securing significant improvements in output from existing human and physical resources in UK manufacturing.[2] Indeed several studies of production methods in British companies supported by much technical literature and many 'awareness' programmes[3] have indicated specific measures which could raise productivity, reduce manufacturing costs and increase profits, thereby increasing the flow of funds for investment in innovation and new industries catering to world markets as well as improving the total climate for investment in manufacturing industry.

Product qualities

1.19 Labour productivity (in terms of value-added per employee) is, however, not just a function of the efficiency of manufacturing production, but reflects the market appeal and value of the products being made, since companies selling high value products on to rising markets may well prove more profitable than those with more efficient and harder-working workforces producing less attractive or lower value products. An important difference between UK and overseas manufacturing industries in this respect is indicated by evidence that British manufacturers have not shared fully in the international trend for advanced nations to trade up-market, that is, to increase the 'value added' represented by their output.[4,5] Studies by the National Economic Development Office and others of the relative selling prices of closely comparable products, have suggested that the UK shows a tendency to 'export cheap and import dear' in manufactured products.[4,6,7] For almost every product group in the Standard International Trade Classification (SITC) the 'unit values' of UK exports are lower than those of exports from other industrially advanced nations, and also lower than the 'unit values' of UK imports of manufactures. In a study of 86 product groups accounting for one-third of British exports, the values per tonne of the British products in 1978 were 20–40 per cent lower than those for comparable German and French products.[4]

[1] See also memorandum from the Secretary of State for Industry to NEDC. NEDC(79)59: Productivity and Manufacturing Industry

[2] Wragg and Robertson: 'Post-War Trends, by Industry in the UK, 1950—73' HMSO 6/78

[3] (a) C New: 'Managing Manufacturing Operations', British Institute of Management, 1976
   (b) D Smith: 'Managing for Productivity' Management Today October 1977
   (c) Centre for Interfirm Comparisons: 'Management Policies and Practices, and Business Performances', IFC 1978

[4] Op cit

[5] Department of Industry: 'International Competitiveness and R&D Policies', mimeo, 1978

[6] D Connell: 'UK Export Performance—some evidence from international trade data', NEDO mimeo, 1978

[7] D Stout: 'International Price Competitiveness, Non-price Factors and Export Performance', NEDO 1977

This disparity, already wide, appears to be growing, as Table 1.7 illustrates for mechanical engineering products.

Table 1.7. Exports and Imports—Mechanical Engineering Index of Unit Values*

UK exports 1970 = 100

	Exports		Imports		Exports/Imports	
	1970	*1977*	*1970*	*1977*	a/c	b/d
UK	100	138	165	290	0·61	0·48
France	99	220	125	246	0·79	0·89
W. Germany	121	297	114	262	1·06	1·13

* $000s/metric tons
Source: NEDO, 1979.

As the table shows, the ratio of the unit values of UK exports to those for imports of comparable products has fallen from 60 per cent in 1970 to 47 per cent in 1977 while the ratio for France, although also less than unity (ie France too has been exporting relatively cheap and importing relatively dear), has been improving and that for Germany has strengthened from 106 per cent to 113 per cent.

1.20 The high 'unit values' of competing exports and of imports into Britain relative to those of British exports suggests that the source of the relative weakness of British producers in world markets has not generally lain in unduly high UK selling prices. There is no evidence of a decline in the price competitiveness of British goods during the period in which UK market shares fell most steeply;[1] if anything and until very recently, the reverse has been true, with producers in other countries often winning sales from British companies despite their higher selling prices. The key differences between Britain and her competitors appear to lie in the differing emphasis given to the specification and qualities of the products made and in the way they are manufactured. While other advanced industrial nations have concentrated on producing high-value, high quality products (in respect of performance, reliability, finish and ease of maintenance) to sell at competitive prices in rising markets, Britain has struggled with a product range for which world demand, including that from home customers, has grown relatively showly; for example, in 1975 the UK and West Germany both sold about 22 per cent of their total exports of metal-forming machinery to developing countries, but whereas the unit value of the British machines was $1,628, that of the German products was $4,951, and the total value of the German sales was over four times greater than that for the UK.[2]

[1] Department of Industry: 'Manufacturing Industries—UK Performance since 1963', Trade and Industry 8/9/78

[2] F Blackaby (ed): 'De-Industrialisation', Economic Policy Papers 2, Heinemann/NIESR, 1979

16

(c) Market trends for manufacturing economies

Implications of spreading industrialisation

1.21 The advanced industrial nations compete for markets mostly with each other but also to an increasing extent with producers from newly industrialising countries. The patterns of trade and competition between the advanced nations and these newly-industrialising countries are changing and will continue to change rapidly as the world becomes increasingly industrialised. As current products and processes mature and more effective designs and production techniques are established, so manufacturing methods become standardised and amenable to automation and routine procedures. The less advanced newly-industrialising countries—which are not in general able to compete in the non-routine, highly knowledge-intensive skills required at the outset of innovative cycles—are at this stage well placed to enter the market with modern plant and with significant advantages in labour and total operating costs over the established producers. The increasing sophistication of industries in some newly-industrialised countries, employing modern plant and new technology, has meant that the area of comparative advantage for the advanced countries is being progressively eroded by this 'product cycle'.

1.22 The strengths of advanced countries lie in inventing and exploiting *new* products and processes, incorporating high levels of human skill and knowledge, most often at the leading edge of technology, and in *continual incremental improvements* to current products and processes through reducing production costs. Their advantages lie particularly in devoting attention to *non-price factors*, for example, in uprating the performance, reliability and general 'fitness for purpose' of their products, improving quality control, providing greater assurance and promptness of delivery, and otherwise attending flexibly and readily to customer requirements before and after sale.[1] The advanced countries must move up-market, in this way, continually seeking new ways to maintain their advantages by identifying, developing and accelerating the introduction of new technologies and potential growth products. They must also be prepared to move out of product areas in which their earlier comparative technical and commercial advantages have been irrevocably lost.

The importance of non-price factors

1.23 Customers' evaluations of value-for-money from manufactured products, particularly for consumer durable and capital goods, have increasingly stressed the relative importance of 'non-price' factors based upon the expected total cost of the purchase over its useable life. Factors in this market trend have been the rising labour costs of servicing, maintenance and repairs, a shortage of skilled technicians to do such work and the rising cost of downtime on highly productive modern plant. Partly as a result, both corporate and private customers have come to insist on long warranties and guarantees from

---

[1] (a) K Corfield: 'Design for Manufacture' NEDO 1979

   (b) J Pilditch: Evidence to CIEP from Allied International Designers

   (c) R Feilden (Chairman) 'Report of Committee of Inquiry on Engineering Design', HMSO 1963

suppliers, and have often proved willing to pay a higher initial price if they are persuaded that later costs and inconvenience will be minimised. Furthermore, progressively more rigorous world-wide standards concerning safety, pollution control, energy consumption and other aspects of product performance have forced products which do not meet these specifications out of many markets. This reflects the international growth in 'consumer power', and in associated legislative controls (particularly those concerning product liability) which penalise inferior designs and unreliable products.

1.24 Studies of the performance of particular groups of UK manufacturers[1] have identified areas where British companies have not adjusted sufficiently in adapting the quality and specification of their products to meet these and other changes in market requirements. Sectoral studies, from shipbuilding to electronic components, have cited opportunities missed and markets lost due to non-price factors. These range from failure of British producers to innovate or to match changed requirements through specific shortcomings in the design or performance of products to a general reputation of British goods for inferior quality, late delivery and unreliability in service (eg over the provision of spares). 'Made in Britain' was once synonymous with high quality, internationally sought-after products. This is still so for products from many UK companies but not for all. Such excellence must be reinstated as the norm for UK manufacturing industry, capitalising upon the successful experience of its best companies. Notwithstanding the shortcomings we have described there is much in current UK manufacturing industry to justify confidence that overall performance could be greatly improved by more companies building upon the 'best practices' exemplified by the leading UK companies and emulating these companies' successes in relating their products to market needs.

Engineering and market trends

1.25 We cannot stress too strongly the need to meet change with change, nor can we over-emphasise how much engineering pervades activities in industry, the home, and even in leisure through manufactured products and systems based on them. The opportunities afforded by recent technological achievements present rich markets to companies with the market perception and engineering capabilities to exploit them[2] but to outline a particular scenario for manufacturing industry in the 1980s and 1990s would be a fruitless exercise. Nonetheless, the central, critical and growing place of engineering

---

[1] (a) K Pavitt (ed): 'Technical Innovation and British Economic Performance', Macmillan/Science Policy Research Unit, 1980

(b) Central Policy Review Staff: 'The Future of the British Car Industry' HMSO 1975

(c) CPRS: 'The Future of the UK Power Plant Manufacturing Industry' HMSO 1976

(d) Department of Industry/Boston Consulting Group: 'Strategy Alternatives for the UK Motor Cycle Industry', HMSO 1975

(e) National Economic Development Office: 'Survey of Investment in Machine Tools' NEDO 1975

[2] (a) D Stout: 'Industrial Policy in the Longer Term—an approach through investment', NEDO/NEDC (74)31

(b) Nabseth & Ray: 'The Diffusion of New Industrial Processes—an International Study', CUP/NIESR, 1974

and engineers within *any* scenario is illustrated by considering emerging developments in:

—the availability and real cost of *basic resources*;
—the evolution and impact of *new technologies*;
—the intensification of *competition* between industrial nations;
—the economic impact of *social and political trends*.

1.26 Fundamental changes calling for engineering-led responses are already being experienced in the demand for and supply of basic resources:

(*a*) *Food*

Continuing (if less rapid) growth in world population, coupled with rising expectations of people in the developing countries, demand engineering-based responses for machinery, chemicals and civil engineering systems for raising agricultural productivity, for manufacturing synthetic foodstuffs for human and animal use and for improving efficiency of food processing, storage and distribution.

(*b*) *Energy*

Rising real costs of conventional energy sources have created an urgent need for engineering solutions to the problems of minimising the energy consumed by products, processes and systems, exploiting hitherto inaccessible or uneconomic fuel sources and developing economically viable alternative sources of energy.

(*c*) *Materials*

The increasing scarcity and rising real costs of industrial raw materials raise new engineering problems in the design and manufacture of products and plant particularly in the optimum use of these materials, in their recycling and in substitution.

1.27 Major advances in technology are radically changing industry's potential to meet these and other market challenges, as well as creating new opportunities in themselves. Particular applications of new technologies, together with new applications for established know-how, are increasingly altering the character and scale of world markets. Among the most pervasive and ubiquitous of these are advances being made in applications of microelectronics; others, to name but a few, include communications, transportation and alternative energy:

(*a*) In *communications*, technical advances in both hardware and software, associated with computing systems and modes of data transmission, are revolutionising the transfer, control, storage, access and display of information. As costs decline and allow economic applications in an ever-extending range of functions these developments will transform business, industry, distribution, entertainment, education, health-care and the home.

(*b*) In *transportation*, the movement of people and freight by land, sea and air is undergoing a revolution built upon developments in vehicle designs, rapid mass-transit systems, traffic control, navigation and safety systems, and other changes deriving from and implemented by engineers.

19

(c) In *products and processes* the choices before customers are continually increasing in number and sophistication, and even the most recent innovations are liable to be rendered obsolete in a short time by competitors' applications of new knowledge and techniques.

1.28 The market opportunities opened by these developments will be enormous. For example, the world market for telecommunications equipment, worth $30bn in 1977, has been estimated at $45bn in 1982 and $65bn in 1987.[1] Competition for world markets will be concomitantly fierce. As more countries industrialise, so the number of competitors for each market will increase but with the advantage in the initial stage resting with the advanced countries. Developments in communications and transportation and international political pressures for free trade will continue to erode distinctions between home and export markets, so that domestic producers must keep abreast of best world practice in the engineering of their products and processes and in the management of both. Competition for markets will be further intensified between established industrial nations, as each seeks to maintain growth in new product areas to provide solutions for the structural unemployment which will inevitably arise as more and more traditional employing industries become obsolete or capital intensive.

1.29 Engineering responses to these market developments must take into account the growing impact of social and political considerations and constraints upon technical decisions. Examples are:

(a) *'Consumerism'*
Not only are the customers for manufactured products becoming more sophisticated in their separate appraisals of the quality and value-for-money of those products, but they are collectively demanding greater controls over their production and performance, as is manifest in the spread of statutory regulations regarding energy consumption, emission and noise levels, safety, and in the introduction into the legal framework in some countries of 'strict liability' upon manufacturers for every aspect and application of their products in use.

(b) *Politics*
The rise of consumerism and the impact of resource and technological developments on people's jobs, their physical environment and their 'quality of life' generally have brought engineering issues into the centre of the political stage and demand a forceful, informed and coherent engineering input to national debates and policy counsels, to ensure that ill-informed and emotional reactions do not predominate in shaping policies and action in these areas.

(c) *International collaboration*
The scale of intellectual and material resources demanded to meet the emerging challenges posed by technological and market changes is now often beyond the capabilities of individual companies, or even individual countries. The engineering expertise of several countries has been mobilised already upon some major projects by initiatives

[1] Arthur D Little Inc, quoted in The Financial Times, October 1979 p.20

either at Governmental level or by private companies (often multinationals). Only those companies whose engineering capabilities are of world class will become involved in these potentially highly-rewarding ventures and collaborations.

The challenges for UK industry

1.30 *The changes outlined above in the competition for world markets in manufactures are inevitable, inexorable and international. Since producers in other countries will undoubtedly respond to the challenge and opportunities presented, the British response must be more energetic and purposeful than it has been hitherto. Britain's survival as an advanced industrial nation depends critically upon her manufacturing companies moving up-market into the production of high quality, high value-added goods, utilising the best of current knowledge and technology, and directed towards areas where world demand is growing or can be generated most rapidly and where competition from newly-industrialising countries is initially least severe.*

1.31 *The response to these developments, which afford unprecedented opportunities for growth and regeneration, demands market-oriented engineering excellence, managed and translated using the best of current technology and know-how into the types of high quality, high value-added goods and services sought by world customers.*

(d) The engineering dimension

1.32 There are few—if any—areas of manufacturing where the competitiveness of a company's products and processes does not depend upon its corporate engineering capabilities. We would not suggest that changes regarding engineering and engineers are all that is needed to achieve the dramatic improvements demanded of manufacturing performance. Account must also be taken of a whole range of complex and inter-related factors, including:

—the size, buoyancy and accessibility of world *markets*;
—the impact of policies and priorities determined in the *political* sphere;
—the availability of *finance* for industry and in particular for innovations;
—the competence of company *managements*;
—the *support and commitment* of employees at all levels for the changes needed.

Each of these factors has been the subject of intensive analyses and reviews. Underlying and largely shaping them all are the intangible influences of British attitudes towards change, industry and engineering, and the legacies of economic and social history. The interplay of these factors has bred an economic and cultural environment in this country frequently inimical to engendering the radical changes needed in national behaviour and priorities. However, the successes of the many British companies which have overcome these supposed handicaps to progress show that changes are feasible, and that they can pay, bringing prosperity to the companies and those who work in them and to the nation as a whole.

21

1.33 Among those manufacturers in this country and overseas who have prospered in world markets, we found a common characteristic in the way they had built upon excellent engineering, integrated into enterprising and forward-looking market and product strategies. Managements in these companies clearly regarded engineering as the common factor linking the inputs of the various specialist functions within the organisation to its overall objectives. Engineers were involved in each stage of the manufacturing process, from the technical appraisal of world market opportunities and the translation of those appraisals to the design of products and systems to exploit the opportunities through to the development, manufacture, sale, delivery and service of the products. There was thus achieved a continuous interplay between marketing, design, research, manufacturing and selling, with all concerned seeking to ensure that the company's products met the demands of world markets.

1.34 The engineering performance of manufacturing enterprises depends not only upon the numbers and qualities of engineers employed but equally, if not more, on the effective priority accorded to engineering in the enterprise, and on *the capability of the organisation as a system for translating engineering expertise into the production and marketing of competitive products through efficient production processes.* This capability involves many of the non-engineering factors mentioned above. *To convey the interaction of engineering with non-engineering factors in determining manufacturing performance, and to emphasise the importance of considering the whole manufacturing system and not just aspects of it, we have adopted the concept of the 'engineering dimension'.* The engineering dimension involves all the factors and activities concerned in relating the technological capabilities and expertise of an organisation, to its overall objectives, which in manufacturing are to prosper through the sale of products and systems in the world market. They should also be borne in mind in government—both national and local—where the importance of engineering and engineers has hitherto been badly neglected.

1.35 *The engineering dimension in manufacturing industry determines the impact of engineers on companies' responses to world markets, particularly in:*
—*assessing and/or anticipating market needs and opportunities;*
—*assessing the company's potential to meet or create these opportunities;*
—*conceiving, designing and continually developing products and systems to meet market requirements;*
—*developing, operating and improving processes for manufacturing such products profitably, making optimum use of materials, energy, capital and human resources;*
—*ensuring that engineering support for products is efficiently sustained throughout product life; and*
—*adapting flexibly to particular market requirements, and responding quickly to changes in those requirements or in the technical potential needed to meet them.*

1.36 *The engineering dimension is understood and well developed in successful manufacturing companies, but there are too few such companies in the UK to produce sufficient wealth to match the social and economic expectations of the nation.*

(e) Summary

1.37 (i) The future of the UK economy and the employment and living standards of its population depend critically upon the extent to which British companies can prosper in international competition for markets for its manufactures.

There is no prospect that growth from natural resources or from other sectors of the economy can generate wealth on the scale which can be provided by manufacturing industries. Past relative declines in UK manufacturing competitiveness and output must therefore be stemmed and reversed if expectations of continually rising living standards are to be maintained and the socially untenable consequences of very high levels of long-term unemployment averted.

(ii) Prosperity for the advanced industrial nations depends on the production of high-quality, high value-added goods, utilising the best of current knowledge and technology. There is evidence that British manufacturers have not shared fully in the international trend among advanced nations to trade 'up-market', and that room exists for greatly improving the efficiency of much of British production. Close attention must be paid to the market appeal of the products of British industry and to the efficiency with which they are made, building upon market-oriented engineering, so that 'Made in Britain' can once again become synonymous with high-quality internationally sought-after products.

(iii) Changes in the world market for manufactured products are increasingly emphasising the need for companies to develop and maintain an advanced engineering capability to meet the challenges posed and to exploit the opportunities being presented; we have no doubt that producers in other countries will respond to this need and it is imperative that UK manufacturers do likewise.

(iv) While engineering excellence is not the only determinant of manufacturing prosperity, the example of the most successful companies shows that it is *essential* to continuing competitiveness. That excellence derives from the effective priority accorded to engineering in manufacturing enterprises, and the capability of the organisation as a system for translating engineering expertise into the efficient production and marketing of competitive products, which capability depends upon companies' understanding and development of the 'engineering dimension'.

CHAPTER II

Engineering changes in industry

(a) Introduction

Engineering in the British culture

2.1 The engineering-based response to world markets is affected by a whole range of cultural, political, financial and attitudinal factors as well as by the inputs of engineers. Weaknesses in any one of these respects have an effect on the others and actions to improve overall performance must therefore come simultaneously on a number of fronts with consistent objectives in view. The regeneration of UK manufacturing industry demands therefore a concerted and continuous commitment to overcoming current inadequacies and meeting future challenges in the engineering dimension through positive support at the national, company and individual level. The assumptions of common interest in the continuing improvement of manufacturing performance and the coherence of response at all levels have been widely remarked upon by many commentators on other countries, notably Germany and Japan and struck us vividly on our own visits. A comparable unity of purpose has been lacking in British efforts to improve manufacturing performance. Policies followed by influential groups within the economy (in the financial system, the educational system, the trades union movement and different Government departments) have often been at odds with each other and with the common interest they should have in a prosperous national manufacturing capability.

2.2 Major features of a successful engineering dimension, less well-established in Britain than elsewhere involved the financing and realisation of technological innovations; the co-ordination of policies to inform and support industry's response to market changes; and the management and organisation of the engineering aspects of manufacturing. In each respect we found deficiencies in this country compared with our competitors, who have shown greater understanding and recognition of the essential role of engineering and engineers within their industrial cultures.

2.3 It is internationally acknowledged that Britain is a country rich in inventiveness and creative talent. Yet, with some eminent exceptions, these inventive talents have not been harnessed effectively by manufacturing industry because, compared with Continental Europe and the large part of the world which has followed its lead, there have been neither the cultural nor the pecuniary rewards in this country to attract sufficient of the brightest national talents into engineering in industry. Great prestige is attached to science, medicine and the creative arts, so that to be associated with their activities is to share in that esteem, but there is no cultural equivalent in Britain, and hence no basis for according similar esteem, to the European concepts conveyed in German by 'Technik'—the synthesis of knowledge from many disciplines to devise technical and economic solutions to practical problems. This 'third culture' (alongside science and art), which underlies the concept of the engineering dimension, is well understood in Continental Europe, in Japan

24

and to a lesser extent in the USA, where the engineer has a standing in his own right since his work is recognised as having social responsibility and economic value. That value is reflected in these other countries by the high earnings of engineers relative to other professional groups and by the presence of engineers in the top policy-making counsels of industry and the nation. Engineering in these countries is thus a first choice of many able and enterprising people, who as engineers make their careers and generate a healthy regard for the engineering dimension not just in manufacturing industry but in the public service, the financial sector and in academic institutions. In this country top jobs in these functions are not as readily accessible to engineers.

2.4 In a survey conducted for us among the general public[1] to establish attitudes to engineering and engineers nearly one-fifth of respondents expressed complete ignorance of what engineers did, about two-thirds (68 per cent) perceived an 'engineer' as someone doing manual work, probably with machinery and only 13 per cent associated the title with design or research work at professional level. Given a definition of a 'professional engineer', half the sample then perceived the title as denoting someone senior, but still only a minority, and then when prompted, thought that a 'professional engineer' would require a degree. It is clear that British engineers are ill-served by a generic title not specifically associated with and reserved to a highly-educated and vital professional group in society. We are not persuaded however that it would be feasible in Britain to protect by law the simple title 'engineer' (as some have proposed) or to devise some new word which will distinguish engineers from craftsmen, mechanics, or fitters. There are already protected distinctive titles for engineers, notably Chartered Engineer (CEng) and Technician Engineer (TEng) but these have not achieved the sought-for public impact. 'Engineer' is internationally accepted in the sense in which we have used it in this report, ie people practising their discipline at a high professional level. The objective of all concerned with engineers and the engineering dimension should be to see a comparable understanding and usage established in this country.

2.5 There is too the misleading national tendency to regard engineering as a subordinate branch of 'science' to be corrected. Action to this end is needed in the educational system. Such action must also be backed by the media—which should revise its indiscriminate use of the term 'engineer' however inconvenient it may be and should ensure that engineering matters are not confused with scientific issues—and by national institutions such as the *Science* Research Council and the *Science* Museum, whose titles belie the fact that they are frequently more concerned with engineering and technology than with science. The award of Bachelor of Science and even Bachelor of Arts degrees to engineering graduates further devalues the separate standing of engineering.

2.6 *It is our firm belief that improved standing for engineers and greater attractiveness for a career among their ranks will only come with enhanced recognition of the nature and importance of engineering* but we do not believe that such recognition can or should be imposed on organisations, institutions

---

[1] National Opinion Polls Omnibus Survey, May 1978. Appendix (G)

or individuals unwilling or unable to structure their activities to further the engineering dimension; nor do we believe that exhortation can of itself succeed in generating a common will for change where none exists. Our aim is to draw to the attention of those involved in determining national policies at every level the critical importance of the engineering dimension and to highlight the relationships within it as they affect industrial success. We have sought throughout to draw upon the effective 'best practices' in this country and others and to propose their extension. *All those involved, directly or indirectly, with manufacturing industry should consciously undertake regular formal reviews of their activities in the light of our observations and recommendations about the engineering dimension.*

(b) Commitment to change

The innovative process

2.7 Continuous innovation has of necessity become a way of life for successful manufacturing companies to cope with the inherent obsolescence of products and production methods in a continually changing technological and market environment. Innovations to meet, or to anticipate, market changes can be grouped broadly under three headings:

—*incremental improvements* to existing products, production methods, and processes;

—*diversification, using existing expertise* and capabilities in different product markets; and

—*radical departure from previous activities,* based on the introduction of products or processes embodying novel applications of technology.

The appropriate innovative strategy will vary with the circumstances of companies and markets. While radical innovations are the most visible and can be lucrative if they are commercially successful, the great majority of engineering progress stems from incremental improvements. The UK has been relatively backward in this respect as compared to her major competitors and has suffered losses in world market shares in consequence.[1]

2.8 There is a direct link between companies' past levels of investment in product and process innovations and their present corporate capability to implement subsequent projects. Where an organisation has an established pattern of commitment to innovation, it can hope to attract and hold a cadre of high-level professional engineers and other technologists, many of whom penetrate the highest levels of management and colour attitudes at these levels to engineering and market changes. Conversely, organisations not sustaining their innovative capabilities are unlikely to attract or retain high-quality engineers to maintain an understanding of the engineering dimension within their top management counsels. Such companies will thus lack the 'corporate expertise' to anticipate and cater for the complex technical and resource implications of an innovative strategy and will consequently be less competent to identify and exploit new concepts in the market.

---

[1] Advisory Council for Applied Research and Development. 'Industrial Innovation', HMSO 1979

2.9 An innovative strategy will succeed only if account is taken of all its technical, financial and human implications, such as the relationship of costs between the conceptual, development and commissioning stages of a project and the likely 'learning curve' for bringing projects to their planned potential. Research and Development is only part of a company's innovative capability, albeit often representing the one prime source of companies' expertise and new thinking about products and production methods. It is at least as important however that adequate resources and attention are devoted to the design, prototype and manufacturing stages of new projects, at which the required levels of expenditure (and risk) are one or two orders of magnitude higher than for the initial research. Nor is Research and Development (R&D) necessarily the beginning of the innovative process. The specification of a technical response to astute appraisal of market opportunities has initiated many successful innovations. The criticisms often made of British R&D efforts—that marketable ideas are not seen through to commercial realisation, or that creative effort is dissipated on projects not adequately related to market requirements—reflect failures by industry to acknowledge the complexities of the innovative process and the magnitude of resource commitment required for successful exploitation of innovative ideas. They reflect also the frequent 'compartmentalisation' of R&D as a function apart from, and often geographically distant from, marketing and manufacturing functions rather than being—as would be preferable—integrated with them. Even the best integrated and balanced innovative schemes are by their nature risky, and for each success there will be tens or even hundreds of failures. This characteristic of innovation is frequently used as an argument *against* risking money on new projects. It should in fact be recognised as one for maintaining a wide portfolio of projects in the expectation that the rewards from the successful few will balance the cost of all the 'might-have-beens'.

2.10 OECD figures for industrial R&D spending among member countries show that between 1967 and 1975 UK expenditure in this category fell, that in Germany and Japan rose markedly and that in France rose slightly; (figures for the USA show a slight fall, mainly attributable to the run-down of the space programme). These movements are mainly due to relative changes in R&D expenditure by private industry, which rose in France, Germany and Japan but fell in Britain (offset in the UK partly by a rise in the level of Government-funded R&D).[1] Industrial R&D activity in the UK, and the technological expertise that goes with it, has become concentrated in those areas upon which public sector support has been focused. Thus 25 per cent of all UK R&D spending (and 49 per cent of that funded by Government) is directed towards defence work, including over half the national research and development effort in aerospace and electronics.[2] 'Glamour technologies' and prestigious projects, particularly in the aerospace, advanced telecommunications and nuclear power industries (all very heavily dependent upon Government contracts) claim more of UK spending than they contribute to national income. As a consequence of the Government-led concentration of R&D activity in

---

[1] 'Trends in Industrial R&D in Selected OECD Member Countries, 1967–75', OECD Directorate for Science, Technology and Industry 1979

[2] 'A defence for arms?' Engineering Today, 5 February 1979

27

certain sectors, proportionately less of the nation's engineering and technical capability is directed toward world commercial markets. While not wishing to see this Government interest reduced (indeed it must be more fully exploited by industry where it can be) we would welcome greater support of R&D in industry by industry since that is the environment which directly fosters the disciplines necessary to meet the vigorous competition of world markets. The UK pattern of R&D effort has been contrasted with the pattern in Japan, Germany and other industrial countries, which reflects more closely the relative contribution of each industrial sector to national value-added.[1]

2.11 Not surprisingly the uneven distribution of the national R&D 'cake' between manufacturing sectors is repeated at company level. In 1975 (the latest year for which figures are available) a total of £1·35bn was spent by private industry in the UK on R&D (mostly development).[2] However 91 per cent of this spending was concentrated in 100 companies and 52 per cent in just 10 companies (all in the aerospace, electronics and chemicals industries). The great majority of British companies are thus maintaining only a minimal level of innovative activity either because these companies do not recognise the value of development work, cannot afford it, or do not take advantage of the sources of technological intelligence open to them. More worrying still the situation has worsened, especially in those sectors which have lost world market shares and whose profits have been hardest squeezed. Since 1969, R&D spending in the mechanical engineering sector has fallen 23 per cent in real terms, while the level of spending in the electrical (including electronics) and motor vehicles sectors has fallen between 10 and 21 per cent. This contrasts with Japan, Germany and France where there have been marked increases in private funding. Nor have deficiencies of 'internal' new thinking and development within British companies been compensated by taking up others' ideas by the purchase of licences and patents, as it has been in Japan and Germany where industry has been assiduous in supplementing its own development work with technological innovation generated elsewhere.[3]

2.12 Thus it would appear that the capabilities of important sectors of British manufacturing industry for generating and transferring new technology within the engineering dimension, whether self-generated or obtained externally, has been seriously weakened. *Companies,* particularly those which cannot afford to maintain their own innovative capabilities, *should examine how to strengthen their access directly or indirectly to research developments from whatever source and large companies should use their capabilities not only to cater for their own innovative requirements but also to encourage innovation in smaller enterprises,* for example within supplying firms. We note that companies in the United States are obliged to publish in their annual reports a statement of their investment in their 'total technical effort'. The American requirement has the merit of forcing companies to an explicit review of these aspects of their activities and capabilities, and *we urge the Government to consider comparable requirements of UK companies.*

---

[1] Seventh Royal Society Technology Lecture—'Science, Technology and Industry', Sir Ieuan Maddock, 12 February 1975

[2] Business Monitor MO14: 1975: Industrial R&D Expenditure and Employment.

[3] See Table 3.7.

2.13 *Government should examine also how industrial enterprises might be encouraged to make better use of the resources and expertise of its several engineering Research Establishments and of publicly-funded research work undertaken in universities and other institutions.* This involves complex issues, since responsibility for the public funding of engineering research and development is divided among several Government departments and agencies. The area of engineering research seems to us better catered for than that of engineering development and applications, and we are attracted to the idea of an Engineering Development Council (on which are represented the Science Research Council, the Research Requirements Boards, and related bodies) to initiate and/or sponsor new products or systems in their development phase so that if successful at that stage they can be taken up by industry for immediate commercial exploitation. These prospects would be best agreed with committed firms since the sums involved at this prototype stage can be considerable. The Advisory Council on Applied Research and Development is concerned with drawing national attention to areas of technological development. *We recommend that they explore the need and possible mechanics for setting up such a Council, in conjunction with appropriate interested bodies.*

2.14 Successive Governments have intervened to encourage innovatory investment by companies and many schemes, involving a great deal of money, have been introduced to this end in recent years. However, the continuing weakness of manufacturing industry suggests that the effort has not been sufficient, or that it has not been directed to the right opportunities. There appears to us to be considerable scope for reducing the fragmentation and dissipation of effort among the various schemes to channel public funds into industrial regeneration, building the schemes into a coherent strategy based upon a common understanding of the engineering dimension and the several stages of the innovation process. In particular, Government support should be much more explicitly linked than currently seems apparent to assisting firms in bringing new developments and prototypes to realisation and launching them as commercial products or processes.

2.15 *We recommend that the Government reviews its machinery for encouraging innovation in British industry* in the light of the observations in the foregoing sections, drawing upon the advice given by the Advisory Council for Applied Research and Development in their report on 'Industrial Innovation',[1] and promoting these through the agency of the National Economic Development Council and its various sectoral committees. The possibility of substantially increasing present levels of financing in consequence of this review must not be precluded; the scale and urgency of the investments required are greater than manufacturing industry can fund itself, or than private investors currently seem prepared or able to finance.

Financing manufacturing innovation

2.16 The investment of human effort and expertise in engineering improvements and innovations requires the investment of money; financial factors

---

[1] Advisory Council for Applied Research and Development. 'Industrial Innovation', HMSO 1979

within the engineering dimension are thus as critical to the outcome as the technical expertise of engineers and managers. A characteristic of engineering-based innovation is that it requires high capital expenditure to execute and returns may not accrue until long after the initial investment; moreover, for every success there are many failures. In short, innovation requires companies to take expensive risks, included in which is the appraisal of world market reaction to the output. These company risks are exacerbated in the UK environment by frequent changes in government policies towards industry and in economic regulators (such as interest rates and credit regulations), inflation, currency fluctuations, labour disputes, and other features. There has in consequence arisen a deeprooted and widespread wariness towards taking such risks in many parts of British industry compounded by the opprobrium attached to business failure (not found in the USA, for example) and by a political and institutional framework conditioned to opposing change rather than sponsoring or supporting it.

2.17 The impact of finance on the behaviour of companies is so all-pervading that it is essential for financial policies to be promoting the desired market objectives. In Britain the priorities determining financial decisions seem often at odds with wider industrial priorities and this has led to a prevalence of short-term, risk-averse investment policies in many companies. Investment agencies such as Finance for Industry and its agency Technical Development Capital Limited have (with others) made a valuable contribution to steering venture capital into new manufacturing initiatives, as have some major British-based multinational companies and Government agencies such as the National Enterprise Board, the National Research Development Corporation, and the Scottish & Welsh Development Agencies. Despite these activities, national wealth is not going into industry in anything like the volume required to reverse its downward slide, and the founding of new high-risk technology-based enterprises has been virtually halted. *The Government should take every possible measure to foster a financial environment more conducive to investment in manufacturing industry, directing it towards designing, making and selling products that world markets want.*

2.18 A view of investment primarily in terms of the long-term benefits is practical only for companies able to keep going until innovative projects begin to pay returns. Heavy commitment of internal funds to long-term projects may render a company vulnerable in the short term. This appears to be a greater problem for British companies than for their competitors in Germany or Japan (and until recently the USA), where the financial environment for manufacturing industry seems quite different; in particular, there seems a much closer liaison and perceived unity of interest in these countries between the banking system, institutional investors and manufacturing enterprises, reflected in a greater willingness to commit adequate funds on 'patient' terms.[1]

2.19 A key factor may be the predominantly non-technical backgrounds from which senior decision-takers in British industry, finance and Government are drawn. Where decisions about risking money are dominated by people

---

[1] Yao-Su Hu, 'National Attitudes and the Financing of Industry' published by Political and Economic Planning (1975)

lacking in technological knowledge, they are likely to be weighted against taking chances on engineering-based projects, since those making the appraisal are inadequately equipped to assess them and therefore tend to place an extra-high risk-premium upon the expected returns. In doing this they are not wholly unjustified, as experiences following decisions taken only on grounds of technical advocacy rather than full commercial appraisal have occasionally shown. Nevertheless, investment policies informed by understanding of the engineering dimension will be less likely to incorporate an undue subjective bias against technological innovations, since they will take greater account of the implications for the company of arriving at a future date without having invested in updating current products and methods in response to market changes. This balance between what might be termed the 'financial' and the 'market' objectives of companies ideally requires that companies have high-calibre staff skilled both in technology and finance, or at least that individuals with the separate skills are brought together in the functions and counsels where their expertise can make its impact.

New technology and jobs

2.20 Antipathy to technology-based change and innovation comes also from company employees and their trades unions. In line with many other commentators, we found that the process of consultation, communication and acceptance of changes worked more effectively, and with far less friction, elsewhere than in Britain. Mutual assumptions of conflicting interests appear to underly communications between managements and workforce in many British companies: in particular, there seems to be an assumption by many on the shopfloor that innovation is essentially for the benefit of management and hence that at best it has little bearing upon the improvement of their own welfare or prosperity. Pride in the product being made, and appreciation of the need to make it better than that of competitors appears to have become subordinated to an uninterested attitude to the employing company as simply a source of weekly income. Consequently it is too frequently the case that changes in products, processes or methods can become the subject of heated bargaining over the immediate material incentives to be offered for the co-operation of those affected, frequently carrying delays in the implementation of changes, retention of obsolete plant and under-use of modern plant and equipment. Many companies and individual managers told us that their time was largely preoccupied with issues such as these. By contrast, on our overseas visits we gained the impression that changes to improve company competitiveness were viewed by employees as supporting the maintenance of real wage increases and were hence welcomed and even demanded.

2.21 Many explanations have been advanced for these differences in attitudes to technology-based change—the fragmentation of trade unions; the persistence of out-dated demarcation procedures; poor leadership and communication from management; the size of industrial units; and the lack of growth in the UK economy and consequent intensity of competition among different groups for shares of an almost static 'cake' of national added-value. Welcome recognition of the vital contribution of new technology to restoring growth in the economy, and thus to the prosperity of everyone in it, was

31

given in a recent TUC policy document (endorsed by the 1979 Congress) entitled 'Employment and Technology', which said that, for Britain to maintain its share of world trade:

'We must use to the full the skills and technological expertise of the workforce; we must increase the rate at which technological advances are adopted by industry.'

2.22 The pamphlet goes on to recommend, however, that trade union co-operation in technology-led changes should be conditional upon assurances regarding the future employment prospects of workers affected by the changes. This reflects the unions' concern at the displacement of jobs which can accompany the introduction of new technologies into products and manufacturing operations. Attempts to forestall the precipitation of unemployment by slowing or 'controlling' the introduction of industrial change are inimical to the protection of national prosperity and to the creation of new jobs. Moreover, those who would oppose manufacturing innovations in order to protect jobs in the short term take no account of the inevitable time when world market changes can no longer be ignored or fended off, and when 'protected' jobs will be lost with nothing to replace them.

2.23 It is not the case that there are a set number of jobs in the economy or that the introduction of new technology takes jobs away from a fixed pool. Innovative technology-based industries, especially those comprising small enterprises, have been the principal source of new jobs in the United States between 1950–78, both through direct employment and by raising the overall level of economic activity;[1] and firms 'committed to innovation as a way of life' have grown at seven times the national average rate in the USA over the past twenty years.[2] A recent study by the Central Policy Review Staff which considered the employment implications of the so-called 'microprocessor revolution' in Britain[3] found that the introduction of new technology had often freed the time of the people employed to concentrate on more rewarding and interesting work which had hitherto been neglected or subordinated to more pressing routine tasks, and that new technologies often generated needs for whole new areas of work. For example, the fastest-growing area of employment in recent years has been that of computer programmers, systems analysts and supporting staff, jobs almost unknown 20 years ago. It is growth in the number and diversity of new manufacturing enterprises to replace obsolete and declining industries which will provide extra jobs, and the need is to achieve this at least on the scale of those displaced in 'traditional' industries. In 1921 the UK economy sustained 16m in employment, with 3m unemployed; in 1978 26m were in employment and 1·5m unemployed. The pattern of industry in 1978 and the products on which it was based were totally different from those in 1921, and the new products

---

[1] 'The Role of High Technology Industries in Economic Growth', Data Resources Incorporated (1977), also 'The Job Generation Process', D Birch, Massachusetts Institute of Technology (1979)

[2] 'Technical Innovation, its Environment and Management', US Department of Commerce (1967)

[3] Central Policy Review Staff Survey Paper NEDC 78(73)—'Microelectronics: Challenge and Response', Memorandum by the Secretaries of State for Industry, Employment, and Education and Science, November 1978

and new technologies introduced in the intervening years—and the old ones disappearing—must be numbered in thousands. *Although we understand their real and valid concern for the immediate effects of technological changes on the jobs of their members, we hope that these considerations will lead the trade union movement to adopt an even more positive policy towards technology-based innovation in manufacturing and to encourage their members to support the introduction of innovations into industry and to participate in their operation.*

2.24 Problems arising from innovations which displace existing jobs can be eased in a number of ways. Some large employing organisations, particularly the nationalised coal and steel industries, have been able to attract and assist new enterprises to employ workers displaced by rationalisation of modernisation measures; others have been able to diversify into new activities employing the skills of displaced workers. A few companies hold close to the Japanese philosophy of 'employment for life' and have accepted responsibility, in co-operation with the unions, for retraining and redeploying displaced workers. Even within such programmes, the new job opportunities created by innovations will, almost by definition, require new skills. It is also likely that many of the new jobs will occur outside manufacturing industry, although they will largely depend upon the wealth created in that sector. *There is clearly a need for a massive programme planned to educate and retrain employees of all ages and all levels if the human skills and support required to implement and sustain new technologies are to match demands for them.* Government and industry must treat this as a common concern and on a scale commensurate with the rate of change involved in regenerating and sustaining British manufacturing industry.

Standards in competitiveness

2.25 A potentially powerful vehicle for raising industry's awareness of the current requirements of world markets and for spreading good practice in specific fields is the setting of technical standards and codes of engineering practice. This vehicle is one which has been used to great effect in some other countries as part of their policies to increase their share of world markets —for example, as it was employed to raise the quality of Japanese exports of manufactures—or alternatively to minimise import penetration into their home markets by imposing high standards which foreign producers have difficulty meeting. The principal, but not the only, body for establishing engineering standards in this country has been the British Standards Institution. The impact of such standards was examined for NEDO by Sir Fred Warner, who found that in many instances manufacturing companies were hindered from producing standardised, internationally-competitive products by the plethora of rival domestic and international technical standards. In particular the Warner Report suggested that the potential for using national standards to propagate best practice in specific areas of engineering and to relate domestic standards to international market needs was hardly tapped.

2.26 We saw in Canada and in West Germany that the professional engineering Institutions were very active in drawing up and disseminating codes of engineering practice covering a very wide range of activities. The UK Institutions (with one or two exceptions) do relatively little in their own right that is comparable, although their members are often the mainstay of BSI Committees. Proposals were mooted by the last Government aimed to exploit the potential for using the machinery of national standards and codes of practice to raise the quality and hence the competitiveness of British manufactured products. We are convinced that a strategy to this end is necessary for the UK to overhaul existing methods of defining and using standards to make a more positive contribution to the rejuvenation of industry. *We recommend that the machinery of the National Economic Development Council and that of the new Engineering Authority which we propose be used to bring together the relevant official bodies, institutions and industrial sectors to develop a national policy for standards and quality, using the Warner Report as a starting point.*[1]

(c)   Establishing engineering priorities

'Awareness brokers'

2.27   It is often said that efforts to regenerate British manufacturing have been constrained by the lack of a national framework or strategy to provide coherence and consistency in policy-making. Some other countries have been able to develop and implement effective national product and market plans for industrial growth, notably Japan, with France also an impressive exponent. For example, the Japanese Council for Science and Technology, chaired by their Prime Minister and representing industry, government, finance and education, formulates a rolling five-year programme of market and technological priorities for the Japanese economy, to which the efforts of all the represented parties are then geared. This machinery is used to ensure that Government-sponsored R&D programmes and other direct assistance to industry, together with private investment by major companies and financial institutions and associated educational policies are related to the same shared world market objectives.[2] There is at present no single acknowledged body in this country geared to identifying such priority areas from within all the alternatives to which companies might respond.

2.28   We have noted the arguments favouring an exercise in Britain to identify the sectors of manufacturing activity offering the best prospects for growth and to direct national energies and resources towards those sectors in the expectation that growth in these would generate growth in the rest of the economy. The effective industrial decisions in this country are taken at company level, and we do not advocate machinery to centralise those decisions. There is a strong case, however, for better machinery to identify national priorities and to inform companies and industry sectors about changes relevant to the engineering dimension, to establish criteria for decision-taking in the context of world markets and to assess the market potential for their technology and new industries.

2.29   To keep up with the volume and diversity of technical and market information available nowadays there has been growth in what might be termed 'awareness brokers'—private and Government-funded bodies working

---

[1] See also 5.40

[2] See Appendix E Overseas Visits

to disseminate information from particular markets or technical areas and disseminate it to clients for whom the information may be considered relevant. Examples of such 'brokers' in the private sector are the many trade-based Research Associations and the various professional technological and engineering institutions. Government-funded activities in this area include the work of the Export Intelligence Service, the Overseas Technical Information Unit, the Committee for Industrial Technologies, the Department of Industry's Microprocessor Applications Project and Manufacturing Advisory Service, and bodies such as the National Research Development Corporation, the Advisory Council for Applied Research and Development and the Design Council. Our discussions with companies have led us to conclude that current proliferation of 'awareness' programmes has lacked impact through a combination of sheer volume, fragmentation, lack of relevance, and basic indifference from industrial recipients. Much valid and potentially valuable work is therefore going to waste which could be built upon were 'awareness' efforts concentrated in priority areas. Machinery to help companies, investors, unions and Government jointly to indentify the most important market changes would fill a valuable, and currently lacking, role. The basis for such machinery exists already in the National Economic Development Council (NEDC), its Office (NEDO) and its Sector Working Parties (SWPs) and Economic Development Committees (EDCs).

An enhanced role for NEDC

2.30 Hitherto, the NEDC and the various SWPs and EDCs have functioned primarily as tripartite fora in which Government, employers and unions could meet to discuss their interests in long-term economic and industrial trends. On the basis of these discussions a number of valuable studies and initiatives have been taken, particularly towards mutual co-operation between companies within particular industries or across related sectors. *However, we suggest that much more effective use could be made of the NEDC machinery were it to be used to establish greater interchange of information about the impact of technological and market changes and the appropriate responses to them from the level of companies to Government and back and through which enhanced mutual understanding and consensus of objectives and policy priorities might emerge.*

2.31 This would entail a shift of emphasis, rather than a radical new departure, for NEDC, and would provide a basis for following up and building upon the work done by some Sector Working Parties, injecting into it the lessons from a number of joint industry-Government exercises such as:

—the Corfield Report on 'Design in Manufacturing Industry', which reviewed the place of the design function in the engineering dimension;
—the Warner Report on 'Engineering Standards and Specifications', which looked at the relationship between technical standards and international competitiveness;
—the work being done by some SWPs to develop closer liaison between UK purchasing and supplying industries, coupled with greater attention to the potential role of Government and public sector procurement for propagating best design and production practices;
—the DOI Microprocessor Applications Project, and the related ACARD report on solid-state technologies;

—the work of the Advisory Council on Energy Conservation (ACEC) and several Department of Energy bodies, and the work and reports of the Watt Committee on Energy;

—the work done by the Committee for Industrial Technologies in highlighting the importance for manufacturing of corrosion control, tribology, materials handling and terotechnology; and

—work done in the Department of Employment's Work Research Unit on the management of technical and human resources to improve productivity and the quality of working life.

2.32 A coherent programme of priorities is needed for actions at national, sectoral and company level geared towards enchancing industry's engineering and market performance. The NEDC and its Office would not be expected to lay down this programme, but rather to adopt the role of catalysts in the process of communication and consensus between Government, industrial companies, the unions and other involved institutions. In this role NEDC and the Office would work very closely with the new Engineering Authority which we propose should be established to maintain a national oversight of British capabilities in the engineering dimension and to propose action to forestall or remedy hindrances to optimal performance. *We recommend the implementation of changes in the organisation of the NEDC machinery to further this role, in particular:*

(*a*) the economic and industrial expertise of the NEDO Office should be augmented with staff who can contribute the required engineering and technological expertise and also generate understanding of the engineering dimension within the Office;

(*b*) a member or members of Council should be nominated with a brief to lead debates and policy deliberations on engineering and industrial innovation;

(*c*) special attention should be given to making the NEDC framework more sensitive to the need to create new industries, often outside the scope of existing SWPs and EDCs, and to propose actions to foster their growth; close links with engineers and engineering developments via the Engineering Authority will be essential to this task.

(d) Managing companies' response to change

Engineering in manufacturing management

2.33 While there are of course many competent and creative engineers working in British industry today, too few—compared with other professional groups—have risen to the top to be 'visible' to the young person making career choices. It was made clear to us on our visits to British companies that there is a felt shortage of able engineers with the personal drive and flair required for the leadership of manufacturing enterprises. Industrial leaders have more often trained in finance and general administration than in engineering and the values and priorities of these backgrounds have thus set the tenor of the British management culture.

36

This lack of technological understanding among top managements has affected the capability of many companies to devise and implement technology-based responses to market changes. A senior and middle management cadre ill-equipped to understand engineering issues is likely to regard them as 'mere technicalities', separate and generally subordinate to the issues of general management, and hence to regard engineers as purveyors of technical services. These notions are reinforced (and justified) if engineers themselves are narrowly educated and lack the wider perspectives and personal skills required to contribute to a range of functions. The consequences are uncompetitive products designed without sufficient reference to market requirements, and inefficient production methods developed with insufficient professional attention to design, specification or operation. Managers who are not trained to recognise these deficiencies will look elsewhere for solutions to the problems they generate—to little avail.

2.34 The failure to recognise and appreciate the value of engineering expertise among British managers has, in the opinion of many commentators, led to an approach to manufacturing significantly different from that adopted by their German, French and Japanese counterparts.[1] This difference was usually described to us in terms of foreign managers' closer identification with the products of the enterprise. By deriving authority from greater understanding of the shared tasks of producing and selling competitively well-engineered goods—as opposed to reliance upon hierarchical seniority and custody of a 'managerial tabernacle'—foreign managers are considered to maintain an inherently better and generally more effective relationship with those under their leadership than do their British equivalents. While this is a subjective judgement, we were impressed with the frequency with which similar observations were made to us by industrialists in other countries with experience of British industry and by others who have studied international management styles.

2.35 It was our experience from visits to a number of innovative and successful companies in Britain and overseas that the impetus for change and progress frequently came from one charismatic individual at or near the top of the organisation. Our findings accord with those of the Centre for the Study of Industrial Innovation at Sussex University;[2] they investigated the process of innovation in a number of manufacturing countries around the world, and found that in the majority of instances an individual 'product champion', almost always an engineer, had provided much of the motive force

---

[1] Alistair Mant: Authority and Task in Manufacturing Operations of Multinational Firms, Study for Department of Industry (1977)
Ian Glover: Evidence to CIEP
Correlli Barnett: Evidence to CIEP and 'Technology, Education and Industrial and Economic Strength', Royal Society of Arts Cantor Lecture, November 1978
Peter Lawrence: Engineers, Management and Status: Comparison between Germany and Britain, study for Department of Industry (1978)
Papers on 'Product Innovation—A Corporate Responsibility' presented at The International Design Engineering Conference, October 1979

[2] 'Success and Failure in Industrial Innovation: Report on Project Sappho', Centre for Study of Industrial Innovation (1972)

for particular innovations. Similar conclusions were reached in a study of innovation in the engineering industry for the Engineering Industry Training Board,[1] which commented:

'The impression was frequently given that new techniques were unused, not because they were inapplicable to the firm concerned, but because senior staff in the firm lacked the necessary knowledge to implement the innovations. The converse was also true. In many cases (in both large and small firms) almost the only factor that distinguished firms using a new technique from those not doing so was the existence in the "innovative" firm of one or two key individuals who had the necessary expertise.'

2.36 A clear perception and understanding of the nature of the engineering dimension and its central place in the fortunes of the enterprise should lead managements to create and develop a supply of able people with a range of skills built upon engineering expertise, who can fill responsible posts in technical functions and also provide a source of technologically knowledgeable managers and future leaders, and to make the fullest use of the contributions made by those people. This structural principle obtains for manufacturing enterprises throughout the world but, with her critical dependence on successful and efficient manufacturing, neglect of the above studies can be afforded less in Britain than elsewhere.

Organising the engineering dimension

2.37 We found little evidence that managers in this country attach sufficient importance to the role of organisational considerations in improving their companies' market responsiveness. Manufacturing is a complex, multi-disciplinary activity, which depends for success upon the balancing of specialist contributions and their co-ordination to satisfy constantly changing market demands. The response of many British companies to these demands is handicapped by lack of an adequate engineering input to marketing and business planning activities and by lack of sufficient market input to engineering activities. Achieving a balance between these and encouraging the exercise of personal initiatives within structured activities must be considered among the most important and most difficult tasks for manufacturing management in Britain. The engineering dimension provides the key to achieving the reconciliation.

2.38 Rapid changes in market needs and in the technology available for meeting them demand a flexible and rapid responsiveness from companies. Recognition of the engineering dimension provides a unifying theme for management to ensure that the contributions of engineers and managers in research, design, development and production functions are effectively integrated to provide that response and are directly related to the company's market strategy. This integration appears to be missing in many companies, in which the efficacy of the engineering dimension has been limited by the 'compartmentalisation' of activities—for example, research conducted with little or no assessment of market needs or products designed with insufficient attention to the demands of production. The functional interfaces in a company are

---

[1] Engineering Industry Training Board: 'Changing Technology and Manpower Requirements in the Engineering Industry', Research Report No 3

critical in disseminating information and know-how between functions and in assimilating that information into co-ordinated activities.[1] Although the essence of the engineering dimension is that the contributions of engineers and engineering be geared to meeting the market objectives of the organisation, engineering and marketing responsibilities are often separated within British companies. An Institute of Marketing survey[2] found that marketing was perceived as synonymous with selling in most companies and that many managements did not stand back from their day-to-day activities to relate the directions that the technology of their products and the market demand for them were taking. Other commentators have observed retrograde effects following the establishment of separate marketing departments within companies when those in technical and line functions have taken this as a cue to abrogate their own responsibility for relating their work to the company's market strategy.

2.39 The compartmentalisation of functional responsibilities was much less apparent in those companies we visited—some in this country but more often abroad—in which the activities of all technical staff were focussed upon the need to ensure that the company's products met the demands—actual and latent— of world markets. Those requirements cut across and meld the functional interfaces within such companies, with the engineering dimension as their unifying theme. Employers we visited in other countries used a variety of methods to develop a wider market awareness and the requisite skills in their engineers, through structuring of their work experience and through the expectations expressed by the employers. It was common in Japan, for example, for novice engineers to spend as much as a year in sales or marketing operations before they began working in research or production functions. In other countries we found the work of engineers in technical functions was consciously integrated into the enterprise, for example by making development engineers responsible for their own financial monitoring or by putting research engineers in direct contact with the customers. Such flexibility in the deployment of engineers requires that the engineers concerned are equipped for wider 'non-technical' responsibilities and most employers believed that these wider skills were generally acquired most effectively 'on-the-job'.

2.40 We encountered a wide variety of organisational innovations designed to co-ordinate and integrate contributions from engineers and other functions in the company. A common feature was a belief that the traditional hierarchical and compartmentalised organisations of companies was no longer appropriate for meeting market changes and other approaches to innovative activities in manufacturing were needed. Various 'organic' types of team groupings have taken the place of conventional organisational structures: for example, in the United States and Sweden much attention is being devoted to mixed-discipline project teams. Although we saw less outward sign in Japan that the hierarchical organisation of work was changing, the cultural foundations of existing hierarchies, based on consultation and committed involvement at all

---

[1] 'British Managers in the Mirror', HL Hansen, published by Binder, Hamlyn, Fry and Co (1974)

[2] Institute of Marketing: Informal Survey of British Industry submitted with evidence to CIEP

levels, make them more responsive in practice than on paper. Nonetheless, some industrialists and educators in Japan are currently exploring organisational methods to engender greater individual and collective creativity among engineers within industry[1], as are some progressive and successful companies in this country.[2]

2.41 One particular organisational feature of the companies we visited in Germany, Japan and the USA was the degree to which working procedures were systematised, formalised and written down—from the initial examination of potential markets right down to the way each operator did his job. The companies concerned placed great importance on these systems, which they considered gave line managers much greater control over such matters as product quality and work flow and also encouraged creativity by providing clearly defined and stable systems within which personal initiatives could be directed at new problems rather than on 're-inventing wheels'. This approach to work organisation may not accord with the British industrial culture, which has traditionally emphasised personal freedom and initiative at all levels. Nevertheless, a number of foreign-based manufacturers have successfully introduced more structured systems into their UK operations and have thereby achieved levels of productivity and quality control comparable to those in their home establishments and higher than UK norms.

2.42 Engineers have a potentially profound influence on the productive efficiency of the manufacturing system and on the quality of working life for a large number of employees. The work of engineers whether in new projects where fundamental changes in the organisation of work are to be made, or in seeking operational improvements to existing systems, has direct and indirect effects on the tasks of other workers in the enterprise, the jobs and systems of which those tasks form a part and the total organisation of work. Engineers must therefore be concerned not merely with technically optimal solutions and systems but with the human and organisational factors involved in the operation of the system in reality and with the process of change by which such innovations are brought about.

2.43 Engineers therefore must expect to find themselves taking part in, and responding to a more participative process of change, through joint discussions of their work and its impact and effects at many levels with workers and their representatives as well as with fellow engineers and managers. This wider role will require that engineers develop appropriate skills in the following areas.

---

[1] See Appendix E, Overseas Visits

[2] Alistair Mant: Authority and Task in Manufacturing Operations of Multinational Firms, Study for Department of Industry (1977)
Ian Glover: Evidence to CIEP
Correlli Barnett: Evidence to CIEP and 'Technology, Education and Industrial and Economic Strength', Royal Society of Arts Cantor Lecture, November 1978
Peter Lawrence: Engineers, Management and Status: Comparison between Germany and Britain, study for Department of Industry (1978)
Papers on 'Product Innovation—A Corporate Responsibility' presented at The International Design Engineering Conference, October 1979

—the ability to express and communicate both verbally and in writing;
—managing and participating in meetings in which engineering expertise is one of the elements contributing to decisions; and
—mastery of cost and budget information.

It is our impression (backed by a good deal of evidence from overseas visits) that engineers in other countries such as Sweden, Japan, and the USA are better prepared by their total career experience in engineering and management to operate effectively in these broader areas within the engineering dimension than are their British counterparts.

(e) Summary of main conclusions and recommendations

2.44 (i) Low and declining profitability among British manufacturing companies have progressively weakened their capacity to respond to changing world markets. Reversal of this trend demands a coherent unity of efforts among all those concerned with the regeneration of British industry—in companies, Government, trade unions, and in the educational and financial sectors—built upon a shared recognition, understanding and commitment to the engineering dimension. There are few signs of this at present among many if not most of those involved with manufacturing industry in the UK, or among the general public. In consequence the engineering dimension has been neglected and starved of talent and resources.

(ii) It is clear that, unlike their counterparts in other industrial countries, engineers in Britain lack the special social standing which attracts young people to aspire to an engineering career, and that they are ill-served by a generic title which in Britain is not specifically associated with and reserved to a highly educated and vital professional group. Engineering is further regarded misleadingly as a branch of science, rather than as a culture and activity in its own right. Improved standing for engineers and greater attractiveness for careers among their ranks must be sought through fostering enhanced recognition of the nature and importance of engineering within the British economy.

(iii) Technological and market changes demand continual innovations in both products and processes. Although Britain is a nation rich in creative talent it has been weak in the commercial realisation of its own engineering-based innovations or in the adoption of innovations originating elsewhere. *We recommend* that Government and individual manufacturing companies, jointly and in collaboration, review their policies and activities for stimulating engineering-led changes in industry, seeking to ensure that these are understood and seen through as related and interdependent stages in the innovative process. In particular we recommend (*a*) Companies should examine how to strengthen their access directly or indirectly to research developments from whatever source, large companies using their capabilities not only to cater for their own innovative requirements but also to encourage innovation in small

41

enterprises; (*b*) Government should consider imposing requirements upon companies regarding the publication of information about their 'total technical efforts' similar to those required in the United States; (*c*) Government should examine how industrial enterprises might be encouraged to make better use of the resources and expertise of its several engineering Research Establishments and of public funded research.

(iv) Companies must overcome the antipathy which many have shown towards investing in new technology to improve their productivity and profitability through the adoption of current technology and by encouraging a balanced appreciation of the 'opportunity cost' consequences of *not* investing in the engineering dimension for the future. The Government must endeavour to create a financial environment more supportive of companies' efforts in this respect.

(v) Only an attitude of total and sustained commitment to market-oriented innovation on the part of all those involved in industry can bring about a revival in our national economic fortunes. In particular, the all-too-frequently demonstrated resistance to such changes from employees and trade unions has handicapped industry. The unions' valid concern over prospects of disrupted or displaced jobs must be tempered with recognition that the likelihood of mass unemployment is greater from industries *not* innovating than from their doing so. At the same time, employers and Government have a responsibility to minimise the effects of the personal disruption and displacement which can accompany industrial innovations, particularly by retraining people for new areas of work.

(vi) Efforts to regenerate UK manufacturing have, in the view of many, been constrained in the past by the lack of a national framework within which priorities and strategies for meeting market changes can be determined. *We recommend* that the machinery of the National Economic Development Council be re-oriented and modified to establish greater interchange of information about the impact of technological and market changes and the appropriate responses to them, from the level of companies to Government and back; through such means an enhanced mutual understanding and consensus over objectives and policy priorities might emerge which will contribute towards the required greater coherence of actions on different policy fronts.

(vii) Innovation is a way of life in successful companies, for which it is essential that they have both the leaders and the 'corporate expertise' to sustain continual change. It is the responsibility of companies to develop engineers with the personal capabilities and experience to lead and assume responsibility at a strategic corporate level. The skills of general management and leadership must be grafted on to the skills and experience derived from considerable knowledge and identification with the product existing or

42

emerging. Companies should endeavour to foster the rise of 'product champions' and to develop a corporate capability of innovative individuals identified with and dedicated to relating a particular product and its production techniques to its specific market.

(viii) Product knowledge, however, is only one of the bases of a successful engineering dimension. Companies geared around the needs of the engineering dimension overcome the compartmentalisation of function and experience which hinders the necessary integration of marketing and production in many other organisations. Firms must endeavour to overcome the widespread 'not invented here' mentality by such measures as ensuring that their engineers obtain a breadth of experience and outlook, appropriate utilisation of outside technical information services and fully utilising 'awareness brokers' in industry, Government-sponsored organisations and the academic world.

(ix) Companies with a strong engineering dimension tend to have an innovative and flexible approach to organisation structures as vehicles for achieving the most appropriate fit between the available human and other resources and the process of converting raw materials via manufacturing to finished products for the market. As production factors and market needs change so too must the organisational structure for attaining the goals of the enterprise. Companies which effectively recognise the systems nature of the engineering dimension demonstrate a sensitivity and alertness to the need for balancing technological and market changes with complementary changes in organisation not shown by the majority of UK companies. This is achieved in some instances by a formalisation of procedures which clarifies and makes more widely accessible the operating system of the enterprise.

CHAPTER III

The Supply, Demand and Deployment of Engineers

(a) The current stock and future supply of engineers

Introduction

3.1 Our terms of reference required us to consider the requirements of industry for engineers, the extent to which these needs were being met and the use made of engineers by industry. Before addressing these questions we must distinguish statements about *needs* from those about *demand*. Employers' demands for engineers refer to their stated requirements to fill identified jobs, either existing or to be created. They are thus more specific—though not always more reliable—than statements about industry's needs, which usually refer to judgements about the numbers of engineers required to achieve corporate national goals. It is thus not incongruous to suggest that, ' . . . in the light of national economic needs', some organisations might need more engineers than they currently demand, while questioning whether other employers are not demanding more engineers than a wider view would suggest they need. With these points in mind we considered the numbers, distribution and qualifications of the current stock and supply of engineers against employers' demands and against national needs regarding the engineering dimension.

The current stock

3.2 Many of the submissions to us jumped from recognition of current weaknesses in manufacturing to prescriptions for improving the future supply of engineers, mostly by means of actions to be taken within the educational system. While we agree that such measures are required, changes aimed at improving the future output of the educational system cannot have any significant impact upon manufacturing performance within a decade or even longer. It is therefore essential that at least as much attention is paid to enhancing the effectiveness of the contribution made by the *existing* stock of engineers as to improving the future supply. If Britain is to remain among the advanced economies the timescale within which manufacturing performance must be radically improved is to be measured in years, not decades. Long-term improvements in the supply of engineers will be to no avail—indeed may not occur—unless the contributions of the current stock of engineers are harnessed to greater effect than hitherto. The pattern set through the employment of the current stock is a key determinant of the numbers and quality of future entrants to engineering. Manufacturing employers are in competition for the services of engineers with many others within and outside industry in this country and abroad. It is vital that they attract and keep a high proportion of the stock of engineers to further the engineering dimension.

44

3.3 There are no comprehensive and up-to-date data on the numbers and distribution of engineers in this country. The last Census of Population was taken in 1971. Table 3.1 summarises the 1971 Census data for engineers and for comparison also shows the numbers and distribution of scientists.

Table 3.1. Engineers and scientists in employment—UK
1971 Census

| Industrial Classification* | ENGINEERS | | | | SCIENTISTS | | | |
| | 1st degree and equivalent or above | | HNC/HND etc | | 1st degree and equivalent or above | | HNC/HND etc | |
	(000's)	(%)	(000's)	(%)	(000's)	(%)	(000's)	(%)
Agriculture, forestry and fishing	0·68	0·3	0·36	0·2	0·60	0·4	0·05	0·2
Mining and quarrying	3·94	1·6	5·46	2·8	0·70	0·5	0·14	0·7
Manufacturing	92·86	38·9	100·92	51·3	44·46	29·9	10·99	53·7
Construction	22·73	9·5	21·39	10·9	0·68	0·5	0·04	0·2
Utilities	14·59	6·1	11·22	5·7	2·13	1·4	0·82	4·0
Transport, communication and distributive trades	12·92	5·4	11·47	5·8	4·70	3·2	0·82	4·0
Insurance, banking, finance and business services	9·24	3·9	3·24	1·6	5·23	3·5	0·26	1·3
Professional and scientific services (including education)	49·61	20·8	23·39	11·9	78·06	52·6	5·64	27·6
Miscellaneous services	4·22	1·8	3·40	1·7	2·40	1·6	0·31	1·5
Public administration and defence	27·02	11·3	15·34	7·8	8·51	5·7	1·28	6·3
Industry inadequately described or work places outside UK	0·94	0·4	0·57	0·3	1·05	0·7	0·10	0·5
Total	238·75	100·0	196·76	100·0	148·53	100·0	20·46	100·0

* As defined in the Central Statistical Office publication 'Standard Industrial Classification'. HMSO (1968)

The table shows that in 1971 there were 238·8 thousand people in employment with qualifications in engineering or technology to degree level or higher, and another 196·8 thousand with HNC/D in similar disciplines. More people in each category were employed in manufacturing than in any other sector. The differences between the patterns of employment for graduates and 'Higher National' holders should be noted; over half of the stock of HNC/D holders, but under 40 per cent of graduates, were in manufacturing in 1971. Another 21 per cent of engineering and technology graduates, compared with 53 per cent of the science graduates, were employed in 'professional and scientific services' (engineers mainly in higher and further education but many of the scientists also in schools) and 11 per cent in public administration and defence (compared with 6 per cent of scientists).

3.4 Since no intercensal survey was taken in 1976, it will not be possible to ascertain accurately, what changes have occurred since 1971 in the numbers and distribution of engineers until the results of the 1981 Census are available. Such data as have been collected, for example by the engineering Institutions or the Engineering Industry Training Board, are variously partial in scope. Data from employers is not collected on a national basis, and what is available is of variable quality. The Council of Engineering Institutions (CEI) undertakes a biennial survey of those engineers registered with the Engineers' Registration Board, of whom there were 195,500 Chartered Engineers and 51,400 Technician Engineers in September 1979. The CEI survey and those conducted by other Institutions are not based on random sampling, and exclude the many practising engineers who are not registered with them. We consider the lack of adequate information about the numbers and distribution of engineers employed in the UK economy a serious deficiency in view of its importance to the efforts of employers, educators and Government to match national supply and demands for this crucial group of manpower.

3.5 There should ideally be a continuing national inventory of engineering manpower, which would monitor changes in the numbers and distribution of the stock of engineers and related manpower and also the flow of new recruits into engineering employment. We accept that such an exercise mounted in isolation from other population surveys might be considered prohibitively expensive of time and money. As a minimum measure, *we therefore recommend that all future official surveys be structured to collect the information which would permit such an inventory to be built up.* This would apply to the 10-yearly Census of Population, to intercensal surveys undertaken by the Office of Population Censuses and Surveys and to other exercises such as the regular EEC Labour Force Survey. This inventory would not of itself bring about a closer alignment of actual with 'desirable' distributions of engineers, but would—in conjunction with the changes at the company level we shall recommend later—give employers a clearer picture of the supply of engineers against which they could frame their recruitment and salary policies. Responsibility for maintaining this inventory and for proposing policy initiatives in its light should lie with the proposed new Engineering Authority, working in close collaboration with the Office of Population Censuses and Surveys and other official bodies such as the Manpower Services Commission.

Movement within and out of engineering

3.6 Our surveys of engineers[1,2] showed at the time of the survey a high degree of individual mobility in those aged under 30 between employers, between functions and between engineering and non-engineering occupations. Although much of this movement is two-way there is a clear trend for engineers, as they get older, to move away from the design and specification

---

[1] Policy Studies Institute: A General Survey of Professional Engineers.

[2] Policy Studies Institute: A Survey of Former Students of Engineering and Science.

46

work in which many begin their careers into more general management or other 'outside' work. It emerged from replies to our survey that many young engineers currently employed in primarily technical functions foresaw themselves progressing in their careers in posts in which they would not directly be applying their engineering knowledge. A review of career patterns confirmed a small but steady shift from engineering practice, mostly into management and teaching positions. To this outflow must be added losses due to retirement and other reasons. A steady supply of new entrants to the current stock is thus required simply to maintain the present numbers in engineering practice.

3.7 The Census data show that people initially qualified as engineers are to be found working in almost every sector of the economy, both as engineers and in many other roles. We undertook a survey of 500 (self-classified and self-selected) ex-engineers to ascertain whether there are significant differences between the experiences of those working as engineers and those who have 'lapsed' from their original discipline. Few additional general conclusions (to those from the main surveys[1-2]) can be drawn from this survey, but it did emerge that most respondents were graduates, and that they tended to earn rather more than graduates of similar age still employed in engineering practice. Many of the respondents were critical of their earlier experiences in engineering practice in terms of job satisfaction, status and pay; a number said that they had left engineering jobs because they positively disliked engineering. The survey of 'lapsed' engineers served primarily to confirm something we found already well acknowledged in other countries, that an engineering background provides an excellent basis for a wide variety of rewarding career opportunities in the modern economy. This factor has important implications both for the future supply of engineers, who need not feel that they are prepared only for a technical career, and also for employers, both in the private and public sectors, seeking to recruit from that supply who should consider engineers for a whole range of technical and non-technical posts.

The supply of new engineers

3.8 Until the last 10–15 years the majority of UK engineers qualified through the so-called 'part-time' route, studying while they were fully employed—usually within manufacturing industry—for Institutional or exempting examinations. A small minority of these completed their academic formation with a degree. The expansion in numbers entering full-time higher education during the 1960s resulted in a sharp diminution of the numbers coming through this part-time route and most engineers now come through full-time degree courses at universities or polytechnics, as has long been the case in other industrial countries.

3.9 Figure 3.1 illustrates the shift in routes to academic qualification, with an increasing majority of young engineers with degrees and most of those engineers now aged over 40 having come through a 'part-time' formation.

---

[1] Policy Studies Institute: 'A General Survey of Professional Engineers.'
[2] Policy Studies Institute: 'A Survey of Former Students of Engineering and Science.'

Figure 3.1. Routes to academic qualification

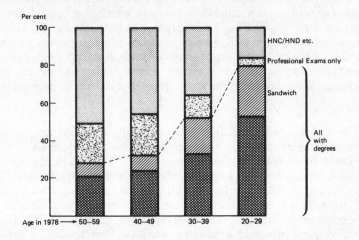

Source: PSI Survey

3.10 Table 3.2 shows the numbers emerging from the graduate route since 1969.

Table 3.2   Engineering and Technology:* 1st Degrees Awarded:† UK

		Universities			Total
	Males (000's)	Females (000's)	Total (000's)	CNAA‡ (000's)	(000's)
1968–69	6·6	0·1	6·7	1·0	7·7
1969–70	7·2	0·1	7·3	1·2	8·5
1970–71	7·5	0·1	7·5	1·7	9·2
1971–72	7·5	0·1	7·6	1·8	9·4
1973	7·3	0·1	7·4	2·0	9·4
1974	7·4	0·2	7·6	2·0	9·6
1975	7·2	0·2	7·4	2·2	9·6
1976	6·8	0·2	7·0	2·1	9·1
1977	7·2	0·3	7·4	2·4	9·8
1978	7·7◄	0·3◄	8·0◄	2·8	10·8◄

* The figures given are from published sources. They do not match those for 'Group III' in DES Statistics (which cover all Engineering and Technology) because surveying and certain technologies outside the direct remit of the Committee (amounting to 0·7 thousands for Universities and 0·7 thousands for CNAA in 1978) have been excluded.

† To Home and Overseas Students.

‡ The number of women obtaining these CNAA degrees is very small (about 50 in 1978).

◄ Estimates.

48

In 1978 about 11,000 students graduated in engineering and technology from UK universities, polytechnics and colleges, representing an increase over previous years (with a higher proportionate increase in CNAA awards). The proportion of all home graduates who have followed an engineering-based course has in fact declined since 1972 (reflecting the rising number of girls in higher education and the increasing proportion of all students following newer degree courses in social, administrative and business studies).

As Table 3.3 shows, the 'part-time' route culminating in Higher National awards is still important, catering for over 7,000 people each year and a further 4,000 with full Technological Certificates.

Table 3.3   Engineering & Technology—Other qualifications Awarded UK

	HNC (000's)	HND (000's)		Full Technological Certificate (000's)
			1968/69	4·2
1969	8·3	2·2		
			1969/70	4·7
1970	7·4	2·5		
			1970/71	4·8
1971	7·0	2·8		
			1971/72	5·3
1972	6·5	2·5		
			1972/73	6·2
1973	6·0	2·1		
			1973/74	5·0
1974	5·8	2·0		
			1974/75	5·4
1975	5·5	1·7		
			1975/76	5·0
1976	5·5	1·7		
			1976/77	4·8
1977*	5·6	1·7		
			1977/78	4·0
1978*	5·7	1·8		

* Estimates.

This table covers subjects approximately within CIEP remit.

TEC: No higher awards yet made.

Source: DES: Education Statistics of the UK; City & Guilds of London Institute.

3.11 These changes have brought with them major implications for the supply of new engineers which have entailed important adjustments—not yet fully assimilated—by employers. In particular, from a situation in which entry to a 'part-time' engineering formation in a manufacturing company direct from school was a natural progression for a significant proportion of able young men, their modern counterparts have the following options at these stages:

(a) to continue their full-time education after school;

(b) to study a whole range of subjects other than engineering; and

(c) to enter a wide range of attractive engineering or non-engineering careers from an engineering degree.

49

Engineering must now compete for its recruits by attracting them to undergo an engineering formation rather than follow another option and then to enter manufacturing rather than another sector.

3.12 Since the supply of engineers now comes predominantly through degree courses at universities or polytechnics, there are more critical decision 'gateways' affecting the supply of potential and actual recruits to engineering than in the past. The first decisions determining whether a young man or woman will become an engineer are effectively made while he or she is at school. It first requires a decision from the pupil (and his or her parents) to remain in education long enough to take A-level or other entrance examinations. In this respect we regret that proposals to provide financial incentives to staying on at school to 18 have not been implemented. For those pupils who do stay in education after 16, it requires that they take an appropriate mix of examination subjects. Entrance to an engineering degree course normally requires that candidates have passes in both mathematics and physics at GCE A-level or Scottish Higher grade (although 10 per cent of entrants to universities, and nearly half of those entering polytechnics offer other qualifications). This demands a positive decision from potential engineers to include mathematics and physics among their O-level or Scottish O-grade courses, a choice made at the age of 13 or 14 when it is too early to expect most young people to be committed to any particular career. Many girls, especially in co-educational schools, drop mathematics and/or physics in favour of other subjects at this stage or later when choosing their A-level specialisms, often because their options are limited by time-tabling arrangements. The number of pupils taking mathematics and a science subject at A-level or Higher level has changed little and if anything have fallen over the last decade,[1] while the proportion of these going on to study engineering in universities and polytechnics has grown and is now nearly 40 per cent.

3.13 The apparent objection of many pupils and their parents to specialising at an early age in mathematics and physics (or another physical science) is that they consider it unduly narrowing of their horizons. We believe, as do many careers advisers, that this combination of subjects is in fact one of the least limiting choices since it allows entrance to a greater range of technological and non-technological occupations than a VIth form specialisation in, say, humanities; this should be stressed to pupils by their teachers and careers advisers, who should strongly encourage them to continue study of mathematics and physics at least until O-level. The problem of specialist subject choices arises from the particularly restrictive nature of English and Welsh VIth form study, and are not shared by Scotland, where pupils can combine mathematics and physics with three or four other 'Highers', nor by continental Europe where school pupils study for a broadly-based 'Abitur' or 'baccalaureat'. There is no suggestion among university teachers in Scotland or on the Continent that a broadly-based school curriculum has entailed inadequate

---

[1] Department of Education and Science: Statistics of Education, Vol. 2.

standards of proficiency or that the intake into engineering has in any way suffered from it.[1]

3.14 Much attention has been devoted—for example in a 1977 Report published by the British Association for the Advancement of Science (BAAS)[2]—to possible means of expanding the pool of potential engineers in England and Wales by dropping the strict 'mathematics plus physics' A-level requirement in favour of more flexible arrangements—perhaps accepting A-levels in engineering, electronics or general science in place of physics; accepting qualifications such as OND (Technology) or the new TEC Diploma in lieu of A-levels; providing 'bridging courses' for candidates with the aptitude but lacking appropriate examination passes for an engineering course; or allowing relevant working experience in place of academic attainments for otherwise acceptable candidates. All of these alternative routes into engineering are already open to some extent, and a sizeable proportion of those currently graduating from engineering degree courses have in fact come through them. The BAAS report noted however that the availability of these other routes to admission was often not widely advertised by engineering departments and that in consequence the potential for expanding entry through them was limited. *We echo the BAAS recommendation that engineering teaching departments and those advising pupils in schools should clearly advertise all routes to entry.*

3.15 The second decision point affecting the flow of new engineers is the one at which young people with the option to enter engineering choose to do so. Factors in this are the level of understanding and interest in engineering among young people; their appreciation of the opportunities open to them following an engineering formation; and the relative attractions of those opportunities. Much recent effort has been directed towards the first two factors through schools-industry liaison schemes, better careers advice, programmes to provide teachers and senior pupils with industrial experience and a host of other valuable schemes. However, it is significant that in other industrial countries the demand from young people for an engineering education is consistently high and the competition for places fierce without any exhortative programmes of this kind. This is because an engineering formation is well recognised in these other countries as an assured route to a variety of attractive and rewarding careers. This suggests that 'demand-pull' from the perceived intrinsic and material incentives to follow an engineering preparation is at least as important in attracting more and better people into engineering as is 'supply-push' from schools-based awareness programmes.

---

[1] Scottish Education: children enter Scottish secondary schools aged about 12 after 7 years in primary school. In their fifth year able pupils take higher grade examinations which are the entry qualifications for a range of tertiary education. Entrants to engineering degree courses would have four or five Higher passes at grade A or B in a range of subjects. A high proportion of pupils study for a further year for the Certificate of Sixth Year Studies in one or two subjects before entering higher education. See also 4.13.

[2] British Association for the Advancement of Science: 'Education, Engineers and Manufacturing Industry'. A Report to the British Association Co-ordinating Group, August 1977.

3.16 Our survey of young engineers[1] suggested that the considerations entering the reckoning in career choice mostly concerned the intrinsic attractions of engineering jobs (perceived salary prospects, career prospects, work interest, etc). An American study[2] claims to have demonstrated that the principal determinant of changes in the demand for engineering and other university places is the relative starting salaries of current graduates in various disciplines. This leads to two observations. Firstly, those concerned to attract more young people into engineering should ensure that the intrinsic and material attractions of an engineering career are good and are well publicised and that pupils are informed of these attractions at the critical ages when subjects are chosen for A-level or Highers[3]; and secondly, employers concerned to maintain a supply of high-calibre engineering recruits should ensure that their employment policies for engineers provide adequate incentive and differentials over other disciplines both to attract new blood and to hold their required share of the current stock.

(b) Demand for engineers

Employers' demands

3.17 The available evidence regarding employers' demands for engineers is piecemeal and anecdotal and it is difficult to formulate any overall picture of the demand/supply situation from it. Evidence to us from some employers and trade associations suggested that there are insufficient engineers in Britain for current demands and that manufacturing industry faces a chronic and growing shortage of engineers at all levels and for the whole range of engineering disciplines. As examples, members of the Electronic Engineering Association[4] said they were suffering a shortfall of at least 10 per cent of engineers overall and were having to decline business opportunities for lack of engineering resource; the Chairman of one major company[5] stated publicly that his company needed, and was constrained by the the lack of, 600 engineers; another company[6] said they were experiencing a 10 per cent shortage of experienced

---

[1] Policy Studies Institute: A Survey of Former Students of Engineering and Science.

[2] Massachusetts Institute of Technology, Centre for Policy Alternatives: 'Improved Methodologies for Forecasting new Entrants in Science and Engineering', September 1978.

[3] A comparison of the starting and subsequent salaries earned by young engineers and young scientists showed engineers significantly better off than their science contemporaries (who would have had a similar background of school subjects followed). Policy Studies Institute. A Survey of Former Students of Engineering and Science.

[4] Electronic Engineering Association (Evidence to CIEP. Paras 4.6–4.8) 'The electronics industry has, for the past eight to ten years, been unable to meet its requirements for engineers. This shortage of key engineering skills is inhibiting employment of other skills and is a major constraint on output.' 'An EEA Survey (held in 1977) revealed shortages ranging from 10 to 40 per cent.' 'A survey (mid–1977) produced results relating to all engineers and indicated that one quarter to one third of the reported vacancies had been outstanding for over six months.'

[5] Chairman of British Leyland. Speech to Institution of Mechanical Engineers—9 November 1978: 'We are short of engineers because there just are not enough to go around in British industry today. Spen King, BL Cars' Director of Advanced Technology, tells me that the 600 engineers we need will take three years to recruit at the present rate.'

[6] Correspondence between GEC and the Manpower Services Commission, (quoted with permission): 'General Electric Company, an employer of some 12,000 graduate engineers and scientists, has told us that it is unable to recruit sufficient experienced engineers and scientists to meet its requirements and that the shortfall is around 10 per cent with the problem being particularly acute in the electronics field.'

engineers; a major recruitment agency[1] told us of other companies seeking to recruit large numbers of engineers for mechanical and production engineering functions; and it was reported that the Ministry of Defence[2] had been unable to spend its full budget because supplying companies could not recruit sufficient engineers to meet defence contracts. Data collected by the Department of Employment[3] showed notified vacancies rising for professional engineers of almost every discipline. Further evidence of unsatisfied demands is shown by the negligible unemployment among engineers, despite recent high aggregate unemployment and minimal levels of industrial and economic growth.

3.18 There are evident problems of shortages of engineers to meet specific current demands in parts of British industry. The most frequently notified of these shortages is of electronic and software engineers; this is an international problem brought on by the very rapid growth of technological developments and applications in these fields. The market and technological trends described earlier have induced companies in other industries within and outside manufacturing to increase their advanced engineering capability, with consequent increased demand for design and systems engineers, particularly in the mechanical engineering sector.

3.19 Without wishing to minimise the problems faced by many employers, we are reluctant, by generalising from these particular reported shortages, to postulate an overall national requirement for more graduate engineers to meet current demands. Our reservations derive from three observations:

(a) 'shortages' often proved to be, not of applicants, but of acceptable candidates with the qualities required; in some instances there was an incongruence between the calibre of person sought and the salary offered which deterred applicants;

(b) the implications of the changed balance in the numbers coming through the 'part-time' and 'full-time' formation routes to engineering have not yet been fully assimilated by all employers, nor have all young engineers and those educating them responded to them; and this has contributed to impressions of shortages;

(c) employers were mostly reporting current or immediate problems and few based their statements on assessments of long-term corporate manpower requirements judged against current capabilities and future market plans; moreover, employers content that they have adequate, or even excess, numbers of engineers are less likely to publicise their situation than those facing difficulties (see also 3.33).

---

[1] Management Selection Ltd (MSL)—meeting with CIEP 30 January 1979, MSL Engineering Ltd said: that mechanical and production engineering had exhibited severe shortages with firms reporting requirements ranging from 30 up to, in one instance, 1,400 engineers.

[2] Ministry of Defence, Procurement Executive, quoted at Conference on Management of Procurement, Bath March 1979.

[3] Notified vacancies and applicants to the Professional and Executive Register (Department of Employment).

The engineering qualities demanded

3.20 Our discussions with employers revealed that the shortages they perceived were sometimes more concerned with the experience and personal qualities they sought than with absolute numbers of engineers. Few employers doubted that the quality of the best British engineers was as high as that of any in the world and this view was echoed by employers in several other countries who backed their belief with a willingness, indeed often enthusiasm, to recruit engineers from this country.[1] There was however a widely held belief among home employers that this high quality does not extend in sufficient depth among the current stock and prospective supply of engineers. Concern was repeatedly expressed to us from all sides (i) that there were too few high-calibre engineers and hence intense competition for them; (ii) that the remaining body of graduate engineers lacked the qualities of practical application and understanding of industry associated with those who came through the old part-time route; and (iii) that those engineers with potential for technological or managerial leadership are lost to manufacturing employers in favour of public-sector employment, 'glamorous' research-based high-technology activities or opportunities overseas. Certainly many engineers are employed in these areas, but we have no way of telling whether these include a disproportionate number of the most able engineers.

3.21 Not surprisingly, all employers wish to employ the cream of the engineering stock and inevitably this cream is too thin to meet all the demand. Some have responded to this situation by advocating priority for efforts to increase the numbers of highly able students entering engineering by, for example, raising academic entrance requirements, if not to engineering teaching departments then to the engineering Institutions. This is the policy now adopted by the three biggest Institutions (Civils, Electricals and Mechanicals). In our view such proposals offer no real solution to the problems of improving the number of high-calibre recruits to engineering. Very good students (in academic terms) have been entering engineering schools in fair numbers. We do not believe that in current circumstances an arbitrary stiffening of entry requirements in the face of current levels of student demand for engineering places will raise these numbers much, if at all, whereas it may well deter others with weaker school results but with suitable personal qualities to become good engineers. Academic performance at A-level has been shown[2] to be an incomplete predictor of an individual's degree performance in engineering. Many employers[3] made the observation that their best engineers sometimes had poor academic qualifications, and that they preferred to recruit a well-rounded individual with perhaps a 2.1 or 2.2 degree than an academically bright but personally less capable PhD or 1st-class honours man.

---

[1] The PSI survey and other data (such as that collected by OPCS and published in 'International Migration', HMSO 1976) have suggested that most UK engineers going to work overseas do so on contract and intend to return home when their contracts are completed. However, a study by the Institute of Manpower Studies (Survey of Emigration of Electronics Engineers (1978)) indicated that some key individuals were emigrating and observed the disruption which can follow the loss of such people from project teams.

[2] T J Heard (BP Research Fellow, Durham University)—'The mathematical education of engineers at school and university'.

[3] Evidence to CIEP from Electrical and Electronic Manufacturers Training and Education Board (EEMTEB)
  also Appendix D: Visits to Organisations Employing Engineers

3.22 In continental Europe, Japan and to an extent in the USA, the demand to become an engineer is such that only able and determined candidates can gain entry to courses, and employers in these countries are thus able to recruit from a large and high-calibre 'pool' with quality in depth. A similar solution must be sought in Britain by raising the attractions of engineering through attention to the career prospects and rewards for *all* engineers, including (but not exclusively) the academic elite.

The mainstream of engineers

3.23 A great many employers expressed dismay at the difficulties they found in recruiting the 'mainstream' of engineers with the experience and ability to apply and maintain best current technology in day-to-day operations. This shortage was frequently linked to the decline in numbers coming through the route to professional engineering practice by a mix of part-time study and working experience. Since the post-Robbins expansion in opportunities for full-time study for a degree, industry has had largely to rely for its engineering recruits upon the graduate stream, few of whom—it is alleged—possess the skills of practical application and the understanding of industry instilled by the part-time route.

3.24 The rapid expansion in the proportion of young people obtaining higher education inevitably means that many will be employed on work not previously done by graduates. This is not inherently a bad thing, and may indeed have positive virtues, for example in training the graduate or employing him in work which requires or would benefit from a higher level of engineering input than has previously been the case. Problems arise when employers, perhaps with little experience of employing graduates, have tried to fit newly-graduated engineers immediately into established job patterns and structures, expecting of them the same contribution as was provided by previous generations of 'part-time' route engineers. Not surprisingly, they are disappointed. These employers have yet to adjust to the shift towards a more academic system of producing engineers, and to recognise that the current mainstream graduates are different from, but not worse than, earlier generations of practical engineers *provided they are given the support through training and structured experience to complete their formation.* At the same time, those responsible for the formal education of engineers and the graduates themselves must recognise that graduate engineers are required not only for leading new technological advances but also for much 'mainstream' engineering work concerned with the application and management of the best of current knowledge and expertise.

3.25 Difficulties in adjusting to the shift from the 'part-time' to the 'full-time' route are, again not surprisingly, felt mainly in those industries and in those functions which relied most heavily upon the old system. They are felt more, for example, in the mechanical and heavy electrical engineering industries than in the electronic and chemical engineering industries which have always recruited mainly graduates. Within manufacturing companies two functions in particular—production operations and design (particularly detail design)—are commonly held to have suffered from these changes.

3.26 The *production function* is the heart of any manufacturing enterprise. It bears responsibility for the management of much, usually most, of the company's fixed and working capital and its workforce, for ensuring that the company's products are up to standard in quality and meet specifications and that they will be available on time and in the numbers required. To a large extent it also determines the cost of these products. It does not appear to be widely understood that the production manager has a vital part to play in the creation of business policy, as well as responsibility for running the main cost centre in the business. In this latter connection considerable demands are being placed on production management as a consequence of the extremely rapid technological changes taking place. To fulfil these responsibilities, production needs engineers of high calibre and yet has commonly been presented as the 'Cinderella' function in British industry—poorly paid, overloaded with thankless responsibilities and unattractive as a career prospect.[1] Several recent surveys have suggested that production is often the province of people with low-level qualifications and with little experience in other functions or other companies, who are inadequately equipped to bring to bear the new knowledge of best practices from elsewhere which market forces require companies to assimilate.[2] Our own survey[3] showed that graduate engineers were more likely to work in what the Policy Studies Institute (PSI) classified as 'specification functions' (eg R&D) than in the supervision of production operations, and that 'operations' or 'support' functions were largely the province of non-graduates. It has been suggested that low expectations of the role of production management cause the job to be undervalued in some companies and thus to attract a lower grade of man. This generates a vicious circle whereby descending expectation chases lower performance.

3.27 Although 25 per cent of our sample of recent engineering graduates[4] were working in production operations, employers[5] reported some reluctance among graduates to work in production and also union resistance to even their temporary placement in foreman posts. Engineers responding to our main survey[3] who were currently supervising production operations were paid above the average (age-for-age) for engineers in the whole sample; they generally received better fringe benefits and bonus payments than other engineers; they had higher expectations of promotion; and they expressed a higher level of satisfaction with the content and status of their jobs than the sample as

---

[1] BIM (British Institute of Management) Survey—'The Career Development of the Production Manager in British Industry' 'The low proportion of graduates in production management can in part be attributed to deliberate company policy. Some companies employ very few graduates in this function, others avoid recruiting them directly from university.' 'A number of companies that recruit graduates will not recruit them directly into production.'

[2] Newcastle Polytechnic Survey (The Engineer 21 June 1979 p 30) 'Our findings seem to suggest the existence of a "conservative culture" among the respondents. A vast majority of them prefer to recruit their production managers from within the ranks of their operatives, paying little attention to other external sources including graduates.'

[3] Policy Studies Institute: A General Survey of Professional Engineers.

[4] Policy Studies Institute: A Survey of Former Students of Engineering and Science.

[5] Appendix D: Visits to Organisations Employing Engineers; also preliminary results of survey work by Prof P Heriott, City University, on attitudes and intentions of undergraduate engineers (correspondence).

a whole. It is clear that the needs of the production function for highly able engineers and managers *are* being reflected in the incentives offered by some employers and working in production is no longer a second-best option in those companies. We are encouraged to note this change taking place in parts of UK industry, since the survival of some of our industries is dependent upon the ability of their production management to equal or better the performance of their overseas competitors. We would urge that more emphasis be placed on the demand for engineers in production and on the positive benefits and advantages they can gain, so that more able engineers might be attracted to work in this vital area.

3.28 Another area where there is apparently a shortage of adequate engineering manpower is in the general field of conceptual or overall engineering design. This function has been handicapped in two ways. Firstly, relatively few graduates work at present on the drawing board in design offices since their education and training in the UK does not in general prepare them well for such work although they may become concerned in the theoretical and computational work related to design. Secondly, detail drawing offices have traditionally been manned by those who have followed the part-time HNC route and their numbers have decreased. To some extent the problem is being alleviated by the introduction of computer-aided design (CAD), particularly for the routine work in detail drawing offices, but a high quality input from graduates with a flair for design is still required, both at the drawing board and in the preparation of CAD programmes. *We applaud the action being taken by the Technician Education Council and the Design Council in developing programmes designed to give technicians a design-oriented training,* although we recognise that the potential impact of such programmes is currently constrained by the limited number of technicians available.

The shortage of technicians

3.29 Many employers told us that they were facing acute difficulties in recruiting appropriately qualified staff for engineering support and first-line supervisory posts. Companies can generally carry on operating for a time, albeit sub-optimally, with reduced professional engineering input, but cannot operate at all if they cannot fill the routine jobs essential to the continuation of day-to-day operations. For this reason, any shortage of technicians will be rapidly felt within current activities, whereas a shortage of engineers limits capability for the future and so may sometimes be considered less pressing. Employers are thus obliged to place priority on recruiting whoever they can for technician jobs; and newly graduated engineers are one obvious source. The shortage of technicians has thus exacerbated the problems of 'underemployment' and consequent dissatisfaction among graduates placed in relatively low-level routine work. This so-called 'technician gap' affects the market for engineers in several ways. On the one hand it may exaggerate the apparent demand for engineers from employers recruiting whoever they can for support work; conversely it may imply that current demands for engineers are understated because employers cannot find the support staff to justify the employment of expensive graduates. Either way, it is clearly a debilitating factor within the engineering dimension.

3.30 Factors contributing to the national shortage of technicians include:

(a) the expansion in higher education opportunities, which has attracted many young people into degree courses (not necessarily in engineering) who might formerly have entered industry as technicians;

(b) the growth in employment opportunities in the service sector, offering a wide variety of career alternatives to school-leavers who might otherwise have trained as engineering technicians;

(c) the diminution of pay differentials between unskilled workers and technicians in recent years, which has eroded the incentive to seek extra training and promotion from the shopfloor.

3.31 Our remit was to consider the supply and qualifications of 'professional and technician engineers' and did not extend to reviewing the problems of technicians although, as we have seen, technicians are also important to the engineering dimension. We have therefore not entered into any detailed examination of the apparent acute shortages of technicians, the factors responsible, nor the measures which might be taken to improve the situation (although our later recommendations on engineering formation should help by improving the prospects for progression from a technician formation). A serious weakness will persist within the engineering dimension, regardless of what is done for engineers, so long as this 'technician gap' persists. *We therefore recommend that the Manpower Services Commission, the Technician Education Council, the Scottish Technician Education Council, the National Economic Development Council and—in due course—the new Engineering Authority, initiate urgent action to review and where necessary increase the supply of engineering technicians, and to review their formation in relation to the engineers whom they support.*

(c) Employers' attitudes and employment policies

Recognition of needs

3.32 Companies which have an inadequate engineering presence in their policy-making counsels will be poorly placed to recognise their needs for engineering expertise, to specify those requirements in terms of different levels of engineering qualifications and to assess whether the engineers they employ are being used to the full. Some of the evidence to us[1] criticised UK employers

---

[1] (i) Royal Institute of Naval Architects—evidence to CIEP

'... However one of the causes of decline has been the inability of the industries themselves to develop a coherent attitude and strategy towards, and plan for, the recruitment, training, employment and career development of professional engineers in all relevant phases of the industries' work.'

(ii) Institution of Electrical Engineers—evidence to CIEP

'... A significant proportion of engineering graduates are engaged in work appropriate to technician engineers. This is sometimes because employers do not, or cannot, provide opportunities for the promotion of young engineers who have the capacity to undertake responsibilities appropriate to chartered engineers. In such cases the employers are not exploiting the full potential of their young engineers.'

(iii) Institution of Mechanical Engineers—evidence to CIEP

'... We were, however, even more concerned by the charge that all too few job descriptions bear real comparison with the actual task—the successful candidate finds himself given work quite different from that which he is led to expect. At best, this suggests an inability on the part of personnel managers either to define a vacancy or to specify and recognise the type of engineer to match it.'

on each of these counts, suggesting that many fail to recognise their needs for engineers, 'not missing what they have never had', and that others do not distinguish adequately the level of person they need when framing their demands. The engineering Institutions quoted from recruitment advertisements inviting applications from people holding 'a degree, HNC/D, City & Guilds, or the equivalent'. The qualifications sought and the salaries offered suggest that these employers may have been seeking technicians, and were casting their net widely to bridge their 'technician gap', but the accompanying job specifications and responsibility levels often suggest that employers would be prepared to recruit technicians to professional posts. Advertisements phrased in these terms suggest that some employers are not able to (or do not) identify and specify clearly their requirements for engineering manpower.

3.33 Other witnesses suggested that shortages were sometimes a consequence of employers' inefficient utilisation and deployment of their current stock of engineers at all levels. At our regional meetings,[1] many individual engineers expressed frustration that they were under-employed in their current jobs. A particular complaint came from engineers working on public-sector contract work, who asserted that the pricing basis of such contracts encouraged employers to hoard skilled manpower in numbers and quality greater than were needed immediately or even in the longer term. Suggestions of inefficiencies in the use of engineers were supported by some employers,[2] and were echoed in the written and oral evidence to us for instance the Engineering Employers' Federation[3] endorsed the suggestion that many employers could get a more effective contribution from the engineers they already employed through better organisation of their activities and/or by applying engineers' talents to fuller purpose.

3.34 It is vital to companies' capability to respond to world markets that they recognise their needs for engineers as the key to the engineering dimension, and that they articulate those needs in the form of demands for the appropriate types of people. Employers must however also make the best possible use of the engineers they employ to ensure the optimum return from an expensive human investment (by the State, the employer and the individual engineer) in education and training and because of the impact which current employment policies (and the levels of satisfaction or dissatisfaction they engender) can have on the future supply of engineers. While some employers clearly acknowledge this and the responsibilities it places upon them, many others

---

[1] CEI—Finniston Inquiry Regional Meetings: CEI Summary at Appendix C

[2] eg Mr Kenneth Corfield at BIM Symposium on 11 January 1978—'A Focus on Manufacturing Industry'.
'Many a well trained engineer is engaged in boring repetitive work which with a little more understanding and assistance from top management he could be planning for others to execute.'
'Many a creative and highly versed engineer is acting in a supervisory capacity which others could be doing.'

[3] Engineering Employers Federation (EEF)—evidence to CIEP (Para 1(ix(a))).
'. . . there is a suspicion that some of the shortages reported arise from poor manpower planning and bad use of qualified staff.'
EEF meeting with CIEP 11 June 1979.
'Proper utilisation of graduates was also lacking because of the misunderstanding of their value.'

still do not. There is a need for a sustained major programme to stimulate more widespread understanding among employers of the nature and pervasiveness of the engineering dimension, and in particular of the potential benefits to them from employing engineers in a range of activities. There is at present no effective source of initiative for such a programme, although some of the bigger Institutions have begun to take steps in this direction.[1] *We recommend that the proposed new Engineering Authority (see Chapter VI) should undertake this task on a national and continuing scale.*

Pay and prospects for engineers

3.35 Three issues recurred with metronomic regularity in the evidence to us from engineers and their spokesmen—pay, prospects and status. A strong impression was conveyed to us of a body of engineers depressed and frustrated at being undervalued and underpaid in manufacturing industry. As we have noted, the image projected of the rewards from an engineering career is of crucial importance in its effects on current recruitment and on the flow of future entrants to engineering, and so it is essential that the facts behind this image are carefully examined. Figure 3.2 shows the distribution of salaries and Figure 3.2 shows the distribution of salaries and earning for the whole sample of engineers surveyed by PSI in Autumn 1978 at a time when salaries were subject to pay restraint.

Figure 3.2   Earnings: all respondents (UK and overseas) (September/October 1978)

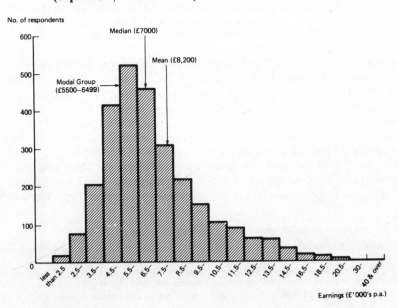

Source: P.S.I. General Survey

Earnings = Basic salary plus *cash* earnings (eg overtime, shift money & allowances, bonus, profit share). No allowance made for fringe benefits.

---

[1] Institution of Electrical Engineers—evidence to CIEP; Institution of Mechanical Engineers, oral evidence to CIEP.

The median salary (£6,400) and median earnings (£6,700) quoted by PSI *for those living in the UK* are not inconsistent, after allowing for sampling and timing differences, with those from other surveys such as the biennial CEI Survey of Engineers.[1]

3.36 Means, medians and modes[2] tell us nothing about the distribution of earnings about them, nor about the patterns of engineers' earnings after account is taken of differences in age, qualifications, responsibility and occupation. We have already observed that engineers are to be found working in a very wide range of activities in almost every sector of the economy, either as practising engineers or as managers or teachers using their engineering expertise to greater or lesser degree. Not surprisingly, this variety of working experience and of educational background is reflected in the pattern of engineers' earnings.

3.37 Figure 3.3 (page 62) shows the distribution of engineers' earnings for those working in the UK, for the age groups 20–29, 30–39, 40–49 and 50–59, giving the proportion of each cohort earning particular levels of income.

The most obvious observation is the wide spread of earnings in each age group; even those engineers under 30 include a number earning high incomes. Looking at the age/earnings pattern, while the modal earnings rise relatively little—and in fact fall between the 40–49 group and the 50–59 group—the spread of earnings increases with the age of each group, and the 40–49 and 50–59 groups each include a substantial proportion with high earnings.

3.38 Table 3.4 summarises the distribution of engineers' earnings by age and qualification.

Table 3.4   Earnings by educational route and by age
(September/October 1978)

| Age Groups | Degree | | No Degree | |
	Full-time (£000's)	Sandwich (£000's)	Professional Exams (£000's)	HNC/HND etc (£000's)
20–29	5·3	4·9	5·3	
30–39	8·6	7·8	7·8	7·7
40–49	10·7		9·6	8·2
50–59	10·9		8·9	8·3

Source: PSI General Survey—all respondents.

[1] CEI Surveys of Professional Engineers.

[2] The average (mean) salary is arrived at by totalling all the salaries earned by the group concerned and dividing that sum by the number of people in the group. The median is arrived at by arranging all the individual salaries in order from the highest to the lowest; the median salary is that earned by the individual in the middle of such a ranking. The modal salary is that earned by the greatest number of people in the group concerned.

Figure 3.3 Earnings by age: engineers living in the UK (September/October 1978)

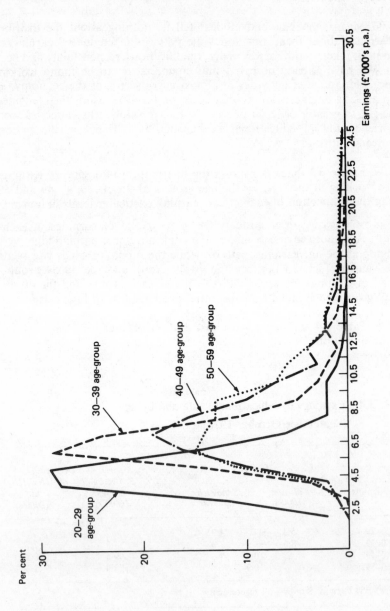

Source: PSI General Survey.

It emerges that the trend over time from the 'part-time' route to a primarily graduate profession is reflected in earnings and that, while initial qualifications appear to have little effect upon earnings among the younger age group, among older engineers (aged 40 and over) those holding a degree tend to earn markedly more than their contemporaries with Higher National or Institutional qualifications (but without degrees). Nevertheless, from Figure 3.3 it will be seen that a large number of older engineers without degrees also earn high salaries.

3.39 A commonly quoted assertion in the evidence was that engineers in private industry fared less well, in terms of earnings, than their contemporaries in the public sector. Table 3.5 shows the breakdown of earnings patterns between private and public sector employment.

Table 3.5 Earnings in the public and private sectors (September/October 1978)

| Age Group | Average Earnings | | Standard Deviation* about Average | |
	Public Sector (£000's)	Private Sector (£000's)	Public Sector (£000's)	Private Sector (£000's)
20–24	4·0	4·0	1·2	1·3
25–29	5·2	5·7	1·2	2·3
30–34	6·6	7·1	1·8	2·6
35–39	7·3	8·1	2·7	3·6
40–44	7·7	8·6	2·2	4·0
45–49	8·2	9·4	2·5	5·2
50–54	8·5	9·2	2·9	5·4
55–59	8·1	8·0	2·6	3·4
All ages	7·2	7·7	2·6	4·3

* The Standard Deviation measures the spread of earnings about the average.
Source: Policy Studies Institute: A General Survey of Professional Engineers.

The figures in the above table relate to September–October 1978, and the comparison is affected by the timing of salary awards under Phase 4 of the Pay Code. It will be seen (a) that the mean earnings are closely comparable in the two sectors; and (b) that the spread of earnings in private industry is greater than that in the public sector, and therefore that there is a greater concentration around the mean among public sector employees.

3.40 There is no ready answer to the assertion that engineers are underpaid, nor to the counter-view that they fare relatively well. Good engineers can do well from an early age while a large number of others—mostly middle-aged and with lower academic qualifications—have been caught in what an American employer called 'a flat spot, career and salary-wise'. Although 62 per cent of the engineers responding to the PSI survey[1] expressed themselves 'very' or 'fairly' satisfied with their salaries and other benefits, over a third (34 per cent) were 'not very satisfied or not satisfied at all'. It is noteworthy that those with the higher qualifications (graduates) were slightly less satisfied with their salaries and markedly less satisfied with their status than were those who came up the old 'practical' route.

[1] Policy Studies Institute: A General Survey of Professional Engineers.

3.41 Much play was made in some of the evidence to us of the low earnings of engineers relative to other professional groups. PSI[1] attempted some comparisons between the salaries and earnings of engineers and data relating to other professionals, and concluded that on the whole engineers, in fact, do not fare badly in comparison with 'peer groups'; the recent report of the Royal Commission on the Distribution of Income and Wealth similarly showed that among 48 occupational groups, the earnings of electrical and mechanical engineers ranked in the top six.[2] On the other hand we saw a number of published 'league tables' of salaries for different groups in all of which engineers were shown to be earning less than other groups. We have reservations about all these surveys, which do not relate earnings to responsibility on a comparable basis. International comparisons are very difficult to draw, but we certainly heard no complaints from engineers in other countries that they were underpaid relative to other groups.

3.42 The complaints we heard about engineers' earnings were frequently linked with assertions that engineers fared badly in the promotion stakes, and that they were not accorded their due status at work or in society. Many older engineers complained that they had been 'forced' to quit technical engineering jobs altogether and to enter general management or other jobs to progress their careers and their living standards. It is noteworthy that those questioned by PSI who had moved out of technical engineering into other areas (particularly those who had moved into general management) appeared far from unhappy about their move. When asked about the intrinsic satisfaction they obtained from their jobs the overwhelming majority of engineers currently in general management expressed themselves more than satisfied, while those currently in 'hard' engineering posts were less enthusiastic in their responses. The 'population' of engineers surveyed by PSI covered people across the whole age spectrum, with a range of levels of qualification (and personal abilities) and in a wide range of sectors, occupations and career experiences. When asked about their expectations of promotion with their current employer within the next few years most of those currently under 30 not surprisingly considered their promotion prospects 'very high', but expectations fell off rapidly among the older age groups, especially those who were currently in 'engineering practice' posts; this difference perhaps represents in part the lower, and possibly out-of-date, qualifications of many older engineers and also the efforts of employers to 'bring through' good younger people, especially graduates.

3.43 Our concern is to attract growing numbers of highly able young people into engineering. It is clear from experience among the current stock that the prospects in terms of earnings and career progress for some can be good; but equally there is a larger number whose real incomes and careers have not progressed as they might have hoped and who have in consequence vociferously shown their frustration. These engineers claim that their contribution is undervalued by employers; while the employers counter that their ability to pay all their employees is constrained by the profitability of the enterprise,

---

[1] Policy Studies Institute: A General Survey of Professional Engineers.

[2] Royal Commission on the Distribution of Income and Wealth, Report No. 8, Cmnd 7679 October 1979—Table 7.1.

and that within that constraint people are paid what they are worth. There are grounds for doubting, however, whether the systems applied in industry for the invidious tasks of assessing the relative 'worth' of people or their different posts adequately reflect the real value of engineers' contributions to the enterprise. Since the reference standards upon which most current job evaluation systems are based derive largely from current perceptions of business priorities—which we criticised earlier—they are not likely adequately to reflect the full value of individuals' contributions to the engineering dimension. Companies with a clearer concept of the value of the contributions made by engineers compared with those in other disciplines will apply more appropriate evaluation criteria when setting salary scales and placing engineers on them.

3.44 Industry must establish the rewards and prospects for good engineers which will attract more of the country's most able young people into a lengthy and demanding engineering formation and thence into manufacturing industry. However, some engineers, while capable of an excellent contribution within primarily technical work, do not have the aptitudes or wish to develop their careers in wider managerial jobs and hence are excluded from the higher rewards available in those roles. Some companies, recognising the current dilemma and its implications for their future technical capabilities, have paid special attention to their employment and career development policies for engineers and a few have introduced separate salary scales and career ladders which offer increased opportunities for people to progress their careers as *technical engineers* within the organisation.[1] This simultaneously lessens problems of recruitment for 'hard' engineering practice, and raises the morale of engineers in the organisation, as we saw in some very large and also in some quite small companies. *We recommend that all employing organisations undertake a comprehensive review of their salary and career provisions for engineers to ensure that, having regard to their key roles within the engineering dimension, engineers are not undervalued. We further recommend that the new Engineering Authority keeps these matters under review so that information and advice can be provided to employers on a continuing basis.*

Engineering manpower audits

3.45 Complaints by employers about shortages of able engineers and by engineers about their pay and status are to an extent symptoms and consequences of the underlying attitudes which have shaped industry's employment policies for engineers. A manufacturing company's most valuable assets are the people it employs, particularly those with the knowledge and ingenuity demanded by the engineering dimension. It should follow that employers spend at least as much time and expense developing their investment in engineers as they do in developing and maintaining their fixed and financial assets—indeed, much more so, since people can be an appreciating asset while physical assets depreciate and are worthless on their own. However, as we saw in Chapter II, engineers appear to be regarded too often in Britain primarily as purveyors of technology, to be kept 'on tap' within technical departments and called on only when technical problems arise.

---

[1] See Appendix D: Visits to Organisations Employing Engineers.

3.46 The supply of highly qualified people cannot be turned on and off to meet changing exigencies within industry. Of some major engineering companies currently advertising for hundreds of extra engineers, one employed virtually no graduates at all until 1970, while two others each laid off over 1,000 engineers in the early 1970s. These, and many others, are now trying desperately to fill a shortage of qualified engineers in middle-management positions, but are handicapped as a direct consequence of their earlier policies, and in the process have contributed to the reputation of manufacturing as an insecure employer and to the slump in recruitment to engineering courses in 1973–74 (currently being felt as a diminished supply of graduates). The lesson has been well learnt by some major employers who have now introduced 'steady state' graduate recruitment policies, independent of short-term business exigencies, based upon comprehensive programmes of systematic manpower development. Yet we visited some other companies which kept only rudimentary information about their current stock and deployment of highly qualified technical manpower and did not appear to regard this lack as a problem. Even among those companies with adequate personnel information, few integrated their manpower development and recruitment policies closely with the technical implications of the company's forward market plans in the way that understanding of the engineering dimension would imply (and as we encountered in a number of companies overseas).[1]

3.47 Recognition of engineers as assets means that it is in employers' direct interests to deploy those assets to the full. Employers should therefore monitor the performance of engineers, rewarding them adequately and ensure that their assets appreciate through structured career development and continuing education programmes. There will also be active employer involvement in ensuring a future supply of well-prepared recruits to their wealth-creating capacity. *Practices used with great benefits to these ends by some employers, in Britain and abroad, and which we recommend should be widely adopted by companies engaged in the engineering dimension include:*

(a) regular analyses of the numbers, deployment and mix of currently-employed technically qualified manpower, especially engineers, to ensure that recruitment, training and deployment policies are founded on informed judgements, relating this exercise to the forward strategic planning of the enterprise;

(b) periodic reviews of the deployment of individual engineers to ensure that each engineer's job makes full use of his talents and develops his potential breadth of activity by bringing him into regular contact with colleagues in different but related functions as well as with customers and other professionals outside the company;

(c) frequent opportunities for managers and the engineers concerned jointly to assess each individual's career progress and development, to ensure that he is being used to the full; that he is not stagnating for want of new challenges; that he is given every opportunity to update or extend his capabilities in the current job or in another position; and also to identify people suitable for promotion or for retraining in new technologies in anticipation of future needs.

---

[1] See Appendix E: Overseas Visits

3.48 We have adopted the term *'engineering manpower audits'* for these practices taken together, to convey their contribution to maintaining and developing companies' human assets. Such audits are intended as a means whereby the best employment practices regarding engineers, as applied in leading companies, may be extended and adopted more generally in British industry. *To ensure that this is done consciously and is recognised as company policy, we recommend that these audit procedures be initiated, and the results discussed on a regular basis at main board and management committee level within all manufacturing companies.* As with the reviews of salary and career structures recommended above, the Engineering Authority should play an active role in encouraging the spread of engineering manpower audits.

3.49 We have noted earlier the American requirement that companies disclose information on their 'total technical capability' in their annual reports.[1] We believe that companies should also refer explicitly in their annual reports to shareholders and employees to the condition of their human asset base and to their policies for building upon it, since the information given in most current reports—number of employees, directors' emoluments and Chairman's thanks to his employees—hardly suffices to inform about this key indicator of the company's health. The information obtained through manpower audits and the actions arising from them will have benefits both at company level (informing and improving employment policies) and at the national level (for improving companies' capabilities and inclination to participate in the policy-making and consequent actions of the proposed new Engineering Authority).

(d) Future demands and supply

The pattern of demand

3.50 There are undoubtedly serious shortages of engineers in some areas of industry (an impression confirmed by the very low unemployment among engineering graduates at a time when graduates in other disciplines are in relatively less demand). The shortage can in some cases be alleviated by better deployment of engineers currently employed, but against this there are suggestions that current demands may understate employers' *needs* because the potential benefits from employing qualified engineers are not adequately appreciated. Industry has continued to employ as many graduate engineers as were available (plus an increasing number of applied scientists in engineering jobs) despite the marked overall fall in manufacturing employment and the stagnation of industrial output over the past eight years.

3.51 *We believe that, having regard to the increasing rate of market change and the complexities of technological innovations, more engineers at all levels will be required in future than are employed in Britain today and manufacturing employers will have to compete with others at home and overseas for the services of the best.* There is little doubt that the demand from manufacturing industry for engineers will continue to expand as market pressures require an engineering-based response from companies, especially once manufacturing

---

[1] See 2.12

67

output rises from its current stagnant levels. Competition may be expected from employers in other sectors of the domestic economy who will also be required to respond to technological developments and will be seeking to expand their engineering capabilities. Moreover, employers in other countries, particularly in the USA and within the EEC, will face the same market pressures and will be seeking to recruit extra engineers; already a number of UK engineers have been attracted to overseas employment by the high salaries offered.

3.52 We have not attempted to quantify national requirements for engineers of different types and levels in the future. Since it is not realistic to anticipate with any confidence any specific future industrial scenario, it is equally unrealistic to attempt to quantify future engineering manpower requirements except in the most general and indicative terms. Our scepticism of such forecasting is strengthened by the lack of any adequate data base for assessing *current* demands and requirements. We nonetheless firmly believe that the demand will exist to provide employment for as many engineers as can feasibly be produced for many years to come and we see no danger of creating an over-supply of engineers. A technology-based education will always be an asset to the individual in the modern world, since it provides the foundations for a great variety of careers within and outside engineering.

The prospects for supply

3.53 The future flow of graduates from engineering degree courses depends on several variables: demographic trends; the proportion of school leavers entering higher education (which is virtually static); the proportion of those choosing an engineering career; and the proportion of entrants to such courses who eventually graduate ('wastage' is currently around 20 per cent overall, mostly among students with weaker entrance qualifications).

Figure 3.4. Population aged 18—United Kingdom

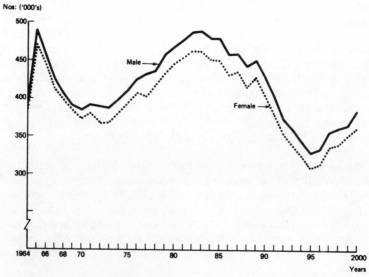

Source: Government Actuary's Department.

68

3.54 Figure 3.4 shows the past and projected numbers in the UK 18 year-old age cohort rising since 1972—largely explaining recent increases in home admissions to engineering courses—continuing on an upward trend until 1983, and falling gradually until 1989 and then steeply until 1995.

Table 3.6 Entrants to universities, polytechnics and other colleges, to read for first degrees in engineering*—UK

| | Admissions to universities | | | | | | Enrolments on CNAA degree courses (1st year) | | Total Entrants (000's) |
| | Home | | | Overseas | | | | | |
	Males (000's)	Females (000's)	Total (000's)	(M + F) (000's)	Total (000's)	Overseas as proportion of total %	Total M + F (000's)	Overseas as proportion† of total %	
1969–70	8·6	0·2	8·8	0·7	9·4	7	2·6	9	12·0
1970–71	8·6	0·2	8·8	0·8	9·6	8	2·7	11	12·3
1971–72	8·5	0·2	8·7	0·9	9·6	9	2·9	13	12·5
1972–73	7·7	0·2	7·9	1·2	9·1	13	3·2	14	12·3
1973–74	7·0	0·2	7·2	1·4	8·6	16	3·2	19	11·8
1974–75	7·1	0·2	7·3	1·9	9·2	21	3·6	24	12·8
1975–76	7·5	0·2	7·7	2·2	9·9	22	4·2	31	14·1
1976–77	7·8	0·3	8·1	2·4	10·6	23	4·8	30	15·4
1977–78	8·4	0·4	8·7	2·5	11·3	22	5·1	28	16·4
1978–79	8·6	0·5	9·0	2·2	11·2	20	5·1	26	16·3

* The figures given in this table are from published sources (UCCA, UGC, CNAA and DES). They do not match those for 'Group III' in DES Statistics (which cover all Engineering and Technology) because surveying and certain technologies outside the direct remit of the Committee of Inquiry into the Engineering Profession, (amounting in 1978–79 to 1·1 thousand for Universities and 1·5 thousand for CNAA) have been excluded.

† Estimates.

69

Unless this demographic decline after 1983 can be offset by a comparably steep increase in the proportion of school leavers entering higher education (of which there is little sign) this implies a fall in the total number of graduates after 1985–87. This in turn will be reflected in falling numbers of new engineers *unless* engineering can claim an increasing proportion of all home students. There are at present only slight signs of such a trend. However engineering still claims a lower proportion of all home male students than it did before 1973.

3.55 Table 3.6 shows that admissions to engineering and related degree courses have risen in recent years, and in 1978 totalled over 16·3 thousand. Employers can expect some rise in the numbers graduating from 1979 until the late-1980s. The recent levels of output of graduate engineers (see Table 3.2) represent those who began their course in 1973–75, when the intake to engineering degree courses dropped markedly below former levels. However a more detailed examination of admission trends, juxtaposed with the demographic projections for the 18-year old age cohort in Figure 3.4 reveals worrying trends. Admissions of *home* students rose at a steady rate of around 500 additional entrants each year, since 1974–75 and 1977–78, but have still only just regained the intake levels of ten years ago. However a rather steeper rise, of around 700 additional entrants to universities a year between 1974–75 has come from increases in the number of overseas students which has nearly trebled over the past decade and now accounts for nearly 25 per cent of all engineering undergraduates (20 per cent of the latest university entrants, and 26 per cent of those to polytechnics). The increase in overseas admissions has levelled off over the last two years and in view of the recently proposed changes in regulations relating to fees it is very likely that their numbers will fall further in future years.

3.56 Recent intake levels suggest that about 14,000 engineers may graduate in future each year, compared with the 1978 output of around 12,000 graduates. The potential increment which this might imply for the UK stock of engineers is constrained by the proportion of overseas students (most of whom return home upon completing their studies), the proportion of all students not completing their course, and the forecast fall in total home student numbers after 1983. The potential will only be realised if the demand from home school-leavers (boys and girls) to enter engineering courses can be stimulated to rise sufficiently to offset these constraints. We believe the likelihood of this depends largely on the attractions of engineering-based careers which employers offer.

3.57 As Figure 3.4 shows, the number of 18-year olds in the population will continue on its current upward trend until 1983, and will decline thereafter. Nonetheless the number of 18-year olds in 1989 will be the same as it was in 1978. There is therefore absolutely no reason why the number of engineering graduates need drop until 1992 or 1993. Indeed if we can improve the engineering participation rate (which is subject to the limitations on the pool of young people adequately qualified at entry—see paragraph 3.12) we could foresee a slight increase in the number of engineering graduates, even with some undergoing a longer academic formation period than at present. We thus have fourteen years in which scope exists to increase and improve the stock of engineers. No time must be lost in realising this scope, otherwise human resources which can be used to save us from national decline will be squandered.

Attracting more women into engineering

3.58 Our adoption of the masculine when referring to engineers in this report is not just a stylistic convenience—less than $\frac{1}{2}$ per cent of the current stock of engineers are women. Engineering has thus been recruiting from only half of the population. Girls now comprise a little over 3 per cent of all engineering students, which is a marked improvement on past showing but is still minimal when it is considered that most of the increase in total numbers of students in sixth forms and higher education over the past decade has come from girls and that 42 per cent of graduate scientists from universities are women.[1] We would welcome an increase in the proportion of women graduating in engineering and urge all concerned to work towards this goal.

3.59 There is no intrinsic reason why women should not become engineers, as many have proved. Few engineers' jobs entail heavy or dirty work; indeed, one of the reasons that some people are keen to attract women into engineering is that they might help demolish the myth of the 'boiler-suits and spanners' image which engineers have long been trying, with limited success, to shake off. Reasons why more women have not entered engineering include:

—*sex differentiation in the curriculum*: conventional school programmes for girls, reinforced by attitudes of parents and teachers, tend to steer them away from educational choices which might lead to engineering careers;

—*the lack of precedents*: girls may know women who are doctors or solicitors and will certainly know women teachers, but they are less likely to know, or even to know of, women engineers;

—*working patterns*: the need to keep abreast of continually developing technologies is sometimes a deterrent to women who envisage breaking their careers to raise a family—and employers may be reluctant to provide expensive training for women who might leave work soon after they have qualified. Women engineers share with other working women with dependent children the problem and expense of employing childminders if they wish to return to work, a problem exacerbated by the lack of any tax relief upon such expenses.

3.60 *Among the recommendations suggested in evidence to us[2] which we endorse whole-heartedly, are:*

(a) the many schools/industry liaison schemes should make special efforts to ensure that teachers and careers advisers are properly informed about the many opportunities open to girls from an engineering formation;

---

[1] DES Statistics of Education: Vol VI (Universities)

[2] Notably evidence from the Women's Engineering Society (WES), Equal Opportunities Commission (EOC), and the Engineering Industry Training Board (EITB)

(b) schemes such as the IMechE/ICE/IEE's 'Opening Windows on Engineering' which enable enthusiastic young engineers to talk about their work in schools, should be expanded placing special emphasis on involving young women engineers;

(c) engineering departments in universities and polytechnics should enable and encourage women (as well as men) who have developed an interest in engineering after they have embarked upon maths or science courses to transfer to engineering after their first year, providing such bridging programmes as may be necessary;

(d) women wishing to maintain their expertise and confidence in a technical field during a break from full-time practice should be provided with opportunities to work on a part-time basis, employers would thereby be increasing their prospects of longer term returns on their initial training investment;

(e) the MSC, through the Industry Training Boards, should initiate a scheme whereby women re-entering engineering practice after a break could be attached to a company for a practical on-the-job retraining course of, say, six months with a nominated tutor.

Overcoming continuing constraints

3.61 Measures to increase the future supply of engineers will inevitably take many years to produce benefits felt on any scale within industry. In the meantime firms are likely to face continuing constraints from shortages of engineers and support staff to fill their growing requirement for an engineering input to their activities. It will be essential for employers to make optimum use of the contributions of the current stock of engineers, drawing on all available sources of engineering expertise. We considered four such sources: consultants; technical intelligence from overseas; university and polytechnic departments; and applied scientists and mathematicians.

3.62 There is an extensive network of private and publicly funded technical consulting and research organisations in this country, available to provide companies with advice on a wide range of engineering problems. The attractions of the variety and high level of much consultancy work, and the high salaries many consultancy firms pay, enable these bodies to employ very able engineers; (some companies told us that they had lost their best engineers to consultants and agencies, and had then to buy back the services of their ex-employees from them). The advice of consultants can be especially valuable to small firms, which employ relatively few professional engineers 'in-house'. It has been suggested (for example, in the ACARD report on 'Industrial Innovation')[1] that such firms claim to find consultancy services prohibitively expensive, or difficult to select, although the Association of Consulting Engineers provides a source of expert advice and both the Design Council and the Department of Industry (via the Manufacturing Advisory Service) run schemes to give small firms access to subsidised or even free consultancy advice. Consultancy services must not be regarded as an indulgence or a luxury

---

[1] Advisory Council for Applied Research and Development (ACARD)—'Industrial Innovation', HMSO; December 1978

by firms short of engineering expertise but—when needed—as equally essential as new capital plant.

3.63 We noted in Chapter II the notorious insularity within parts of UK industry towards ideas from outside whether from other organisations in this country or from overseas. This is in contrast to the willingness of companies in Japan, Germany and the USA to take up and develop promising marketable ideas from any source. As Table 3.7 shows, while Britain has long been a net earner on royalties from patents and licenses, Japan and Germany have run substantial deficits on their public accounts which have been repaid many times over from exports of products and processes derived from imported ideas.

Table 3.7 Receipts and payments for licenses and patents

		1973	1976
		$m	$m
Japan*	—receipts	82	175
	—payments	661	799
		$m	$m
West Germany*	—receipts	219	306
	—payments	602	806
		£m	£m
UK	—receipts	201	387
	—payments	160	296

Sources: * IMF Balance of Payments Yearbooks, quoted from 'Second Report of the Select Committee on Science and Technology 1977–78: 'Innovation, Research and Development in Japanese Science-based Industry' HC682–1, 1978.

† Central Statistical Office; 'UK Balance of Payments'.

British companies seeking potentially exploitable ideas and know-how from overseas can draw upon a variety of sources, in particular the Overseas Technical Information Unit in the Department of Industry, which collates and disseminates market and technological intelligence (including information about opportunities for collaborative ventures and licensing arrangements) collected by Technology Attachés to British embassies in several industrial countries. *We recommend that the activities and services of the OTIU be given greater publicity, and that they be expanded if industrial interest subsequently justifies this.*

3.64 A significant proportion of the nation's engineering resource is employed within the higher education system, where it is at present largely untapped by industry. This is in contrast to the situation in Germany or Holland (for example) where we found evidence of day-to-day collaboration and interchange between engineering schools and industry on a scale found in relatively few UK teaching departments.[1] A variety of schemes in Britain seek to build up links between academic engineering and industrial practice,

[1] CIEP Survey of UK Engineering Departments (Appendix F); also Appendix E

73

for example the Teaching Company scheme, but these cannot substitute for the full-time placement of staff in each others' environment—teaching staff in industry or engineering staff in teaching departments—for extended periods. We fully recognise the practical difficulties for both sides of such secondments, but nevertheless it is our view that mutual benefits would arise from an expansion of the number of secondments on these lines. Firms could learn of current developments in engineering science and the teaching staff would benefit from experience of current engineering practice. *We recommend that the Government —and in due course the Engineering Authority—greatly extends current schemes for two-way exchanges of staff between industry and engineering schools* (removing constraints such as problems regarding pension rights).

3.65 Where the skill or knowledge constraints experienced by companies are quite specific they can sometimes be met by people possessing the particular skills required, even though they may lack the wide knowledge and perspective of fully qualified engineers. For example, the education of mathematicians and others provides a good grounding for computer-related applications, while much of the knowledge acquired through a physics degree is potentially applicable in the electronic engineering field. Many such people, initially trained as scientists, already make a substantial and valuable contribution to the engineering dimension. *This should be encouraged by the establishment of a number of six-month or one-year conversion courses through which people whose initial formation was in suitable subjects can develop specific engineering skills.* Completion of such a course could be taken into account if the individuals concerned later wished to extend their formation and become qualified as engineers.

Conclusions on supply

3.66 The supply of new engineering graduates over the past two or three years has been lower than in previous years, reflecting a slump in admissions to engineering degree courses in 1972–74 (in turn reflecting the manifest insecurity of engineering employment in 1971–73). Output of engineering graduates is now rising again and is likely to continue rising until the mid-1980s. Thereafter it is probable that the number of new engineers available for employment will fall rapidly unless a significant increase in the proportion of all students entering universities and polytechnics can be induced to follow engineering courses. We fear that by the late 1980s a serious shortfall is likely in the supply of new engineers relative to continuing high demands from employers. It is imperative therefore that the national stock and supply of engineers is used as effectively as possible and that employers actively explore and make use of every alternative source of engineering expertise. It will be essential, at the same time, that a system of formation for future engineers, highly attractive both to students and to prospective employers be developed.

(e) Summary of main conclusions and recommendations

(i) The information currently available about the stock and distribution of engineering manpower, and changes in it, is quite inadequate. This data is essential to employers, educators and the Government in their efforts to match national supply and demands for engineers.

We recommend that official surveys should in future be structured to collect, inter alia, the information which would enable an up-to-date national inventory of engineering manpower to be built up.

(ii) A drift of many engineers out of engineering practice and into engineering-related activities during their careers, added to retirements from the stock, implies a significant annual requirement for new engineers simply to maintain current numbers in engineering practice. Since most engineers now enter engineering employment through the higher-education system, conscious decisions are needed at an early age from potential engineers in order to obtain the necessary qualifications at school and afterwards. We regard as the *key* determinant of the future supply the relative intrinsic and material attractions of engineering against other careers. Nonetheless *we recommend* that schools act to ensure that the maximum number of pupils retain the option to become engineers, for example by retaining the study of mathematics and physics to the age of 16+.

(iii) Many employers have complained of shortages of engineers. However, assessment of their complaints is complicated by the *ad hoc* nature of their reports, the mixing of demands for numbers and demands for qualities, and the use of graduates on sub-professional work. Neither the employing nor the education systems have yet fully adjusted to the implications for engineering of the post-Robbins expansion in higher education. The remedies for current deficiencies lie in raising the quality of the whole body of graduate engineers, including (but not exclusively) the academic elite.

(iv) The contribution of engineers within the engineering dimension is attenuated by the national shortage of technicians, which has meant that many highly qualified engineers have been underemployed on lower level support work.

We recommend that the Government investigate the shortage of technicians and introduce corrective measures as a matter of urgency.

(v) Evidence of ambiguity in some employers' stated requirements for engineers, and reports that engineers are often used to limited purpose suggests the need for a major national programme to stimulate employers' awareness of the engineering dimension and the benefits to firms obtained by using engineers to effective purpose.

We recommend that such a programme be among the responsibilities of the new Engineering Authority which we propose.

(vi) Evidence about the relative pay and career prospects of engineers is mixed. While some engineers undoubtedly do well on both counts many others are unhappy that their rewards compare poorly with those of other professional groups and do not reflect the full value of their contributions to the economy.

We recommend that employers appraise whether their salary and employment structures fully recognise and reflect the value and contribution of engineers within their enterprise, and consider improved salary and career structures for engineers, as already introduced in some organisations, in relation to the potential benefits to be derived.

(vii) Manufacturing companies must recognise engineers as key assets within the engineering dimension and act upon their shared interests in developing and making best use of those assets.

We recommend that the current best practices to this end be generalised among UK organisations through the adoption of 'engineering manpower audits' initiated and supervised at Board level.

(viii) Total demand for engineers from manufacturing and other sectors will increase to require many more engineers than are currently available. There is no danger of producing too many engineers, since an engineering formation can lead to a wide range of careers in and outside engineering.

The national objective should be to produce as many engineers as possible.

(ix) Taking account of demographic projections the prospects of a sustained increase in current numbers of graduates after the early 1990s are slim. Nonetheless scope for increasing current numbers of engineering graduates over the next decade comes from generating increased demand for places from home entrants (including girls) and minimising wastage through 'drop outs', *all of which we recommend*.

(x) It is likely that shortages of engineers will persist in the medium term (although they may be ameliorated by increasing graduate numbers for the next few years). This makes it vital that employers make optimum use of the stock available and maximise engineers' productivity by all possible means.

CHAPTER IV

Engineering Formation for the 1980s and Beyond

(a) Introduction

4.1 In this chapter we propose means of ensuring that future British engineers receive a full and balanced 'formation' to prepare them for careers as practising engineers. We have adopted this term, in preference to the more usual education and training, to convey the progressive process through which a young engineer develops his or her technical and personal capabilities. This process starts while he or she is still at school and is taken much further during his or her time in higher education, but it can only be properly brought to fruition in the working environment in which he or she will practice as an engineer. For this reason we lay special emphasis on the role of employers in structuring and supervising the experience gained by young engineers in their first years of work, which are in many ways the most critical in the package. The academic years should seek best to develop in students the analytical and scientific foundations on which they will build their practical skills and also to prepare them to begin synthesising and applying what they have learnt from the time they enter employment. The formation process thereafter is one which will continue throughout each engineer's working life, but we have concentrated on the process up to the point of transition at which the young engineer can show himself or herself ready to assume responsibility in his or her own right as a qualified engineer (albeit a junior one).

4.2 Even if the changes which we shall suggest for improving the formation of future engineers were to be implemented at once, it would still be six or seven years before the first fruits of the revised system were able to begin careers in industry, and even longer before they were able to make their impact in significant numbers. The country cannot afford to wait this long before introducing measures to improve the engineering dimension. So, whilst efforts to strengthen the formation of the future supply of engineers must begin urgently, equal attention must be given to the needs of those already practising as engineers, and those joining them from the existing formation system, to enable them to develop their potential to the full. In a constantly changing world, learning and development must be a continuous process throughout the engineer's career. We shall suggest how this might be provided for through greater in-career 'continuing formation' for current and future engineers.

(b) The current formation of engineers

Factors at secondary school

4.3 The formation of the prospective engineer begins at school. The skills and outlook acquired at this stage directly affect individuals' subsequent formation in the higher education system and during employment and thus their

77

attitudes and approach to work as engineers. We commented earlier[1] on the part the schools play in shaping attitudes and how these affect the cultural standing of engineering, and on the impact of policies followed in schools on the supply of future engineering manpower. In this Chapter we are concerned with the impact of schools' education on those who may become engineers.

4.4 The criticisms repeated most frequently in the evidence to us concerned the standards attained by school leavers in mathematics and physics. We received submissions from educationalists[2] alleging variable and often inadequate standards of attainment amongst engineering students in mathematics and physics, which made the subsequent teaching of the basic principles of engineering much more difficult and required that course time be devoted later to remedial teaching in these subjects. These shortcomings in the teaching of mathematics and physics (and other science subjects) at school level are widely held to be due to shortages in the supply of qualified mathematics and science teachers. We received evidence to the effect that these shortages have been felt more acutely in England and Wales because of the wider distribution of able schoolchildren among establishments since the move to comprehensive secondary education. The problem is exacerbated by variations in the content of what students are taught in their A-level mathematics and physics syllabi; there are, for example, over 60 different A-level mathematics syllabi. The teaching of mathematics in schools in England and Wales is currently under review by the Cockcroft Committee[3]. *We hope that they will recommend specific actions towards a major effort to improve the provision and standards of mathematics teaching in schools. We urge the Department of Education and Science to consider devoting similar attention to the teaching of science (especially physics) in schools.* We note that in Scotland reviews of syllabi (which are common to all schools) in mathematics, physics and engineering science have recently been completed or are currently taking place.

4.5 We also received a substantial volume of evidence both from educationalists and employers concerning the generally poor communicative skills—both written and verbal—of many engineers and engineering students, and their narrowness of outlook.[4] Effectiveness for an engineer demands a high level of skill in communication, plus a basic understanding of social affairs and the exercise of judgement and discrimination in non-technical matters. We pointed in Chapter III to the advantages which a broader school curriculum might produce in enlarging the pool of potential candidates for engineering.[5] Another advantage might be to ensure that those entering engineering courses had studied, say, economics or a language (as well as mathematics and physics) during their senior school years and that they were thus better equipped for an engineering formation and career.

---

[1] See 2.5

[2] Evidence from the Committee of the Engineering Professors Conference (CEPC) to the Committee of Inquiry into the Engineering Profession; Paragraph 9

[3] Committee of Inquiry into the Teaching of Mathematics in schools

[4] See Appendix D: Visits to Organisations Employing Engineers

[5] See 3.12

Schools industry links

4.6 Instilling an appreciation and understanding of industry and technology is a highly desirable, if not essential, requirement of school education both for potential engineers and also for all the others who will live and work in a technology-dominated world. This was acknowledged in the 1977 Green Paper on 'Education in Schools'[1], which cited as one of the principal aims of school education:

'to help children appreciate how the nation earns and maintains its standard-of-living, and properly to esteem the essential roles of industry and commerce in this process.'

Although significant attention has been paid in recent years to the development of links between schools and industry, much remains to be done to generate a full understanding of such issues through the curriculum and hence by those teaching it.

4.7 The tenor and content of what is taught to children in schools is to a large extent established by the examination syllabi for the main curriculum subjects. Efforts to relate the curriculum more closely to the aims described above can be either constrained or encouraged by the policies adopted by the Examining Boards. We have not been able to undertake a study of the extent to which examinations syllabi in subjects like geography, history, economics or the sciences are geared to encouraging pupils to develop their awareness of the nature of the modern economy and the pervasiveness of technology in its development. *We commend the moves which have already been made in this direction by some Examining Boards, and urge that these and others regularly monitor their syllabi to ensure that they meet and keep pace with these desiderata.*

4.8 Many good schemes seek to kindle the interest of schoolchildren in the world of engineering and industry—so many, in fact, that to cite examples would be invidious. Schemes range from those which bring young engineers to talk careers to those collaborative programmes between teachers and outsiders which introduce a 'real life' flavour in the day-to-day syllabus, especially in mathematics and science subjects. The diversity of these schemes is a strength, but it has led to an unevenness of coverage across different schools. Local Education Authorities have an overall responsibility to consider schools/industry liaison, but often lack the necessary industrial contacts. The Science and Technology Regional Organisations (SATROs), which bring together edu-cationalists and industrialists at local level, can help here in providing 'clearing houses' for information about schemes and programmes and by liaising between individual schools and local companies. *We recommend that the Departments of Industry and of Education and Science ensure the availability of adequate funds for existing and new SATROs to develop in this role.*

4.9 *We would like to see every secondary school involved in one or more schools/industry scheme, and every company developing links with at least one local school.* Companies not yet so involved, will be pleasantly surprised at

[1] 'Education in Schools. A Consultative Document' Cmnd 6869, HMSO 1977. Paragraph 1.19v

the benefits to be derived from such links and at the talent which can be exposed. Within the schools, additional encouragement should come from subject teachers, careers specialists and careers officers. At present there are insufficient qualified careers advisers[1] and very many pupils obtain no proper careers counselling at all (as our own surveys confirmed).[2] Good careers advice from an early age is an excellent way of generating an appreciation of a wide range of jobs. Measures which would encourage a more positive and informed presentation of engineering to pupils in schools include:

(a) *greatly improved careers advice from people with the time and experience to do the job properly,* drawing on joint industry/education expertise through the for example Engineering Careers Information Service[3] and the Industrial Society;

(b) *short secondments of teachers into industry,* such as are available under the jointly run I Mech E/IEE Teachers Fellowships[4] scheme;

(c) *more emphasis upon industry and technology in teacher training courses* (which should be easier now that many such courses are run within polytechnics);

(d) *greater publicity* from the Institutions and the Industrial Training Boards *for the many opportunities for support and sponsorship,* eg from companies, and from the new National Engineering Scholarships scheme, *for students of engineering.*

Entry to higher education

4.10 Much has been made of alleged shortcomings in the quality of those entering engineering, for example in studies by the British Association for the Advancement of Science[5] and the Parliamentary Select Committee on Science and Technology[6], (although it must be said that we heard similar complaints—albeit to a much lesser extent—about young engineers in other countries). It is alleged in particular that the distribution of academic talent among entrants to engineering degree courses is excessively weighted to the lower end of the ability scale. While no-one disputes that UK engineering courses attract a good proportion of those with very good scores at A-level (or Scottish Higher), there is concern that the long 'tail' of candidates with relatively poor examination results has depressed the academic centre of gravity of the engineering student population. Fear has been expressed that the acceptance

---

[1] Correspondence with the Department of Education and Science

[2] Policy Studies Institute. A General Survey of Professional Engineers and A Survey of Former Students of Engineering and Science

[3] Engineering Careers Information Service, sponsored by the Engineering Industry Training Board, the Engineering Employers Federation and the Confederation ·of Shipbuilding and Engineering Unions, endeavours to attract the right calibre of people into all types of engineering by means of various types of publicity

[4] Evidence to the Committee of Inquiry into the Engineering Profession from the Institution of Mechanical Engineers and the Institution of Electrical Engineers, on Teacher Fellowships

[5] 'Education, Engineers and Manufacturing Industry. A Report to the British Association Co-ordinating Group.' British Association for the Advancement of Science, 1977

[6] 'Third Report from the Select Committee on Science and Technology: University/Industry Relations' HC 680, HMSO 1977

of students with poor qualifications causes the more able to reject engineering and further that the engineering schools cannot provide appropriate teaching to cater for such a wide range of student abilities.

4.11 To an extent, this situation can be seen as a consequence of past attempts to increase the supply of qualified engineers by increasing the supply of places, particularly during the late-1960s and early 1970s. As the provision of engineering places increased faster than demand from able students, so heads of engineering departments have been faced over the last ten years with the choice of leaving places empty in their departments (thus jeopardising future funding), of accepting overseas applicants (of whom the numbers have risen steadily), or of using the UCCA clearing house system to recruit home candidates whose qualifications were inadequate to gain a place the first time round. They have often followed the two latter courses, thereby adding to the number of overseas and less able home students, whilst the number of academically more able home students has remained more or less constant.

4.12 Some of the major engineering Institutions have responded to this trend by proposing raising the academic requirements for their corporate membership; for example the Institution of Civil Engineers has agreed on a points system which will make entry to full membership difficult to obtain for candidates without good A-levels and the Institutions of Electrical and of Mechanical Engineers are considering restricting future membership to candidates offering high performance at degree level. In our view these proposals provide no real solution to the problem of improving recruitment to engineering whatever they may do for the membership. Very good students have been entering engineering schools—for example over 21 per cent of the 1978 university intake offering three or more A-levels had 13 or more points—and we do not believe that an arbitrary stiffening of entry requirements will raise these numbers much, if at all. There is a danger that potential engineering students would be deterred by higher Institutional entry requirements from pursuing an engineering formation, even though they may well have the aptitude and ability to become capable engineers. Pertinent to discussion of the 'quality' of entrants to engineering courses is the observation that nearly a quarter of engineering students have worked in industry before entering their course.[1] These include many who left school before completing A-levels but who now hold alternative entry qualifications such as Ordinary National Diplomas and Certificates. It would be folly to discount the experience and practical education of these people as inferior to the academic examination performance of the student who continued study in school, which a policy of simply raising academic entry standards would imply.

Current engineering education
4.13 We showed earlier[2] that until the 1960s most engineers obtained their formal education through part-time study or block release while they were working in industry. Only a minority—less than a quarter—took full-time

---

[1] Courses see 3.8.
[2] Policy Studies Institute: A Survey of Former Students of Engineering and Science.

degree courses. These proportions were changed during the 1960s, following the expansion of university places after the Robbins Report[1], the conversion of the Colleges of Advanced Technology (CATs) to university status, and the rise of the polytechnics and other colleges offering degree courses. The trend towards an all-graduate engineering profession was reinforced in 1971, when the CEI decreed that a degree would be required for all future Chartered Engineers (with very limited exceptions). A 3-year full-time degree or a 4-year sandwich course has now become the normal educational route for aspirant engineers in England and Wales. In Scotland ordinary engineering degrees may be awarded after three or four years of study with the Honours degree taking four years; selection for the Honours course may take place after two years although this varies according to the pre-requisites of the degree programme. Sandwich courses can take between $3\frac{1}{2}$ and five years according to the class of degree.

4.14 Degree-level courses in engineering are offered at 48 universities and university colleges, 28 polytechnics, and 12 other institutions, although the size of establishment varies considerably among these. Some have small intakes of 50 students each year (or even less) while the largest ex-CATs take over 600. The 18 biggest schools (those graduating over 200 students a year) provide some 70 per cent of the total output. Over 16,300 students embarked on engineering related degree courses in these institutions in 1978—about 11,200 in universities and another 5,100 on CNAA courses in polytechnics[2], etc. On past indications around 80 per cent of this number will graduate in engineering, which suggests that the number of engineers graduating in 1981 will be around 13,000—compared with the 1978 output of around 10,000. Demographic trends and participation rates lead us to hope for some further increase in the numbers of home students graduating until the late-1980s, but total numbers will probably decline since new admissions of overseas students are forecast to fall steeply. After 1983 the intake of home students will probably also decline unless a major increase in the overall proportion studying engineering can be achieved.

4.15 In this context it is interesting to note that the number of engineers expressed as a proportion of the relevant age cohorts is not markedly lower in Britain than in most other industrial countries with the notable exceptions of Germany and Japan. Table 4.1 gives the comparisons:

---

[1] Report of the Committee on Higher Education; chaired by Lord Robbins, Cmnd 2154, HMSO 1963.

[2] See Table 3.6.

Table 4.1. **Engineering graduates as a proportion of relevant age group (first degree)**

		%
UK	1978	1·7
Sweden	1977	1·6
France	1977	1·3
USA	1978	1·6
Germany	1977	2·3
Japan	1978	4·2

Note: These figures include both home and overseas students
Source: Unesco Yearbook updated.

4.16 The recent announcement of cuts in the funding for higher education from 1980 onwards, linked to proposals that fees for overseas students be charged at an 'economic' rate to make up the deficit, raises the prospect of substantial reductions in the annual provision of funds for engineering education. Some 40 per cent of overseas students study engineering and it seems probable to us that their numbers will fall steeply once the higher fees come into force. If, as seems probable, the practical effect of these policies is that overall home student numbers are frozen at about current levels, this might entail some engineering departments having to turn away acceptable home applicants over the next four or five years. *We would deplore any such consequences since this would mean that current opportunities for increasing the numbers of engineers graduating over the next decade (see para 3.52) will be lost forever and the consequences will be with us for many years.* The national capacity to prepare engineers should be built up further, not run down, at this critical stage in Britain's economic history.

4.17 Most British degree courses are specialised, with students registering on discipline-based courses in aeronautical, civil, mechanical, electrical, chemical or other branches of engineering from the outset. Some universities and CNAA institutions offer broadly-based 'unified' degree courses in which students study engineering science over a wide field for two years, usually concentrating on a particular field in the third and final year. However the system usually requires students to commit themselves to a specific type of engineering, when applying for admission, at a time when they can have only a limited appreciation of its various branches or of their own aptitudes.

4.18 Engineering education has been the subject of a good deal of critical comment in previous reports and in the evidence to us. Complaints commonly voiced, especially by employers, are that the education of engineers is unduly scientific and theoretical; that newly-graduated engineers lack awareness of 'real life' constraints to text-book solutions; that they are oriented too much towards research and development work and are not interested in working in production or marketing functions; and that they lack understanding of the factors in the commercial success of their employing organisation.

4.19 Much of this criticism is accepted by the engineering professoriate, and in their evidence to us the Committee of the Engineering Professors'

Conference (CEPC) agreed that *most current first-degree courses are not generally well-matched to the requirements of industry*. The following extract from CEPC's submission describes the main features of full-time British engineering courses:

'The 3 year degree is mainly devoted to engineering science, though in some courses, especially in sandwich courses having integrated practical experience, a somewhat greater emphasis is given to design. Generally however, the time available in the academic part of all courses is insufficient for professional topics and for the study of engineering practice, although most courses allow some exposure to the elements of management studies, including economics. The central aim of most university departments is to give a rigorous treatment of engineering science which emphasizes fundamentals so as to provide their graduates with the ability later in their training and their careers to tackle real engineering problems in an original and flexible way . . . . Students thus typically reach the graduation stage with a knowledge of engineering science and of analytical tools but they usually have little experience and skill in their application to engineering tasks as they occur in practice; they are also often without an understanding of the constraints under which engineering work is conducted in practice. Under the present arrangements, the development of this experience and these skills in professional practice must be developed after graduation in industry.'

4.20 This appraisal was frequently echoed in the evidence we received, although such comments were applied far less to sandwich courses, which intersperse formal teaching with periods of working experience; about 30 per cent of new engineers currently graduate from sandwich courses. Employers have expressed themselves keen to recruit sandwich graduates but, paradoxically, a major constraint on the expansion of these courses has been the difficulty of finding industrial placements for students, especially for those not initially sponsored on the course by an employer. Our firm view is that formal engineering teaching should be closely oriented to practice and applications in the manner which we discuss later. In addition we believe it is preferable that engineering students obtain an understanding of engineering practice within the working environment from the early stages of their formation. In an ideal world all engineering students would obtain this industrial experience through some form of sandwich course although opinions vary on whether the 'thick' or 'thin' models are most appropriate. However, we are forced to the conclusions that this must remain a long-term objective. In the meantime efforts must be made to ensure that full-time courses aim to impart as much as possible of the understanding of the place of engineering within the whole engineering dimension, obtained from the best sandwich courses. The formation packages proposed later in this chapter are designed to achieve this.

Current engineering training

4.21 It has been widely accepted in this country—for example in the membership criteria set by the professional Institutions—that an academic institution cannot by itself provide a complete formation for an engineer, and that engineering practice is best learnt where engineering is done. The initial formation process must therefore be completed with a period of industrial training and working experience. Qualities which employers claim to seek from graduates are almost invariably expressed in terms of personal attributes such as 'motivation', 'ability to work in a team', 'ability to communicate', etc, in addition to technical knowledge. Very few say they seek a 'finished' engineer—that is, one who can fit into their activities from day one—and a number told us that they were against the engineering schools attempting to teach undergraduates specialised applications or general management studies which were almost always out-of-date and/or irrelevant to the company. *It should follow— and in the best companies does—that employers accept responsibility for developing the abilities of newly-recruited engineers and completing their professional formation. Too often this does not happen.*

4.22 In the past, when graduate engineers were relatively few, the recognised way for an engineering graduate to obtain this practical training was through a graduate apprenticeship, and places with outstanding companies (such as Metropolitan-Vickers, BTH and English Electric) were keenly sought. Many senior engineers in industry today proudly claim a double pedigree—from their university and from the company where they served their graduate apprenticeship. Other engineers who followed the 'part-time' HNC route to professional status obtained excellent training 'on-the-job': Rolls-Royce's premium apprenticeship scheme, for example, supplied many of the company's top designers during and after the war.

4.23 Much of the evidence submitted to us, and our own surveys, suggested that the quantity of formal training obtained by engineers has progressively diminished over the last 20 years. The part-time route to qualification has declined markedly, and now provides only a fraction of past numbers. As far as graduates are concerned, their structured formation all too often ceases when they begin work. The Industrial Training Act established a number of Industrial Training Boards, part of whose remit extended to encouraging the provision of training to graduate engineers within industry. Their impact has been limited; for example the Engineering Industry Training Board reported that only 30 per cent of graduates from full-time courses—or 50 per cent of total graduates when sandwich course students are included—entering industries within their scope received training to their standards[1]. Only a minority of those questioned in our own survey of young graduate engineers[2] stated that they had received formal training after graduation specifically for their first professional post. Many graduate recruits are 'thrown in at the deep end' without further training, almost always in technical jobs where their university experience is notionally relevant, on the principle that 'cream will rise to the top'. In fact the 'cream' is often the first to get frustrated for want of encouragement and opportunities to develop their capabilities.

---

[1] Engineering Industry Training Board (EITB). Evidence to CIEP. Paragraph 21 and '. . . Since so many full-time graduates enter industrial employment without formal training to EITB recommendations, they have little opportunity subsequently to consider jobs other than the one they have been recruited for. The graduate given broad based initial training over a period of 18–20 months has a better chance to move to a job to fit his talents and inclination and the industry's needs'.

[2] Policy Studies Institute. A Survey of Former Students of Engineering and Science.

4.24 The move to an all-graduate profession in recent years has thus not been accompanied by satisfactory training for graduates in crucial elements of engineering practice and applications. *It is small wonder that industry complains of graduates who are not practically inclined when the formation received by so many graduates neglects this training.* The capabilities of outside agencies to counteract this trend have greatly weakened. The effective decline of the levy/ grant system which the Industrial Training Boards used to encourage post-graduate training has deprived them of leverage over employers in this area and while the professional Institutions and the Engineers' Registration Board specify criteria for post-graduate training as part of their membership requirements, the majority of their corporate members enter on the basis of 'experience in lieu of training'.

Recent developments

4.25 There have been a number of valuable attempts to improve the balance and relevance of engineering education in recent years. Engineering departments in universities and polytechnics keep their courses continually under review, introducing new aspects and new approaches and instilling extra science and technology into courses which over the years have become more and more demanding. Many departments have attempted to give greater weight to design training and have also sought to bring in fresh approaches to laboratory and project work. Another important development has been the introduction of economics, operational research and other business techniques along with the technical engineering content. We support the inclusion of such subjects in the initial formation of all engineers to the extent that all require an understanding of management principles at the start of their careers, but we consider it essential that this is designed to enhance, and not to detract from, a sound technical foundation. As their careers progress engineers may require further general management training to varying degrees according to their particular career paths; so far as their initial formation is concerned we believe that such topics should be introduced on the following basis:

(a) the student should be brought to understand the various constraints of cost, time, market and human considerations under which engineering is actually carried out, and the compromises and judgements required from its practitioners;

(b) the student should be given enough practical examples of these constraints to give him confidence in his ability to recognise engineering problems in their industrial and commercial context; and

(c) the student must be given a general understanding of how the engineering dimension relates to industry and business.

We shall make proposals later for achieving this within the degree course and immediately after graduation.

4.26 A major recent initiative, which aims to attract more highly able students into engineering and to prepare them as 'high fliers' for industry, has been the establishment by the UGC of new 'enhanced' courses at ten institutions, including two polytechnics.[1] The 'enhancement' of these courses refers in most cases to the inclusion in them of a substantial component of business topics and engineering management plus some required experience in industry rather than the extension of engineering practice which we wish to see. The structure of the courses varies greatly between institutions, and some appear much more promising than others. It is too early to pass judgement on the impact of the new 'enhanced' courses as measures to induce more highly-able recruits into engineering, since none have yet graduated any students. However, as experiments, contributing towards a more practice-oriented education for engineers, we welcome the 'enhanced' courses; *but we would wish to see a critical review of the lessons to be learnt from them after they have graduated, say, their first three generations of students.*

4.27 Various attempts have been made to integrate the theoretical and practical elements of engineers' formation. Several universities and polytechnics have achieved close integration with industry on the industrial part of undergraduate sandwich courses and in some cases performance in this part is assessed jointly with employers and counts towards the degree award. A few departments have undertaken a radical review of their traditional engineering courses in collaboration with employers, and have developed new courses structured more closely to teaching engineering practice and to producing engineers with an understanding of engineering in its industrial context. *We strongly commend these joint initiatives between organisations and universities to develop engineering courses with enhanced industrial relevance and hope that more organisations will come to see the mutual benefits of such collaboration.* Our later proposals for formation packages are aimed at encouraging such collaboration.

4.28 Further developments undertaken to counteract shortcomings in current engineering formation have been taken at post-graduate level: for example the SRC/DOI Teaching Company scheme, involving close co-operation between selected companies and universities in planning the 'internship' of young engineers in industry; support by the Control Engineering Panel of the SRC for 'action research in integrated production systems'; a Manufacturing Fellowships scheme run by the Engineering Industry Training Board; and the Total Technology courses sponsored by the SRC. The SRC in particular has been striving to meet criticism that its activities have lacked relevance to industrial needs, but its scope to take such initiatives is limited—in particular, it cannot fund undergraduate developments or post-experience short courses—and it cannot be expected to do very much more in this field than it currently attempts.

---

[1] Institutions offering UGC 'enhanced' courses:

Universities: Birmingham	*Polytechnics:* Sheffield
Brunel	Trent
Cambridge	
London, Imperial College	
Manchester (UMIST)	
Oxford	
Queen's, Belfast	
Strathclyde	

Formation overseas

4.29 Our terms of reference required us to consider the position of engineers overseas, particularly, in the EEC. In fulfilling this remit we looked especially closely at engineering formation in the countries we visited to see whether their practices offered any pointers to possible improvements in the British system. Descriptions of engineering formation in several overseas countries are contained in Appendix E. More detailed accounts are available in other reports.[1]

4.30 The main model of engineering formation in continental Europe is what might be called 'the *German model'*. This system has been in operation in West Germany, Scandinavia, Holland and Switzerland. It distinguishes two streams of engineers, known in West Germany as the Ing Grad and the Dipl Ing. Both are considered professionals and the ratio between the numbers graduating in the two streams has been of the order of 4:1. The Ing Grad student follows a four year course at a Fachhochschule (FH) usually after at least two years' working experience since leaving school. The FH course is strongly practical in orientation and includes substantial training in industry. The Dipl Ing student takes a course nominally lasting five years (though many students require six or seven years) usually at a Technische Hochschule (TH) or a Technical University (TU), entering straight from school after completion of the 'Abitur' at age 18. All holders of a satisfactory 'Abitur' have a right to entry to a TH or TU, but the drop-out rate in the early years of the course from those who cannot stay the pace is high. The first three years of the course are largely devoted to engineering science) although the student is required to spend at least six months working in industry during this period and the last two years to professional engineering practice in a particular discipline. Theoretical and practical instruction is given mostly within the TH and TU, relying heavily upon the close integration between these institutions and industry, and in particular on the substantial industrial experience required *by law* of engineering professors. Both streams are regarded by the State and by employers as 'finished' (that is qualified) engineers once they leave the education system: the Dipl Ing has a flying start to his career and is generally expected ultimately to reach a more senior position than the Ing Grad, although many Ing Grads in practice have highly successful engineering careers and reach top jobs.[2]

4.31 Formation in *France* does not purport to produce a 'finished' engineer to the same extent as the German model, although a French engineering graduate is similarly deemed by the State to be qualified. A distinctive feature of the French system is the prestige and career opportunities attaching to the elite state award of Diplome d'Ingenieure. There is fierce competition

---

[1] 'First Report on the education and training of engineers on the Continent of Europe, with special references to courses in total technology.' Professor A W J Chisholm, University of Salford, June 1975.
'The recruitment, deployment, and status of the Mechanical Engineer in the German Federal Republic.'
Professor S P Hutton, P A Lawrence and Professor J H Smith, University of Southampton. European Society for Engineering Education (SEFI) Guide, 1978.

[2] See Appendix E for details of recent developments in 'German model' courses.

to win a place at one of the 150 or so designated schools of engineering (especially the top nine or ten 'Grandes Ecoles') to study for the Diplome d'Ingenieure because this qualification virtually guarantees a rewarding and influential career within the managerial 'cadre' of French industry and public service. Entry to the engineering schools is through rigorous entry examinations, groups of schools setting their own examination for which candidates prepare through two years' study of mathematics and physics following completion of their 'baccalaureat' at age 17 or 18. By contrast, all baccalaureat holders have a right to enter a university course. The Diplome d'Ingenieure course lasts four or five years and emphasises the analytical and conceptual aspects of engineering as a foundation upon which the individual can build later in his career. The first few years after graduation are usually spent in junior or technician posts to complete the formation package, but promotion thereafter can be very rapid.

4.32 The *Japanese* system of engineering education was originally modelled on the French 4-year course—modified by experience of American methods—with even fiercer competition than in France for entry to the top engineering schools. Japanese engineering formation emphasises postgraduate 'on-the-job' training and development within companies, to which the graduate recruit owes complete and often life-long allegiance. An important feature of the system is the vast number of young people taking engineering courses, with an annual output in excess of 70,000 graduates reflecting the relatively large 18 year-old age cohort in Japan, and their very high participation rate in higher education, as much as the popularity of engineering.

4.33 The system of formation in the *United States* embraces a great variety of opportunities for engineering education. A wide range of institutions offer engineering courses, usually four years in length with some colleges also offering Bachelor of Engineering Technology courses leading to careers supporting the professional level: the Technical Institutes; the vast State Colleges and Universities; the 'Ivy League' colleges; and the world renowned Institutes of Technology in Massachusetts, Illinois and California. There is a substantial throughput of engineering graduates, around 75,000 in 1975. Courses vary considerably in their emphasis in the balance between theory and practice, with minimum standards ensured by a national system of course accreditation (details of which are given in Appendix H). An engineering education is seen in America as providing a ticket to a wide range of jobs, either practising as an engineer or in other functions, and this has contributed to the popularity of engineering among school leavers. An important element of the system is the almost universal willingness of employers to develop the graduate engineer by providing early career challenges and continuing formation opportunities.

4.34 As these brief descriptions indicate, there are important differences between the approach to engineering formation in other countries, and several features distinguish them from the UK system. In particular, it is significant and noteworthy that engineering education in other countries is often provided in specialist institutions, outside and frequently more exclusive and academically prestigious than the universities. In Europe most of these special institutions claim a pedigree originating from the Technische Hochschule and the Grandes Ecoles established in the early nineteenth century (or even earlier) in Germany and France, founded to further perceived national needs and based firmly upon the philosophy and concepts of 'Technik'—the synthesis and practical application of knowledge—rather than those of scientific scholarship. Many commentators have attached great weight to this feature of engineering formation outside Britain, contrasting it with the British pattern wherein the formal academic study of engineering grew up in universities historically founded upon the twin cultures of the liberal arts and pure science and was aligned with science to gain academic acceptance.

4.35 This view of engineering science as an offshoot or application of science is held to have underlain many of the current criticisms of engineering formation in Britain today; in particular, engineering courses constructed on the basis of teaching *first* the underlying scientific analysis and theory and *then* the potential applications of it, build into engineering formation a dichotomy between 'theory' and 'practice'. This dichotomy does not arise in courses built upon the philosophy of 'Technik' which places everything taught firmly in the context of economic purpose. Theoretical teaching is from early on linked to its potential usefulness within the overall theme of an engineering system, be it mechanical, electrical or process. The final years of 'German model' and French engineering courses are then concentrated upon specialised projects designed to focus and bring together what has been learnt about various aspects of a particular system. The debate which has continually dogged engineering teachers over the appropriate balance in engineering formation between theory and practice is a non-issue within the continental mode of engineering teaching. We would hope that our proposals in the next sections will help render it a non-issue in this country too.

4.36 The separation of engineering from the rest of the higher education system in other countries reflects a second major difference in national attitudes to engineers. In France and Germany, and later in the other countries which followed their example, it was acknowledged that a continuing supply of high-calibre engineers was a requirement of primary national concern and priority and as such something to be ensured and regulated by the State. The nearest to a parallel acknowledgement in this country of the national interest in ensuring and maintaining the engineering capabilites of industry came when the Colleges of Advanced Technology were established in the late 1950s, but these were absorbed into the university system within ten years and have now largely lost their unique position.

4.37 A third important feature of the German model (although apparent also in France and in the USA) is the clear differentiation within the system between extended and intensive courses with high academic requirements designed to prepare a relatively small cadre of potential leaders within engineering practice and shorter courses with a lower level of analytical and theoretical content designed to prepare the majority of mainstream engineers. This differentiation has served to keep the formation provision in line with the varying aptitudes and career requirements of potential engineers in a manner which happens largely by default—if at all—within the British system.

4.38 There are two other important differences in the entry to engineering courses in continental Europe. Firstly, all entrants have had a broadly-based school education, culminating in either their 'Abitur' or 'baccalaureat' embracing five or six subjects at sixth-form level; only in France is there a specialised entrance requirement and that comes after the 'bacc'. Secondly, competition to secure or maintain a place on an engineering course is much greater than for most engineering schools in Britain. In France and Japan this competition comes before entry, in other countries at the end of the first year. There is certainly no reflection of the image sometimes encountered in this country of engineering as a 'soft option' for academically-weak candidates unable to secure a university place in another science subject.

Summary of current formation

4.39 While there are many strengths in the British system of engineering formation, we are forced to the conclusion that the quality and balance of the initial formation of engineers in Britain's major overseas competitors (to the point when they emerge as fully fledged engineers capable of assuming professional responsibility) is generally superior to that currently offered in the United Kingdom. This deficiency to a large extent reflects the relatively restricted and narrow British conception of engineering as a branch of applied science, which militates against an effective marriage between theory and application. The British system does not give students sufficient grounding in the synthesis of technical, human and financial considerations nor does it adequately encourage the development of the wider skills and outlook required of engineers within the engineering dimension. In consequence employers have often taken the attitude that few engineers are properly equipped to take on broader managerial responsibilities and have employed them instead as providers of technical services, thereby closing the vicious circle.

4.40 Various praiseworthy attempts have been made to break out of this vicious circle through new approaches to engineering formation but these isolated and piecemeal efforts have not so far managed to bring about an overall improvement. In spite of recent decisions by the three biggest Institutions to work for better accredited courses and more comprehensive standards, the Institutions on the whole have had neither the resources nor the sanction to overcome the underlying weaknesses of the British system of formation for engineers; neither can those in academic engineering departments in universities and polytechnics hope on their own to remedy all the deficiencies of the current system. What is required is a concerted national effort involving engineering teachers, employers and engineers themselves (through their Institutions) to establish new and more effective formation machinery. In the next section we recommend how this should be achieved.

(c)   Proposals for a new model of engineering formation

Overview

4.41 From our investigations and the evidence given us, two characteristics emerge as essential in any formation system:

(*a*) it should provide an integrated mix of theory, application and experience from which intending engineers can emerge with an appreciation of engineering as it is practised, well-equipped and confident to begin contributing effectively;

(*b*) it should cater for the differing requirements of the main body of engineers, those who demonstrate exceptional potential for leadership in engineering and for a large group of supporting engineers.

4.42 No single route is capable of providing the formation appropriate for every engineer, and *we recommend three principal routes* as illustrated in diagram 4.1 opposite. These are:

(*a*) a route leading to the qualification of '*Registered Engineer*' (*R Eng*) for the main body of engineers, based upon a new first degree programme leading to a Bachelor of Engineering (B Eng) plus a programme of structured postgraduate training and experience;

(*b*) a route leading to the qualification of '*Registered Engineer Diplomate*' (*R Eng (Dip)*) for those showing early potential for engineering leadership, based upon new first degree programmes leading to a Master of Engineering award (M Eng) plus a programme of structured postgraduate training and experience;

(*c*) a route leading to the qualification of '*Registered Associate Engineer*' (*R Eng (Assoc)*) for those engineers who will work mainly in support roles, based upon Higher National or TEC (Higher) programmes plus appropriate structured experience and practical training.

4.43 To maintain standards of qualification at these three levels *we recommend a system of statutory registration of these formation qualifications based upon the accreditation and assessment of the formation packages, to be carried out by a new statutory Engineering Authority* discussed in detail in Chapter VI. *Use of the titles Registered Engineer, Registered Engineering Diplomate and Registered Associate Engineer, and their accompanying designations R Eng, R Eng (Dip) and R Eng (Assoc) will be reserved and protected by law.* We consider it important that the academic awards leading to these statutory qualifications make clear by their titles that they are engineering awards, and that they are clearly distinguished from other arts or science degrees. We therefore urge upon university and polytechnic governing bodies that the degree titles they give for engineering courses accredited for a B Eng or M Eng are amended accordingly—and that non-accredited courses are *not* given these titles.

4.44 The distinction between R Eng and R Eng (Dip) is intended to provide two coherent and complementary formation streams for engineers. The R Eng formation is designed for those with the aptitude and capabilities needed by the main body of engineers in industry. The R Eng (Dip) formation is designed to provide a more advanced formation for the minority who demonstrate a high level of intellectual, creative and personal qualities which indicate a potential to lead manufacturing activities and to develop new technologies.

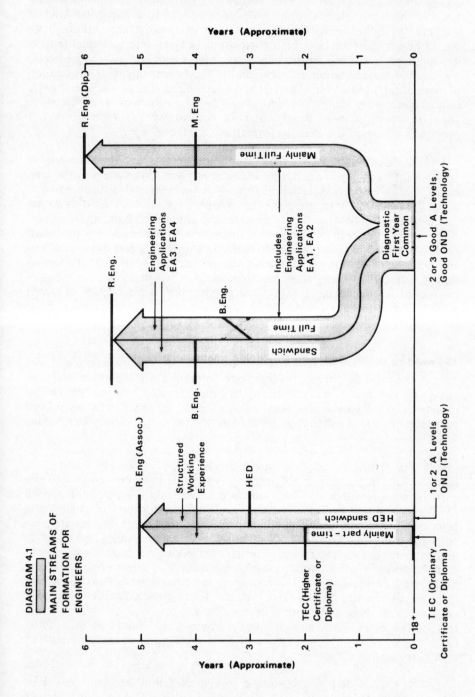

DIAGRAM 4.1

MAIN STREAMS OF FORMATION FOR ENGINEERS

Years (Approximate)

R. Eng (Dip.)

M. Eng

Mainly Full Time

Engineering Applications EA3, EA4

Includes Engineering Applications EA1, EA2

R. Eng.

Diagnostic First Year Common

2 or 3 Good A Levels, Good OND (Technology)

B. Eng.

Full Time

Sandwich

B. Eng.

R. Eng (Assoc.)

Structured Working Experience

HED

HED sandwich

Mainly part-time

1 or 2 A Levels OND (Technology)

TEC (Higher Certificate or Diploma)

TEC (Ordinary Certificate or Diploma)

18+

Years (Approximate)

6   5   4   3   2   1   0

6   5   4   3   2   1   0

4.45 The new structure we are proposing will go far towards producing qualifications more relevant to the needs of industry than the current system. Each of these formation streams is designed to lead to a particular level of qualification rather than to particular levels of employment—although we would expect there to be a high correlation between levels of qualification and employment. *While our proposals are framed with particular reference to the needs of manufacturing industry*—and thus relate mainly to the formation of mechanical, production, electrical and electronic engineers—*we are strongly of the view that the same philosophy should be adopted across other disciplines* since the intergration of theory, practice and application upon which our proposals are based is crucial to formation for all engineers.

4.46 We have recommended these 'formation streams' and their component parts on the basis of our analysis of the existing formation system in the UK, in the light of our consideration of formation overseas and of proposals put to us. We have sought to overcome the 'compartmentalisation' existing within the current system between theory, practice and application building on current best practices rather than trying to overturn them. Nonetheless, our proposals demand changes in the approach to teaching engineering and in the relationship between engineering departments and industry. In particular, the formation of future British engineers must include a substantially greater input of experience in engineering practice and applications, a major part of which must be provided by industry itself.

The route to qualification as a Registered Engineer (R Eng)

4.47 The 'R Eng' stream will provide formation for the main body of engineers, and as such will constitute the principal route into the engineering profession. *It will involve two closely related stages, one based on an educational institution and one in industry, taking in total upwards of five years,* (see diagram 4.1).

4.48 The B Eng programme within the R Eng package will incorporate new elements of training in Engineering Applications to be woven into the curriculum in two themes which we have called 'EA1'—an introduction to the fabrication and use of materials, and 'EA2'—application of engineering principles to the solution of practical problems based upon engineering systems and processes. These are not intended as discrete modules, but as intergral parts of restructured and re-oriented engineering courses. Business techniques relevant to the application and realisation of engineering solutions should be incorporated into the course on the criteria set out in 4.26 above through case studies and worked projects. Entry standards will be broadly on a par with those for existing degree courses, that is 2 or 3 A-levels (or the Scottish equivalent), although these requirements should be interpreted flexibly, particularly for candidates offering working experience as part of their entry qualifications.

4.49 The whole B Eng programme should be firmly set in a context of purpose, with the primary emphasis on the synthesis of basic subjects and on developing students' design and problem-solving capabilities. This should be taught through progressive project work incorporating such elements of engineering science and mathematics as are required to provide a foundation for instruction in practice and applications. Design practice should be a prominent and unifying theme of the course, (as is achieved in continental engineering formation) and not an isolated expertise through the strong emphasis, particularly in the later years of their courses, on a specialised project which focuses the more general engineering theory and applications previously taught. The aim should be for a more detailed confrontation with the specific engineering problems in a particular field which will make the students' knowledge and practical skills operational. This approach should characterise the EA2 aspects of the B Eng course with the integrated study and detailed understanding of a complete engineering system or process the final objective.

4.50 In considering the appropriate length of the B Eng course we were concerned (*a*) to make the best use of existing capacity to maximise the numbers graduating, (*b*) to keep down the total costs of engineering education, and in particular (*c*) to get young engineers working and learning in industry as soon as they were capable of making a contribution. At the same time, we were all concerned that the basic instruction in engineering courses should not be skimped to make room for the development of teaching of engineering applications. Most existing 3-year engineering courses already include elements of workshop practice and project work, so that the incorporation of EA1 and EA2 within the B Eng course need not of itself imply much addition to the length of courses. Moreover, we believe that a critical review of the engineering science and mathematics content of many current BSc (Engineering) courses will identify material being taught which is superfluous to the working requirements of mainstream engineers, and which could without loss be dropped to allow more time for teaching in engineering applications (including EA1 and EA2). Thus, although the B Eng course will certainly require more teaching time than the 3×30 weeks of most current full-time courses, just how much more can only be resolved in practice after some actual B Eng courses have been designed and accredited. Nonetheless, most of us are of the view that wherever possible the aim should be to encompass the new courses within three calendar years of full-time study, although some of us consider that a longer period—say $3\frac{1}{2}$ years—will prove necessary. *We recommend that the UGC and other relevant authorities undertake support for both 3-year and $3\frac{1}{2}$-year B Eng courses until a working patttern emerges.* (These periods of study apply to English and Welsh courses, and may differ in Scotland.)

4.51 To gain the R Eng qualification *the B Eng graduate must follow a rigorous programme of planned and accredited training and experience in industry* covering criteria specified under two further phases: 'EA3'—a structured introduction to industry under supervision and involving a range of practical assignments; and 'EA4'—specific preparation for a first responsible post and a period carrying responsibility in that post under decreasingly close supervision. These are described more fully below. Graduates from full-time B Eng courses are unlikely to meet the standards required of EA3/4 in less than two years after graduation, though those from a four-year sandwich course B Eng may need somewhat less. There is a variety of possible permutations of EA1–EA4 within the overall R Eng package, and we would see such variety (within bounds) as a good thing.

4.52 We believe that the introduction of the R Eng formation package will produce substantial improvements over the typical BSc (Engineering) currently available. The B Eng course will place more emphasis upon engineering practice and rather less on the academic aspects of advanced engineering science, which will be more in keeping with the aptitudes and career requirements of the majority of intending engineers. With further training and monitored experience in industry (through EA3 and EA4) the B Eng holder will on reaching R Eng have had a comprehensive and practically-slanted formation built on a sound theoretical base, equipping him to carry professional responsibility and to develop his capabilities further during his career. We believe this model of formation will prove attractive to students and employers alike. Those who apply for B Eng courses will not be committing themselves finally to careers as engineers but will be opening the door to such careers. The technical appreciation and skills of analysis, synthesis and problem solving which the B Eng course will instil in them should also stand graduates in very good stead for a range of non-engineering careers. So far as employers are concerned they will provide a supply of engineers with a mix of practical and theoretical capabilities, in numbers sufficient to meet industry's needs. The R Eng stream is intended to fill the gap which has opened up between qualifications and competence since the decline of the part-time route to qualification.

The route to qualification as R Eng (Dip)

4.53 Further to the requirement for an able main body of engineers, there is a need for a cadre of engineers combining technical capabilities with the personal potential for leading others both in the development of advanced technology and the management of engineering operations.The R Eng (Dip) stream (shown on the right of Diagram 4.1) is designed to prepare engineers for these positions. We envisage this stream providing around one-quarter of future qualified engineers, which in our judgement reflects the likely relative requirement of industry.

4.54 Diagram 4.1 illustrates the main route qualification as a Registered Engineer Diplomate through the academic award of a Master of Engineering (M Eng) degree. We envisage this M Eng course taking rather less than one-quarter of each year's engineering undergraduate cohort and providing most future Registered Engineering Diplomates. There should also be available various postgraduate and post-experience routes available to R Eng (Dip) to enable limited transfers across from the R Eng stream (see 4.62 below).

4.55 The *M Eng degree course would have the following characteristics:*

(a) selection would usually follow *a diagnostic first year* on a common course with B Eng entrants, designed inter alia to identify those with the potential to undertake the M Eng programme and to succeed as engineers at the R Eng (Dip) level. There is evidence that ultimate attainment, at least in academic terms, is better predicted on the basis of first-year performance than it is on entry qualifications and for this reason selection upon entry to higher education would be premature; selection after the first year should take account of *more than academic attainment,* considering also candidates' personal aptitudes;

96

(b) the course would require 3 years of highly intensive study and work after the initial preparatory year, ie *4 years overall,* and would be heavily oriented throughout towards design, synthesis and engineering applications. It would cover more ground in greater depth than most current undergraduate courses and than the B Eng course—seeking, for example, to instil a high level of understanding in several engineering discplines, whereas the B Eng course would concentrate on one broad discipline;

(c) the course would encompass the engineering application phases EA1 and EA2 as in the B Eng;

(d) unlike the B Eng course, graduates from which would continue to be classified Honours and Pass as at present M Eng graduates would not generally be classified since graduation from the M Eng course would in itself constitute high merit.

4.56 Recognition of the variations in the ability range of student intake *between different engineering departments leads to the conclusion that a varying proportion of students (from department to department) should be selected for M Eng courses.* For example, in those departments with a very high quality intake (in academic terms) a high percentage of students would probably show M Eng potential; some other departments with larger but academically weaker intakes might also offer M Eng courses, but for a smaller percentage of their students; while in some small departments there may well be insufficient numbers of students of high potential to justify mounting any M Eng courses. We expect there to be a limited number of establishments or consortia of establishments[1] offering M Eng courses, including several existing and currently developing schemes providing a sound base for the M Eng/R Eng (Dip) route. We should like to see some institutions establishing M Eng sandwich courses.

4.57 The M Eng graduate would be required to demonstrate that he has satisfied the training/experience requirements of EA3 and EA4 to attain R Eng (Dip). As for the R Eng, we would expect EA3 and EA4 to require about two years. Thus the R Eng (Dip) qualification would require a formation of about six years, making it comparable in length with continental Dipl Ing courses.

Relation of B Eng to M Eng

4.58 The philosophy and objectives of both the B Eng and M Eng courses are similar inasmuch as both should be built upon the precepts of teaching for economic purpose and of preparing young engineers with the confidence and competence to begin applying their engineering knowledge to real problems. There should be the minimum of distinction within both courses between theory and practice, and certainly no presumption that the academic stage of formation instils the theory leaving the practice to be 'picked up' in employment. Differences between the two streams will arise in the area and depth of engineering knowledge to be covered and in the nature of the focussing

[1] See 4.8

of that knowledge through EA2. The R Eng might expect, in his early years at least, to find himself working in fairly specific areas of engineering practice, and the B Eng course is intended to prepare him for this while ensuring that he has an adequate analytical foundation and breadth of understanding subsequently to develop his capabilities in a variety of directions. The R Eng (Dip) will be expected to be conversant with a range of engineering disciplines and to have a higher level of expertise; the M Eng course must therefore extend more widely across and to greater depth within engineering disciplines than the B Eng course, and will thus make greater intellectual and personal demands on those following it.

4.59 We have not sought in this report to prescribe outline curricula or syllabi for B Eng or M Eng courses. Many engineering teachers will say that they already follow the criteria set out above and we have observed some UK courses which do achieve, or look likely to achieve, much of what is sought. But much work will be required by engineering teachers and employers working together and through the new Engineering Authority to achieve agreed guidelines for the two courses and to generalise current best practices. In their evidence to us the CEPC, recognising the challenge and difficulty of planning such courses, suggested that *'teaching contracts' should be placed with selected university and polytechnic departments for course development. We strongly endorse this recommendation.*

Formation for Registered Associate Engineer

4.60 For those many engineers who play a vital practical supporting role in industry we recommend a package leading to registration as a *Registered Associate Engineer (R Eng (Assoc)). The academic part of this formation will be based on the new TEC qualifications of Higher Certificate and Higher Diploma in appropriate engineering subjects, equivalent SCOTEC qualifications, and a modified form of the current Higher National Diplomas in engineering* subjects. The mainstream—those qualifying through the TEC and SCOTEC route—will usually have studied part-time and will have accumulated considerable practical experience. It is probable therefore that they will have obtained experience equivalent to the elements EA1 and EA2 of our proposed training package, but they would nonetheless have to satisfy the Authority that their total experience was adequate for them to be registered as qualified for this level of practice. The acquisition of this experience may take three or more years after the TEC (Higher) award. For those who qualify by full-time study and who thus lack practical experience the courses would need to cover the requirements of EA1 and EA2 with supplementary, specified industrial training (analagous to EA3 and EA4).

4.61 The number of Registered Associate Engineers who qualify through the part-time route via HNC or TEC (Higher) awards will eventually be measured in tens of thousands each year. A smaller group, currently about 1,700 per year, study for Higher National Diploma courses and reach an academic standard considerably higher than the basic requirements of HNC or the new TEC Higher Certificate. The HND, which is a sandwich course, has a minimum entry qualification of Mathematics and Physics studied up to A-level, with one of them passed at A-level, or appropriate Scottish Higher passes. However, increasing numbers of entrants have two A-levels often in mixed Arts and Science subjects. We were impressed by the high standing of the HND in industry and believe that it should be preserved by incorporating it into the academic part of the formation for Associate Engineer. The course should be modified and extended to include the elements EA1 and EA2, and might be renamed the *Higher Engineering Diploma* to distinguish it from HNDs in other disciplines. *As both HED and the B Eng courses would be offered alongside each other in the polytechnics, with the possibility of transfers between them, we recommend that both should be validated by CNAA under the aegis of the new Engineering Authority.*

Bridging between the streams

4.62 We attach great importance to maintaining bridging points between our three streams and to providing ladders from technician education and training programmes. There must be many points of entry and transfer and ample potential for mobility across the framework. We simply do not believe that final selection for any stream can be made at one point in a person's development; provision must be made, for example, for late developers, for those who missed earlier opportunities and for those who do not realise early promise. Diagram 4.2 illustrates possible bridges and transfer points. These include:

(*a*) from R Eng to R Eng (Dip), through three routes:

    (i) 'internal' postgraduate study;

    (ii) 'external' postgraduate study;

    (iii) recognition by the Engineering Authority of outstanding achievement in engineering practice;

(*b*) from R Eng (Assoc) to R Eng, for example through a part-time degree course entered (with appropriate credits) from HED level, leading to a B Eng; HEDs might also be admitted to the third year of full-time B Eng courses.

(*c*) from the TEC certificates to B Eng courses (including part-time), possibly with credit for the higher certificates similar to those allowed for HNC in the past (with exemption from the first year).

Practice, training and experience

4.63 Graduates from the new B Eng and M Eng courses will have received some exposure to engineering practice from the inclusion of the elements EA1 and EA2 in the degree course. For those who have followed a sandwich course, this will have been augmented during their industrial placement with significant elements of working experience, some of which should count towards EA3 and EA4. Provided the industrial training elements in such courses are well integrated with the academic programme we would consider such arrangements as ideal. However, until many more industrial placements become available it is likely that the majority of engineers will have followed full-time courses. *We believe intending engineers must complete their initial formation in a working environment to complement the academic phase of their preparation.*

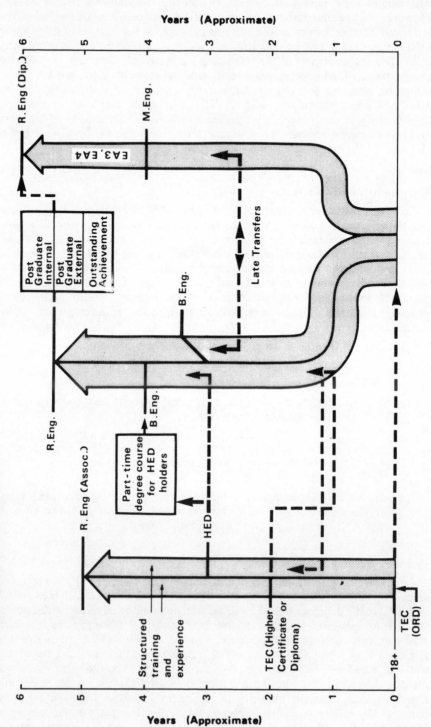

DIAGRAM 4·2: BRIDGES AND TRANSFERS

100

The framework we propose for this industrial phase is embraced in the elements EA3 and EA4. No engineer should be deemed qualified until he has satisfactorily demonstrated that he has met the objectives of both these elements.

4.64 The objectives of EA3 are to develop in aspirant engineers:

(*a*) understanding of the operation of an industrial organisation and the nature and importance of the engineering dimension within it;

(*b*) understanding of systems of communications and control within organisations;

(*c*) personal skills of working with other people at all levels in an organisation;

(*d*) understanding of the organisational and administrative principles of running a business particularly the roles of financial control, costing and marketing;

(*e*) appreciation for the kinds of work in which they can best contribute to the business and most effectively develop their own potential;

(*f*) experience in carrying out engineering tasks to build confidence in the application of knowledge to the solution of real problems.

4.65 EA4 provides the bridge between formal training and the first commission of a responsible post. The nature and length of it will depend very much on the individual and on the job for which he is being prepared. At some stage, the decision has to be made about what that post is to be. Sometimes it is made when the new graduate joins the firm, either because the company is recruiting to fill a particular vacancy or the graduate believes that going directly to a specific job will hasten his progress. However, this can have marked disadvantages. The graduate may have no or little previous industrial experience and be unaware of the nature of many kinds of work best suited to his talents and his interests. The firm may place him in a job which is not the one in which he will make his best contribution to its success. There is also a danger that the broad experience of industry which the trainee should be acquiring at this time may be sacrificed to the specific and immediate interests of the job to be done. We believe, therefore, that whenever possible, the decision over each individual's first substantive post is best delayed till towards the end of the EA3 stage. In any case, the decision should be preceded by a detailed discussion between the graduate and those responsible for his formation, to identify any shortcomings in his ability or confidence to fulfil the tasks to be required of him.

4.66 It could be, if his background and experience is adequate, that the novice engineer is ready to start in a substantive post immediately after EA3, albeit under supervision. In most cases, however, he will require some further development either during or for a period before entering that post. This might be achieved through a variety of means, for example:

—a period spent with a customer using the firm's product so as to become fully versed in the conditions in which it is operated and with problems arising in its operation (such as maintenance);

101

—attendance at a course to become more fully acquainted with the specialist technology involved to acquire a new technique such as computer programming or statistical method, or to improve the trainee's knowledge of financial control or human relations;

—an agreed course of individual study to enlarge the trainee's background knowledge in a particular field:

—a period in a related department in the organisation, eg in marketing for a potential development engineer or in engineering for a potential marketing or sales engineer.

It is emphasised that there may be other quite different needs for any individual, and that the length and content of any particular programme cannot be specified here. The essential purpose of EA4 is to make sure that the individual is as fully equipped as possible to set out on his first substantive post, so that he will approach it with confidence, do himself full justice in it, and make his best contribution to the success of the enterprise; it is no less important that the employer too has confidence that the young engineer can be entrusted with the tasks involved.

4.67 Even after his first substantive post, time will be needed for the new graduate to gain mastery of it. We take the view that EA4 must extend to cover *a period actually carrying independent responsibility in the post under decreasingly close supervision* to allow adequate time for the young engineer to demonstrate his ability to carry it effectively. We envisage the time needed for a graduate from a B Eng or M Eng course to complete EA3 and EA4 and to demonstrate proficiency against the criteria set out above being not less than two years. The appropriate method of assessment of this stage of formation will vary with circumstances, but wherever possible it should draw upon the outcome of extended professional interviews and/or project reports. In drawing guidelines for assessing applications for registration after EA3 and EA4, the Engineering Authority should seek to draw upon the experience in this field of the leading Institutions.

The responsibility of employers

4.68 *Our aim is to see the teaching of engineering practice being undertaken jointly between industry and academic engineering departments with the latter taking prime responsibility for EA1-EA2 and industry being responsible for EA3-EA4.* The provision of postgraduation training along the lines of EA3 and EA4 is essential for the success of the formation packages. We place responsibility for this squarely upon employers. The industrial phase will be vital. It is in employers' interests that they provide this experience to ensure that a sound foundation is laid to enable young engineers to master the increasingly complex and diverse problems which will face them and their employers in the future. Our proposals will depend for success on the readiness of employers to play their role in engineers' formation (before and after graduation) and also upon individual experienced engineers, who must accept responsibility for passing on the benefit of their knowledge and experience by becoming closely and continuously involved in coaching and developing the young engineer during the critical early stages of his career. It follows that practising engineers must participate fully in the provision of EA3 and EA4 within organisations, rather than leaving it entirely in the hands of training specialists. The proposed B Eng and M Eng courses will still be a year or more shorter than their respective analogues in other European countries because it is our belief that *in the British context* the work covered in the last one or two years of continental engineering courses is, of its nature, better undertaken within the working environment. The B Eng or M Eng graduate will have covered a good deal of what the CEPC called 'professional studies in engineering practice', but the onus will be on his first employer—possibly in liaison with his academic teachers— to complete the formation process. We believe that provided industry accepts this challenge and participates to the full in the new formation packages these will produce even better, more capable young engineers than the continental system.

Accreditation and registration

4.69 *A central feature of our new formation system would be that B Eng and M Eng degree courses (including the integrated elements of EA1 and EA2) and the training elements EA3 and EA4 would be subject to external accreditation by a statutory national authority to ensure high standards and continuing relevance. Individual aspirant engineers would be required to satisfy this authority that they had met the full formation requirements before they were registered as qualified with the statutorily-protected title R Eng (Dip), R Eng and R Eng (Assoc).* This will require the establishment of new machinery to set standards and guidelines for the new formation packages, to accredit courses and training and to assess and register individual engineers.

4.70 We recognise that to some extent these things are done already, in particular by the engineering Institutions, by the CNAA and by the Industrial Training Boards. We would hope that all of these groups will continue active in these areas but they must do so with greater concert and unity of purpose than has been the case hitherto and within a coherent national framework. In addition, we would wish to see far more active involvement of employers in the whole formation of engineers. *We recommend the establishment of a new Engineering Authority which would bring together engineers, employers and those with expertise in engineering education and training to promote, accredit and monitor new systems of engineering formation on the model we have recommended and to register as qualified the products of those systems.* The case for establishing new machinery, rather than continued reliance on the existing regime, is argued in detail in Chapters V and VI. Some preliminary observations are, however, apposite here.

Accreditation of academic courses

4.71 Although there will be exceptions, in most cases those eligible for registration as R Eng or R Eng (Dip) should be graduates from accredited B Eng and M Eng courses respectively. *The Engineering Authority itself should supervise the accreditation of these courses,* (much as the Engineers' Council for Professional Development does in the United States).[1] The objective of

[1] See Appendix H

the exercise would be to involve employers and practising engineers with academics in the design of courses, and in ensuring that the teaching and back-up for those courses met minimum and up-to-date requirements of relevance, balance and rigour. A few departments (particularly those at present offering sandwich courses) may be able to meet the requirements for B Eng (or even M Eng) provision with little amendment to their current courses; others will need to make substantial changes. An important function of accreditation will be to indicate to students, schools and employers which courses provide balanced and relevant education. *Accreditation will also provide a means through which the location of M Eng courses could be determined.*

Accreditation of training and experience

4.72 In carrying out its responsibility for registering engineers the Authority will need to satisfy itself about the quality of training and experience as well as the quality of the taught course. *To ensure high standards of post-graduation provision, we propose a system of accreditation of employing organisations.* To be accepted under this system, which would be run by the Authority, an employing organisation would have to demonstrate that it provided:

(a) an operating planned system of manpower development for engineering staff;

(b) a programme of structured training/experience for engineering recruits covering the requirements for EA3 and EA4;

(c) arrangements for trainees to carry out a range of appropriate engineering assignments during their training period;

(d) a system of supervision of trainees by responsible senior engineers during the period until they are qualified.

4.73 We envisage candidates being provisionally registered with the Engineering Authority upon taking up employment after their B Eng or M Eng course. When subsequently applying for full registration, candidates would be required to produce evidence of their training and of the work they had done since graduation and be required to satisfy the Authority as to their experience. The employing firm (or firms, for engineers who had moved or participated in joint schemes) would be required to endorse applicants' experience and fitness for registration. Some graduates will join non-accredited employers. We see no reason why such graduates and their employers should not be able to submit training programmes for that individual for approval by the Engineering Authority. In such cases the acceptance of the individual for registration must be based upon a professional interview or similar assessment.

4.74 Some small firms which may recruit graduates only occasionally and which would thus be unlikely to obtain accreditation can nevertheless provide young engineers with excellent training and experience, possibly working in conjunction with other employing organisations. The new Authority might itself foster the extension of group training arrangements covering smaller firms, especially those not covered by Industrial Training Board schemes.

An excellent model for such schemes is provided by the Scottish Electrical Training Scheme (SETS).[1]

4.75 We recognise that with the marked differences which exist between different fields of engineering and with the rapid advance of new technologies it no longer makes sense to specify a single pattern of postgraduate training for all engineers. For some areas of engineering, and for graduates with little previous experience of industry, formal training to encompass EA3 and EA4 in the two discrete steps described above may be the most appropriate preparation. This would accord with many excellent existing programmes. In other cases, eg in parts of the electronics industry, it may be more appropriate to develop each individual engineer through a series of structured assignments carried out under close and careful supervision. Properly designed training through assignments can be extremely effective but it calls for a planned and well judged sequence and range of jobs under the right guidance. We would expect companies putting forward assignment-based programmes of graduate development to be considered for accreditation on an equal footing to those proposing more conventional training programmes, provided these assignments were seen to satisfy all the criteria for EA3/4 and were carefully monitored.

4.76 We hope that there will be strong pressure from all young engineers and from the Authority to ensure that employers provide appropriate experience to satisfy EA3 and EA4 and we believe that firms which do so will attract the best recruits. There will however be some engineers entering manufacturing or associated industries who are unable to secure the kind of early development prescribed here. It would be wrong for those denied such opportunities at the beginning of their career to be permanently excluded from the register. There will be others who come to practise as engineers whose initial formation was as applied scientists or mathematicians. We would expect the Engineering Authority to devise provisions for late or 'external' registration for engineers (and scientists) who can demonstrate that they have achieved the necessary breadth of engineering experience and understanding to merit registration on a par with those who have come through an accredited formation route. Such provisions should be based upon personal application and judged against very strict criteria, including satisfactorily passing an intensive interview and assessment procedure. Later or 'external' registrands must demonstrate that through achievement they have obtained the breadth of knowledge, understanding and experience required of those registered for accredited formation programmes.

4.77 A substantial group of graduate engineers will seek their careers outside manufacturing—in public authorities, the Armed Forces, and so on. These too will require an ordered formation and we would expect the employing organisations concerned to devise with the Engineering Authority parallel schemes to provide the equivalent of EA3 and EA4 and to facilitate the cross-transfer of personnel between manufacturing and other sectors. The criteria upon which such parallel schemes are based should be closely similar to those

---

[1]Scottish Electrical Training Scheme exists to recruit and train suitable engineering graduates for its nine member companies who span the electrical industry of Scotland.

set out in 4.62–4.66 above, modified for circumstances and context, and they should be subject to similar accreditation procedures. Engineers who have undergone satisfactory programmes under these criteria would be eligible for registration as described above.

(d) Implementing the new system

Teaching the new courses

4.78 The new formation streams will require special emphasis on the teaching of engineering practice. This will be a difficult and demanding task but evidence from Continental Europe and some UK courses indicate that it can be achieved. In particular, we found that engineering schools on the continent displayed major strengths over most of the UK counterparts in three aspects:

(a) their senior teaching staff generally have more industrial experience than their counterparts in the UK and there is more mobility between industry and higher education;

(b) close contact with industry enables more design, research and development and consultancy work of industrial relevance to be undertaken within engineering departments and this is reflected in their teaching programmes;

(c) equipment and facilities in the best European technical institutes are often of such high quality that industry (which has often provided them) comes itself to the institute to use them.

All these factors contribute to an academic environment conducive to and expert in the teaching of engineering practice.

4.79 As we have indicated, there are several worthwhile developments in this direction in the UK, but not as many as are needed. Two important changes are required. First, employers must recognise the need for them to contribute their experience to enable engineering practice to be taught—by more secondment of staff, by further co-operation in teaching companies, greater assistance with teaching and training and by providing more places for sandwich course students. Secondly, on the educational side, universities and polytechnics must develop new approaches to teaching within the two streams; to the assessment of practical as well as academic skills; to collaboration with industry; and to involving their staff in current engineering practice.

4.80 Our survey of staff in engineering departments,[1] revealed closer involvement between industry and engineering education than is commonly supposed and that more academics have close and current links with industry than generally recognised. However, the picture varies considerably from one academic establishment to another and there is room for substantial overall improvement. Some engineering departments claim good relations with industry and experience few constraints in this respect. In other cases collaboration is virtually non-existent either because the will for such collaboration does not exist or (more frequently) because of resource constraints. Often we found a record of efforts towards greater collaboration but that development has been stifled through lack of resources or because of a lack of response from industry. The survey also showed that, whilst most UK engineering teachers have some industrial experience, this is usually

---

[1] See Appendix F

short-term and often of distant memory, suggesting that engineering departments will need more staff with experience of current industrial practice in order to teach the new courses effectively. The survey revealed a number of bright spots in a generally gloomy picture, but certainly shows that much more progress must be made before a satisfactory level of interchange between engineering teaching and current practice is achieved.

4.81 There are several approaches to these staffing problems and to the related issue of expanding academic/industrial collaboration, all of which should be pursued. First, the expertise of practising engineers in industry needs to be made available to academic establishments on a sustained basis. There must be continuous involvement by industry in the new courses, with practising engineers of standing in their companies assuming specific teaching commitments and helping to plan courses as well. The second line of approach to be pursued is to provide for the regular updating of the industrial experience of engineering teachers through industrial sabbaticals. The current stock of engineering teachers is especially in need of such updating according to our survey, but the requirement will continue. Our survey further suggested that the introduction of schemes to facilitate the provision of industrial experience would be welcomed by many engineering teachers. This will require extra funding for participating departments since heavier teaching loads will be created for those not on sabbatical and many extra costs have to be met (housing, travel etc). Such secondments might help to balance the cost to industry of releasing staff to assist in the teaching of engineering practice.

4.82 It is central to our philosophy that responsibility for the formation of young engineers should, from the outset, be shared between teaching establishments and employers. In current circumstances, where there is frequently insufficient recent experience among engineering teaching staffs for sound instruction in current engineering practice,[1] it is likely that in most cases a distinction will remain between those parts of the formation package undertaken within a teaching establishment and those which can only satisfactorily be obtained in employment after graduation. However, a number of good collaborative sandwich courses already incorporate some of what we envisage being covered under EA3 (and even some aspects of EA4) within the period of the first degree; we certainly see nothing immutable about the division between the academic and employment-based phases of the new formation packages. As the body of engineering teachers is strengthened in the way we have proposed and as the links between engineering schools and industry become closer, so we would hope that some co-operative programmes for complete formation packages leading to R Eng and R Eng (Dip) might be developed by university or polytechnic departments in association with particular industrial companies. Such programmes would be subject to accreditation by the Engineering Authority which would ensure that all the requirements of B Eng or M Eng (including EA1 and EA2), plus those for EA3 and EA4, were fully satisfied.

4.83 To encourage engineering teaching staff to retain meaningful industrial contacts, perhaps via the secondments and sabbaticals suggested above, *we recommend the introduction of a system of recognition, accorded by the teaching*

---

[1]See Appendix F

institution and endorsed by the Engineering Authority, for engineering teachers who are registered engineers and who meet criteria laid down regarding their industrial experience, and their continuing involvement with industry, as well as their academic standing. Accreditation of B Eng and M Eng courses should then take into account the number of 'recognised' teaching staff on the course. Such recognition should be subject to renewal, say every five years, and should command additional remuneration in the form of a special responsibility allowance. To develop an easy interchange between educational institutions and industry, senior engineers must be encouraged to return to universities and polytechnics to assist in preparing future generations of engineers. Appointments should be made at professorial or lecturer level on pay scales negotiated to reflect the industrial earnings of engineers who will divide their time between industry and education in this way. The criterion for appointment should be industrial achievement as an engineer.

Formation through research

4.84 The importance of research and development work within the engineering dimension, and within the long-term development of advanced technology in the UK, has been emphasised in Chapter II. We note criticisms of the kind made in a paper by a committee of the Fellowship of Engineering, chaired by Lord Baker,[1] that 'relations between research workers in academic institutions and industry are not close enough, leading to a situation where much research is carried out without input from the ultimate beneficiary'. This criticism is by no means true of all of our engineering schools. Nonetheless we accept the general point that the centre of gravity of university and polytechnic postgraduate work should shift from basic scientific research work towards *engineering research*.[2]

4.85 As we described earlier, many joint university-industry research projects have developed in recent years, particularly through the initiative of the Science Research Council (SRC). These developments are very much along the lines we wish to encourage. However, a less successful feature of engineering postgraduate work in the UK is the one-year taught course, usually leading to the Master's degree. Most of these courses, usually but not always specialist in nature, have been unsuccessful both in attracting home students and in generating industrial enthusiasm. Recruitment of home students to university engineering research schools has been and remains poor for a variety of reasons, not least the low level of grant compared with the remuneration in a first appointment in industry. Overseas students, apparently always willing and eager to obtain a British engineering education, now make up over half of the student body at postgraduate level.

---

[1] 'Report of a Working Party on Engineering Research in Britain; chaired by Lord Baker' 1979 (Paragraph 4).

[2] Defined by Lord Baker in the following terms: 'Engineering research should be considered as the combination of new scientific discovery with the practical design and development of a real product or process of proven, or potentially likely, utility. Involvement by industry is essential at all stages of research, development and design, whether it be done in the physics or materials laboratory as basic research or in an engineering laboratory or drawing office for product design and development'.

4.86 The overall picture of postgraduate instruction and research in university engineering departments and in polytechnics, is thus unsatisfactory, in spite of the efforts of many distinguished engineers who have produced high quality work under discouraging circumstances. We consider nevertheless that there remains a good case for strong research activity in our engineering schools of the engineering type specified by Lord Baker and the Fellowhip of Engineering.

4.87 We show on Diagram 4.3 how engineers who have completed the first level of formation might move forward to higher research degrees. *We recommend that most existing MSc courses which are currently taken immediately after a first degree course should be discontinued.* Taught courses of this level, restructured and reoriented in the way already described, should be absorbed into the latter phases of the new M Eng courses, although parts of them may also be available to the R Eng 'late developer' (as we indicated in Diagram 4.2, and show again in Diagram 4.3 on page 110). We also show on Diagram 4.3 how an M Eng graduate may proceed to an engineering-based research degree, (which we would prefer to call a Doctor of Engineering (D Eng)). Our preference is for the D Eng to be taken after attaining R Eng (Dip), but we recognise the economic and practical difficulties involved. Qualified engineers in well-paid industrial employment will not willingly return to student levels of remuneration. *We therefore recommend the introduction of a number of 'teaching fellowships' at universities to combine research and teaching responsibilities, carrying salaries commensurate with the previous earnings of those recruited.* Such 'teaching fellows' would form part of the 'recognised' cadre of engineering teachers proposed above. We see no place in engineering for the research studentship scheme which, although it may be valid for scientists newly graduated, does not offer remuneration sufficient to attract highly qualified and older R Eng(Dip) engineers back to universities.

Regional consortia for M Eng courses

4.88 For an M Eng course to be viable it will require a minimum intake of some 25–30 students per annum. Many departments will not have this number of students capable of tackling an M Eng course. To cater for able students in these departments we suggest that *regional consortium arrangements be set up linking academic establishments.* For example within such a consortium the Mechanical Engineering Department at University 'X' might offer an M Eng in that discipline, drawing the ablest mechanical engineering students from smaller departments in Polytechnic 'Y' and University 'Z'. Alternatively, several institutions might share the services of key teaching staff, using video and other 'distance learning' technology or expensive equipment. In this way a comprehensive coverage of M Eng courses could be achieved in most regions. This is important given that students might be reluctant to switch to an M Eng course if it meant moving out of an area in which they were settled. Such consortium arrangements already operate for some postgraduate courses and illustrate the attractions of the concept of local pooling of efforts, not least in providing a basis for the economical use of resources, eg in providing facilities for teaching EA1–2 on a joint basis or in 'continuing formation'.

DIAGRAM 4.3 : FORMATION THROUGH RESEARCH

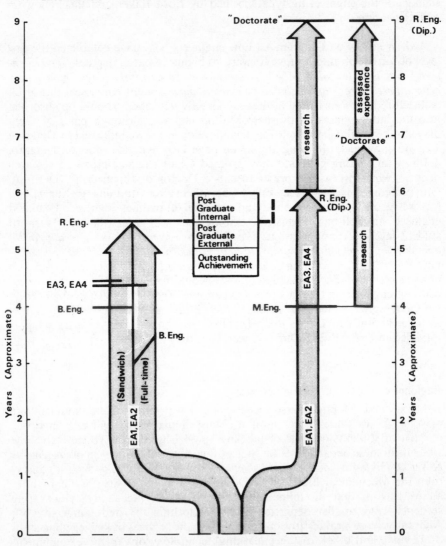

Funding the new proposals

4.89 It was put to us by the Committee of the Engineering Professors' Conference (CEPC) (but by no means endorsed by the engineering professoriate as a whole) that engineering departments in universities should be funded separately. Under the principle of university autonomy, University Senates and Councils are usually left to decide for themselves how they distribute block grants from the University Grants Committee (UGC) between faculties and departments. The UGC occasionally 'indicate' specific sums for, or to take account of, developments in certain faculties, eg to establish a new Chair. However, the CEPC told us that funds 'indicated' by the UGC for engineering development often do not get through in practice to those departments. The 'earmarking' of funds—that is, the prior allocation of specific monies by the UGC which are then not given unless they are used for the stated purpose—was in the CEPC's judgement a stronger measure but still not enough. In their view, based upon their experience of working with the current system, entirely separate funding is required to assure the interests of engineering.

4.90 We considered most carefully these arguments in favour of setting up special funding arrangements for engineering education. While we accept that engineering education overseas seems to have benefitted from being based largely on special institutions devoted to technical education, we see great difficulty in separating engineering from the rest of higher education. Engineering departments currently share various common services and overheads with other departments and they benefit from service teaching from mathematics and science departments. The disruption and extra costs involved in disentangling engineering departments from the rest of higher education would in our view outweigh any potential benefits.

4.91 Nevertheless we see a need for reforms in the framework of funding and administration in higher education to ensure the implementation of our proposals for formation. Although we do not advocate separate funding for engineering education in universities, *we recommend the specific immediate and long-term earmarking of extra funds, via tranches from the UGC and equally effective measures for the maintained sector to accredited engineering departments*. This additional funding must be sufficient to provide generally for the extended and intensified pattern of courses; to provide adequate staffing of the right calibre and experience to facilitate the establishment of favourable student-staff ratios in engineering departments for teaching purposes and to allow adequate staff time for collaboration with industry. It should also allow sufficient provision for up-to-date machinery and equipment, a key and currently badly neglected resource in engineering education. To ensure that these extra resources are deployed to best effect, *we recommend that courses which fail to get, or lose, their accreditation should no longer be eligible for earmarked funds*.

4.92 The polytechnics play an important part in the formation of engineers and it is vital for them also to be able to respond rapidly to changing national needs in this area. About one-quarter of British engineering graduates come through polytechnics and this contribution is further strengthened by the significant number emerging with the Higher National Diploma. *We recommend*

111

comparable earmarking of special funds for engineering formation in the poly-
technics as in the universities, although we understand that their constitutional
position may make this difficult for some of them. We were told in evidence
that the polytechnics, unlike the universities, are subject to a multiplicity of
external controls and that their Governing Bodies are often prevented thereby
from discharging their proper management functions; for example, many of
the 26 Local Authorities responsible for the 30 polytechnics are said to exercise
detailed day-to-day control in a style developed to suit their other wide and
varied responsibilities. For polytechnics to be able to respond to the need
of the engineering dimension and to mount the new formation packages their
governing bodies must be in a position to take action without having to await
approval from a hierarchy of external committees. If the Local Education
Authorities concerned are unable to provide this autonomy, then we believe
that appropriate changes must be introduced. Notwithstanding the proposals
made by the Oakes Committee[1] *we consider there to be an urgent need to
re-examine the management of engineering education in polytechnics. This may
require that their governing bodies are given greater authority to manage their
activities within an approved budget.*

4.93 As far as the funding of industrial experience is concerned, the earlier
and particularly expensive aspects of training specified in EA1 and to some
extent in EA2, which hitherto have been considered the responsibility of industry, will in future be incorporated into the B Eng and M Eng degree courses.
This in itself should release resources within industry to fulfil the requirements for
EA3 and EA4 in the structured way we have proposed. Moreover, much of the
work done by trainees within EA3 and EA4 will be of direct benefit to the employing firm, constituting a direct contribution to its activities. For these reasons *we
take the view that the training expenses associated with EA3/4 provision should
be the responsibility of companies who will benefit from the services of the
engineers concerned,* though we welcome existing arrangements whereby some
firms can obtain help with training costs through Industrial Training Boards,
etc. We envisage the Engineering Authority being in a position to back up
this support with 'pump-priming' funds to stimulate experimental schemes
and to assist group training schemes in getting off the ground.

4.94 The reshaping of degree courses to encompass EA1 and EA2 and
the higher quality and intensity of teaching required, especially for the M
Eng courses, will add to the current costs of engineering education. The cost
of engineering education in the universities and polytechnics is currently of
the order of £200m per annum. Our proposals would in due course add
perhaps £15m-£40m per annum to this (but not at once). In our view this
extra expenditure is modest when set against the likely national returns.
*Notwithstanding current constraints on public expenditure, this price must not
and cannot be baulked.* It may well imply the diversion of funds from other
areas of education or elsewhere within the public sector; if so—and we would
hope it need not be—this must be achieved. The revitalisation of the engineering dimension, and the development of a supply of high-quality engineers
must take priority over other national objectives if the problems identified

---

[1] Report of a Working Group on the Management of Higher Education in the Maintained
Sector; chaired by Mr G Oakes MP Cmnd 7130, HMSO 1978

in the earlier chapters of this Report are not to drag the whole economy further into decline. The foundation of a competitive national engineering capability through an effective system of formation must be an overriding national priority.

4.95 It need not follow that the public purse bears the full brunt of the extra cost. The interests at stake are as much those of industry itself as those of Government, and it would therefore be entirely reasonable for the Government to look to industry to contribute equipment, facilities or people towards the new programmes. We were indeed impressed, when we asked engineering departments about their sources of funding, to find the degree to which some departments were already financially assisted by industrial contracts and similar arrangements. But these arrangements and the amount of direct help from industry to engineering teaching are still much less than we saw in Germany, say, and every effort must be made to increase the flow of funds and support from this source.

Student grants

4.96 Current demographic projections indicate a requirement for a marked rise in the proportion of home students entering higher education who seek to study engineering after 1983 if the number of home engineering graduates is not to fall sharply after 1986–87.[1] No trend in this direction is yet apparent. We believe that a prime stimulus for extra student demand for places will in due course come from the higher salaries and attractive careers available to engineers as employers' demands outstrip the number of engineering graduates entering the employment market. It must be recognised however that there are long time lags in this 'feed-back', and also an element of circularity if employers take the view that they will offer better salaries and good careers to better engineering graduates only after these become available. We therefore perceive the need for a more direct and immediate incentive to raise the level of student demand to study engineering, and *a majority of us recommend that all students accepted on to accredited B Eng/M Eng courses should be assured a bursary of at least £250 per annum over and above their mandatory LEA award for the duration of their course.* This would cost about £10m per annum if current student numbers can be maintained.

4.97 Such bursaries, awarded by the Engineering Authority, would without doubt attract more school leavers to seek entry to accredited engineering courses, hopefully allowing teaching departments scope to apply more rigorous admission standards (which we hope would be based as much on personal aptitudes and commitment as on academic attainments) without jeopardising intake numbers. We make this recommendation independent of consideration of any industrial sponsorship students might be able to obtain. Such sponsorships, in which the value is as much the link it gives students and potential employers as the money involved, should not count against the student's maintenance award or his bursary. We recognise that there would be problems in such positive discrimination in favour of engineering students, but the revolution which current and likely future circumstances demand will

---

[1] See 3.50 *et seq*

not be achieved by baulking at such problems. Nothing will ensure that young people actively consider a career in engineering more than spotlighting the national priority attached to engineers in this way. We must record that some of us demur from this recommendation, considering that it will be divisive (within the student body) to offer differential grants, which may attract students to engineering who have no enthusiasm for the subject, and might make poor engineers.

Relationship of the new to current qualifications

4.98 Engineering practice involves a whole spectrum of contributions, varying by shades in the level of intellectual capability, responsibility and personal leadership skills demanded. These three requirements are mixed in differing ratios, with many jobs requiring only an 'average' intellectual input carrying greater responsibility than others demanding a very high conceptual and theoretical input. Any attempt to draw demarcation lines or bands across this spectrum is thus inevitably arbitrary and liable to incongruities. Differentiation is nevertheless necessary for some purposes, particularly with regard to formation and qualification, as is recognised in all industrial countries.

4.99 Any categorisation of engineers for national economic needs must be based in the first instance on categorisations of engineering practice and the appropriate formation and qualification requirements then based on the needs of each category of practice. Useful classifications of this kind were given in evidence from several Institutions, each of which identified three bands of practice framed in terms of the needs of the particular discipline under consideration.[1] We might paraphrase these classifications as follows:

A(i)   a relatively small number of engineers of the highest technological competence, who inspire others and probably work as engineering innovators throughout their careers;

A(ii) a relatively small number of engineers with the personal qualities needed for them to reach, in due course, the highest levels of industrial and commercial management;

B   substantial numbers of broadly educated and trained engineers with practical competence to take a creative and leading role in innovative engineering and the management of it in industry;

C   an even greater number of suitably well-educated and trained engineers able and competent to operate in the more detailed aspects of engineering and in support roles.

The Institutions' evidence related these bands of practice to the levels of qualification currently recognised by the CEI and its member engineering Institutions, holding that categories A and B were properly the province of Chartered Engineers, and that C was the province of Technician Engineers. Thus A(i), A(ii) and B are currently deemed broadly the province of graduate engineers and C currently the province of HNC/D holders.

---

[1] eg evidence from the Institution of Electrical Engineers, Institution of Mechanical Engineers, and Council of Engineering Institutions.

114

4.100 We would not demur from this formulation in its general form. However, our own formulation took into account three further considerations:

(a) there is a very wide spectrum of demands, in terms of intellect, leadership and responsibility, from bands A(i) and A(ii) through band B;

(b) there is an equally wide spectrum of abilities among engineering graduates;

(c) the decline in the numbers with HNC/D level qualifications relative to graduate engineers and the increasing intellectual demands made by much routine engineering work mean that band C is also becoming increasingly the province of graduates; there are already moves within some of the Institutions to make Technician Engineer a predominantly graduate category.

Our proposals envisage that most of those rising to jobs in band A would in future come through the R Eng (Dip) stream (which would approximate to the 'enhanced' C Eng demanded by Chilver[1], Merriman[2] and Dawson[3]; that band B would be primarily the province of R Engs; and that band C work would be undertaken sometimes by R Engs and sometimes by R Eng(Assoc)s.

4.101 Our structure of qualifications is thus not dissimilar to that envisaged by the more progressive among the Institutions for the future development of the current C Eng/T Eng framework although we believe that the related formation streams leading to R Eng (Dip), R Eng and R Eng (Assoc) will better fit the needs of engineering practice than any development based upon current education and training requirements. The Institutional developments mentioned above have all been conceived independently by different Institutions; they are partial in their scope and even if implemented carry no guarantee that they would operate in a mutually consistent and balanced fashion across all levels of practice nor that their requirements would be flexible to changes in the needs of current practice. Our proposals are for a coherent, integrated, centrally-administered hierarchy of qualifications, based upon a statutory register operated primarily for the purpose of improving engineering practice.

4.102 Registration by the Engineering Authority will be a recognition that an individual has satisfactorily completed his formation and demonstrated his fitness to practise as an engineer, but although the State register is designed to be a strong indicator of *technical* competence it does not seek to verify the *professional* standing of the qualified engineer. This latter entails an assessment which can only be verified through each individual engineer's working record over a number of years as vouched for by his employers and—if he seeks it—his 'professional peers'. We do not propose to confuse the statutory

---

[1] 'Summary of written opinions submitted to the Chilver Committee on matters related to the civil engineering profession' Institution of Civil Engineers 1975

[2] 'Qualifying as a Chartered Electrical Engineer.' Report of a Working Group chaired by Mr J H H Merriman. Institution of Electrical Engineers May 1978

[3] 'Towards a Qualifications Policy for the Future. The Dawson Report on the relevance of the Institutions current qualifications policy in the context of future needs'. Chairman Mr J G Dawson. Institution of Mechanical Engineers March 1978.

award of statutory formation qualifications with this. While there would therefore be no Institutional membership requirement attaching to the new statutory qualifications we would expect the leading Institutions to indicate their support and confidence in the new qualifications—which they will have helped set and administer—by accepting them as meeting the appropriate levels for their membership requirements.[1]

(e) Continuing formation

The need for continuing formation

4.103 The technical and professional development of an engineer does not cease once he is qualified—indeed this is just a beginning. We have recognised a distinction between the *initial* formation of engineers, up to the point when they first qualify as professional practitioners, and *continuing* formation thereafter. If an engineer is to merit continuing status as a professional then he must regard his initial formation as something to be built upon and extended during his career. Indeed the effectiveness and value of his contribution in industry or elsewhere will largely depend on the extent to which he does so. The need for systematic continuing formation for all engineers will persist even after the initial formation of engineers is enhanced in the way we have recommended. Aspects of expertise an engineer may wish to develop include:

—awareness of what others are doing in his own or in related fields;

—knowledge of specialist technologies and techniques not covered in his initial formation;

—knowledge of new technologies and techniques which have arisen since he qualified;

—details of new demands upon the engineering dimension, and their implications (eg health and safety regulations, product liability laws, etc);

—managerial skills, for example in financial control, marketing or industrial relations.

---

[1] **Footnote by Lord Howie**

In Britain, the traditional formation of the engineer and control of the profession has been, nominally at least, in the hands of the engineering institutions. At its best, the traditional formation is sound, and no evidence has come before the Committee to gainsay that, although the value of the formation package varies from Institution to Institution.

With the exception of the construction industry, where a system of 'licensing by consent' may reasonably be said to operate, the Institutions have not succeeded in convincing employers of the value of their formation. That is not to say that their aims have been mistaken, and the aims of the Committee's formation proposals are in harmony with those of the Institutions.

There is one innovation in the Committee's proposals, however, from which some difficulties flow. It is suggested that the existing two tiers in the profession, Chartered Engineers and their equivalents and Technician Engineers, should be replaced by a three-tier scheme. This is a departure from the British tradition, and is also out of key with continental engineering usage.

The proposals demand a substantial recasting of engineering education, and it is hard to imagine an upheaval of this sort being readily brought about. If the upheaval were necessary, the difficulties would have to be faced and overcome. But it is not.

The Committee's aim of producing a more elite cadre of engineers can as readily be achieved by stiffening the qualifying requirements much in the manner which has already been proposed by the major engineering Institutions. This is a much simpler way of reaching near enough the same end. It would also remove some of the difficulties of registering the existing stock of engineers. A scheme of engineering education and formation along these lines is to be preferred to the Committee's proposals.

4.104 Much of this knowledge can be and is obtained in the course of an engineer's day-to-day work through contacts with colleagues in his own and other departments, with customers and with suppliers. Working practice naturally entails a measure of continuing development and regular changes in jobs and assignments foster the development of an individual's capabilities. In Chapter III we suggested how manpower audit programmes can help in identifying people ready for career moves, where they might be moved in their own and the company's best interests and any extra training they might need. Companies which do not or cannot offer employees the prospect of developing their expertise and widening their horizons in this way may well experience unduly high staff turnover, as engineers seek better career development opportunities with other employers.

Current provision and uptake

4.105 Even when careful attention is paid to formation 'on-the-job' the individual engineer is necessarily limited within this by the expertise and scope available within the company and the particular climate or philosophy within which it operates. The need remains for a range of 'off-the-job' provisions to supplement structured experience. Much can be gained through private study; in addition to this, more formal media for post-experience formation include:

(a) postgraduate instruction, mainly through taught Masters courses offered at universities and some polytechnics, usually lasting one year full-time, or longer if taken part-time;

(b) short courses lasting a few days or a few weeks, sometimes on a modular or part-time basis, offered mainly by universities and polytechnics;

(c) seminars, conferences, workshops, short courses etc, lasting from a few hours to a few days, offered by educational and professional Institutions, research associations, private training organisations and often by companies for employees of major customers who will use their products;

(d) 'in-house' education and training given within companies by their own staff or outside teachers.

4.106 With some notable exceptions taught Masters courses entered immediately after first graduation have not made the contribution they should to the engineering dimension, given the resources deployed to mount them. Such courses have been poorly supported by home graduates and very often in consequence cater in practice largely to overseas students. For this reason we recommended earlier (4.85) that most current taught MSc's in engineering be discontinued, although there will still be a continuing need for a number of specialist one year or shorter courses in particular technologies or applications.

4.107 The major current vehicles for 'off-the-job' formation for engineers are short courses, seminars, workshops, lecture programmes and conferences, lasting from a few hours to a few months, provided mainly by private agencies, engineering and management schools, and by engineering Institutions. Despite a commonly-voiced opinion that the provision and uptake of such facilities

117

were lower in Britain than elsewhere, we found this to be an active and growing area involving large numbers of engineers. The 1977 CEI survey[1] showed that nearly one-third of the Chartered Engineers sampled had undertaken at least a one-week course or the equivalent during the previous year; this finding is more optimistic than that reported to us by the SRC[2] that less than 8,000 students had attended short or part-time courses in engineering in 1977–78 but the SRC survey did not cover engineers attending non-engineering courses. The same SRC survey illustrated the enormous number and range of post-experience courses available for engineers. In addition, all the engineering Institutions mount programmes of lectures and short conferences which they told us involve up to 10 per cent of their members each year. The texts of these are usually given wider circulation to Institution members and others.

4.108 While current provisions and participation rates in formal continuing formation are growing, it is our impression that the level of activity in the UK is still well behind that in Germany, say, or in the United States. A notable overseas programme is that arranged by the Verein Deutscher Ingenieure (VDI) in Dusseldorf, which provides facilities and recruits lecturers from industry and academic establishments. Some of these courses are arranged in conjunction with television broadcasts (for example, an 'introduction to digital technology' course, based upon 13 half-hour broadcasts and 4 week-end practical sessions arranged at 10 different centres). We were also impressed in the United States, Germany and Sweden by the extent of and commitment to 'in-house' teaching programmes in some of the larger companies. The same applies to some of the UK firms we visited.

4.109 Few engineers need persuading of the need for them to participate in post-experience formation activities; similarly the providers of courses and seminars in academic or professional institutions are alive to the need for more activities and say that they are inhibited only by the level of effective demand and the availability of resources. While we doubt if many employers would argue against the desirability in principle of continuing formation, a great many find difficulties in freeing hard-pressed staff for more than a short while. Many engineers have complained about this and about the problems of financing their attendance at courses. *Support for a relatively small but increasing number of graduate engineers to take full-time courses in both management and technical subjects is available through the Training Opportunities Scheme, and we recommend that this facility be extended.*

Stepping up the demand for continuing formation

4.110 The main impetus for raising current levels of post-experience formation activities must come from individual engineers and their employers. Good employers will regard engineers as appreciating company assets and actively

---

[1] Council of Engineering Institutions. Survey of Professional Engineers 1977

[2] A survey of part-time and short full-time Postgraduate Courses carried out by the Group for Higher Education Policy Studies at the University of Essex for the Science Research Council 1979.

encourage them to involve themselves in such activities, both to further their personal development and also to maintain the company's corporate expertise. Engineers should demand time and financial support to participate in programmes which will benefit their company as well as themselves.

4.111 We considered possible means of encouraging engineers and their employers in this area, noting what is done in some other countries. In France, for example, employers are obliged to spend the equivalent of 2 per cent of their annual payroll on continuing formation provision[1] and all employees have a statutory right to paid leave for the purpose of study, the period of leave entitlement being related to length of service. Some German Lander have adopted similar 'right of release' laws and we understand that the European Commission is considering an EEC Directive to the same effect. These statutory provisions apply to all employees, although engineers are important beneficiaries. Given the importance of training and re-training of the current stock of engineers in an era of rapid technological development and change, *we recommend that the Government introduce a statutory right to paid study leave for all statutorily registered engineers* (including those currently practising who become registered with the authority—see 5.20 below) *on criteria and lines to be devised by the Engineering Authority.*

4.112 Another lever proposed to encourage engineers to maintain their professional development is the introduction of a periodic review mechanism into the registration system, requiring registrands to demonstrate that they have taken pains to keep their knowledge up to date before they are allowed to continue their registration. We think this is cumbersome and unnecessary. There may well be value however in *requiring registered engineers to commit themselves (through a code of practice) to maintaining their technical expertise as a condition for remaining on the register, and for demonstrable failure to uphold this commitment (eg through incompetent or culpable professional performance) to be grounds for deregistration.*

Stepping up provision for continuing formation

4.113 Providing for continuing formation requires the identification of programmes to meet customer demands; facilities accessible to those interested in the particular course; resources to run courses with the appropriate calibre of teaching staff and equipment; and publicity for the opportunities available. At present the initiative usually lies with the provider, be it an academic institution or a professional body. We heard complaints on both sides about this, from university and polytechnic departments which have arranged courses often after consulting employing companies which then had little support and from engineers and companies unable to find courses suitable to their particular requirements. A recent survey carried out for the SRC[2] found that many employers would welcome a source of reliable information on programmes available. The SRC have proposed an experimental 'regional brokerage' scheme, which could bring together customers and suppliers so that programmes meet agreed requirements.

---

[1] See Appendix I
[2] Op cit

4.114 It would be sensible for a number of centres to build up their activities in this area and become foci for continuing formation provision for engineers. *We recommend that several centres be designated Regional Engineering Centres (RECs) based on groupings of existing engineering schools and other interested organisations and professional institutions.* These could be set up quickly and at low cost to provide a highly effective means of using existing physical resources and teaching capabilities to provide for the needs of industry and engineers in each region and to bring together academic and practising engineers. The number of full-time staff in the Centres would be very small, supplemented by both engineers on secondment and part-time appointments from industry and engineering schools. Models exist for such a framework in the regional management centres, regional computing centres and some Business School consortium arrangements. We anticipate the RECs having a close working relationship with the Authority through which funds could be channelled to them.

4.115 The rapidly growing technology of 'distance learning' provides a ready means for courses to be brought to the student at his place of work and for increasing the impact of the new RECs. These techniques are undergoing rapid development in many countries, notably the USA. They include teleconferencing; interactive programmes using a combination of a conventional TV set, a simple audio cassette and the telephone; and more passive types of audio-visual aid. *The Open University and other agencies are leading exponents of these techniques in the UK, and we recommend that the new Authority, working with engineering departments in universities and polytechnics, companies and Institutions, should evaluate, promote and where necessary fund the initial trial and expansion of these techniques.*

4.116 Continuing formation can be an expensive area of education and training since courses and programmes are often tailored to the specific and narrow requirements of small groups of people and require frequent updating or renewal. Engineering schools profess themselves hindered from laying on ad hoc short courses by the requirement that these be self-financing over and above the school's regular teaching commitments and by the system of UGC funding, which is geared to the number of undergraduate students and takes little account of continuing formation provisions. Since these courses are disproportionately demanding of the time of already hard-pressed staff, the cost in time and money is often more than can be spared. *We recommend that the DES, SED, UGC and LEAs, when reviewing the extra resources needed in the engineering schools to undertake the extra demands of the B Eng and M Eng courses, also take full account of the importance of allowing adequate senior staff time for building up their activities in continuing and post-experience formation, and that in so doing they allocate a 'full-time equivalence' rating to part-time and short course students which fully reflects the costs of providing these facilities.* The DES already provide direct funding for University Adult Education Departments and this model might be followed to fund continuing formation for engineers.

4.117 A large part of continuing formation costs is taken up in preparatory research and the preparation of teaching material (especially for distance learning courses); these costs are incurred long before the courses begin and fees can be claimed and so place a drain on the schools' resources. *We recommend that the Engineering Authority be provided with funds to support preparatory work for selected continuing formation initiatives,* much as the Department of Industry has provided in the last year for the 'start-up' costs of courses in microprocessor applications.

Special categories

4.118 We have considered the required range of continuing formation programmes in general terms only. These requirements are extremely diverse, ranging from narrow problem-specific programmes to broad programmes aimed at extending engineers' horizons and employment prospects. Another spectrum to be covered extends from 'hard' engineering at one end to management subjects at the other. Particular technologies to be catered for range from microelectronics to production techniques, from process technologies to software and design. We have not gone into detail on the coverage of the programmes which ought to attract support; that is best left to those responsible for implementing and co-ordinating the general measures we have proposed. However, certain groups have special requirements which need to be borne in mind. They include:

(a) engineers re-entering the engineering dimension after a period of absence, including women engineers returning to work after raising a family;

(b) scientists and others employed in engineering jobs who may need training in engineering practice;

(c) those engineers whose formation has been predominantly engineering science-based;

(d) engineers changing disciplines;

(e) those upgrading their qualifications, eg promoted technicians; and

(f) people managing or needing a working knowledge of technical operations whose initial formation was inadequate to equip them in this respect, eg 'technological literacy' for non-engineers.

A particular role for the Engineering Authority would be to consider the special needs of these groups and to initiate provisions to cater to those needs.

Summary of main conclusions and recommendations

(i) The formulation of aspirant engineers begins at school in the proficiency obtained in mathematics and physics which are the analytical foundation of engineering and in the outlook and understanding generated through their studies. We hope that the recommendations of the Cockcroft Committee will prove the basis of improvements in the numbers studying mathematics in school and in the quality of what they are taught and *we recommend* the Department of Education and Science to devote similar attention to the teaching of science

121

in schools. *We urge* the various Examining Boards regularly to monitor their syllabi in subjects like history, economics or the sciences, to ensure that they develop in pupils an awareness and understanding of technology and industry within the economy. *We further recommend* that the Departments of Industry and Education ensure the availability of adequate funds for building up the role of the Science and Technology Regional Organisation (SATRO) movements as initiators and co-ordinators in the extension of the many valuable programmes linking schools with local industry.

(ii) To become 'fit to practise' as fully professional engineers, aspirants should have undergone a balanced and well-integrated formation package encompassing formal education, practical training and structured experience in the working environment including the exercise of personal responsibility on the job. Only a minority of British engineers have hitherto received an adequate formation in these terms by the time they are deemed qualified, largely because there has been insufficient input to engineers' formation from employers and from current engineering practice. *We recommend* the introduction of a new structure of engineering formation, operated under the auspices of a new national statutory Engineering Authority, which would bring together practising engineers, employers and engineering teachers to develop models and guidelines for the academic and employment phases of engineers' development, and would supervise and monitor the administration of those models in teaching departments and employing organisations. The functions of the Authority in this regard would embrace the general specification of objectives for the new packages and for each stage within them; the accreditation of establishments offering programmes within these criteria; the assessment of individual engineers completing accredited programmes; and the registration of successful candidates from them.

(iii) *We recommend* a new formation structure, leading to three bands of registered qualification: Associate Engineer, Engineer and Engineering Diplomate. These should be based respectively upon Higher National awards (or the equivalent), new Bachelor of Engineering (B Eng) degrees, and new Master of Engineering (M Eng) degrees, each subject to accreditation by the new Authority. The B Eng and M Eng courses would be oriented much more than most current engineering degree courses to the synthesis, application and practice of engineering in the market environment and would in particular incorporate elements of practical training and project work which we have called EA1 and EA2. The M Eng course would be more rigorous and demanding than the B Eng course, though both would build upon a firm foundation of engineering science and mathematics. There would however be less development of these in the B Eng course than in most current BSc courses. A period of two or more years of structured training and working experience would be required after completion of the degree courses for registration as R Eng or Dip Eng, to meet criteria designed to bring graduates to the stage of 'fitness to begin practice' as qualified engineers; this stage of formation would be conducted within programmes to be accredited by the new Authority and on the basis of two phases of industrial training and development, EA3 and EA4. The B Eng/R Eng stream would be geared to providing most of the professional engineers required for 'mainstream' work, while the M Eng/R Eng (Dip) stream would be intended for the smaller group (perhaps 25 per cent of the total intake) showing early potential for leadership in the development of advanced technology or in the management of engineering operations. The M Eng stream would be selected at the end of a common first year with B Eng entrants. Qualification for R Eng (Assoc) should be based on the new TEC qualifications of Higher Certificate and Higher Diploma in appropriate engineering subjects, equivalent SCOTEC qualifications and a modified form of a current Higher National Diploma in engineering subjects, to be designated the Higher Engineering Diploma (HED). Bridges between the three streams to allow professional progression will be available.

(iv) We estimate that the provision of B Eng and M Eng courses for the current number of engineering undergraduates may add as much as 25 per cent to the costs of engineering education. This is a price which cannot be baulked by Government, if they genuinely wish to improve Britain's future capabilities in the engineering dimension. The Government's recent proposals to cut funding for higher education are to be deplored because they undermine national capabilities to produce engineers at a time when we believe they should be built up. We have rejected as impracticable proposals that university engineering departments should be funded autonomously from the rest of the university sector, but recommend that increased funds be earmarked for accredited courses. Comparable provisions in respect of the maintained sector are not possible within the present constitution of the polytechnics (outside London), since responsibility for the allocation of their funds rests with the various local authorities concerned; *we therefore recommend* that the Government seriously consider reforms in the management of engineering education in the polytechnics to give their Governing Boards greater autonomy to manage their institutions within an approved budget.

(v) Our proposals demand a high level of active support and participation from the employers of engineers. In particular we are calling on them to provide carefully structured programmes of training and development (EA3 and EA4) for all graduate recruits during their first few years of employment, subject to external accreditation of the programmes and of the progress of the individuals by the new Authority. Since the graduates from B Eng and M Eng courses will already have obtained a large measure of basic training, and since they will be equipped to make some contribution to the enterprise virtually as soon as they begin work, *we have not recommended* any further financial inducement to employers to provide EA3 and EA4. We would hope that many employers will participate, through the new Authority, in the design and accreditation of B Eng and M Eng courses, and will also become closely involved in the teaching of them, whether by themselves assisting in some of the teaching,

123

by providing equipment or facilities to local departments, or by providing opportunities for teaching staff and students to gain experience of current engineering practice through secondments, joint industry-academic projects, or sandwich course sponsorships.

(vi) We have attached great importance to increasing the provision and uptake of 'continuing formation' for engineers during their careers, both towards enhancing the contribution made by the existing stock of registered engineers in the short term and as a means for all engineers to keep abreast of developments in their own field or to extend their expertise into new areas. *We recommend* that a condition of statutory registration for engineers should be a personal commitment from them to maintain their technical knowledge, and further that employers should be obliged to provide paid study leave (for periods linked to individuals' length of service) for registered engineers to meet this commitment. *We further recommend* that a number of centres should be designated as Regional Engineering Centres, funded via the Engineering Authority, to act as the focus for continuing formation activities in each region. Among their activities should be encouragement for the development of 'distance learning' schemes for engineers, in liaison with the Open University and national and local media, employers and engineering teaching establishments. The DES and UGC should be required to ensure that engineering schools have adequate resources to free senior staff time for continuing formation activities, in addition to which the Engineering Authority should be allocated funds from Government and industry to help with the appraisal and 'start-up' cost of selected initiatives in this area.

CHAPTER V

The Organisation of Engineers

(a) Introduction—engineering as a profession

5.1 The majority of engineers fulfil the key characteristics of professional occupations identified in the literature,[1] in that

(a) they are required to be expert in a particular area of activity, for which an advanced and extended formation is necessary, and practice in which requires a high level of theoretical foundation;

(b) they have custody of a clearly definable and valuable body of knowledge and understanding;

(c) they accept responsibility and accountability for the decisions they make against recognised values and standards of conduct.

However, engineers differ from other professional groups in three important aspects: the great majority of engineers are employees of companies and other organisations; the nature of engineers' work is not well understood by the lay public with whom they are seldom in direct professional contact; and the range of activities covered by engineers is greater than for most other professions. Whether reflecting these or any other characteristics of engineering in Britain, it was clear from the evidence we collected and from our survey results[2] that the professional status of engineers is not generally acknowledged in this country by the public and by employers to the extent that it is for, say, doctors or lawyers.

5.2 Like those other professions, engineers have over many years formed themselves into associations, the number of which has grown enormously from the founding of the Institution of Civil Engineers in 1818 to the present day through a process of initiation, division and (less often) amalgamation, based sometimes on technical disciplines such as civil, mechanical or electrical engineering and in other areas of engineering activity such as municipal, gas, nuclear or aeronautical engineering. There are now over 80 national engineering Institutions, and numerous other *ad hoc* and local associations of engineers. In 1962, after a long period of negotiations, 13 of the largest Institutions, each holding a Royal Charter, established the Engineering Institutions Joint Council to provide a single forum and representative voice for all professional engineers. This body changed its name to the Council of Engineering Institutions (CEI) on securing its own Royal Charter in 1965. The CEI now comprises 16 Chartered Institutions which are corporation members and

---

[1] Monopolies Commission. 'A report on the general effect on the public interest of certain restrictive practices so far as they prevail in relation to the supply of professional services'. (Appendix on definitions of professions) Cmnd 4463, HMSO 1970

[2] National Opinion Polls Omnibus Survey, May 1978. Appendix G
Policy Studies Institute. A General Survey of Professional Engineers.

another nine with affiliate status. These and their memberships (which include some duplication) are listed below:

Corporation Members of CEI
(as at 1 July 1979)

	Corporate Members	Total Members
Royal Aeronautical Society	7,814	13,258
Institution of Chemical Engineers	5,971	12,035
Institution of Civil Engineers	37,820	59,832
Institution of Electrical Engineers	37,217	74,928
Institution of Electronic and Radio Engineers	7,772	13,029
Institute of Energy	4,813	5,611
Institution of Gas Engineers	3,811	5,787
Institute of Marine Engineers	13,470	19,257
Institution of Mechanical Engineers	51,986	72,654
Institution of Metallurgists	6,407	10,013
Institution of Mining Engineers	2,921	4,187
Institution of Mining and Metallurgy	3,464	4,860
Institution of Municipal Engineers	8,382	10,108
Royal Institution of Naval Architects	4,365	6,698
Institution of Production Engineers	12,852	18,663
Institution of Structural Engineers	10,379	13,974

Affiliate Members of CEI
(as at 1 July 1979)

	Corporate Members	Total Members
Association of Mining, Electrical and Mechanical Engineers	3,250	3,700
British Institute of Non-Destructive Testing	1,574	2,094
Institution of Agricultural Engineers	1,329	2,347
Institution of Highway Engineers	8,266	8,783
Institute of Hospital Engineering	1,536	1,706
Institution of Nuclear Engineers	1,476	1,864
Institution of Public Health Engineers	2,655	3,350
North East Coast Institution of Engineers and Shipbuilders	1,127	1,358
The Welding Institute	2,353	5,012

5.3 The major Institutions were originally formed mainly as learned societies for the exchange of views and the dissemination of information among people with a shared interest in a branch of engineering, from which beginnings they sought also to improve the practice and standing of their branch of engineering. In particular they made efforts to raise the quality of its practitioners in terms of their educational attainments, their practical training and their personal standing in the eyes of their professional peers. This was done through the establishment of membership criteria which specified minimum requirements for education, training and responsible experience and which also imposed a code of professional conduct upon those wishing to join an Institution. Thus the Institutions came, over an extended period, to take on a qualifying function for professional engineers.

5.4 Until quite recently this function of the Institutions offered the main route to qualification for the majority of British engineers. France, Germany and other European countries began early in the nineteenth century (in some cases even earlier) to establish specialist institutes of engineering formation, providing extended full-time courses leading to *statutory* qualifications for engineers. Although there were a few comparable establishments in Britain during the late nineteenth century, until the expansion in higher education provision in the 1960s, most engineers developed their expertise through a combination of working experience and part time education (usually night classes and/or day release). The qualifying activities of the Institutions thus served a valuable purpose, providing engineers with a pattern of formation to follow and standards to aspire to and giving those who satisfied the membership standards of an Institution a qualification which they could show to employers as proof of their attainments. However, the system had some critical weaknesses; in particular

(a) there was little attempt at uniformity of membership requirements among the various Institutions;

(b) the standards set were in each case determined through a balance between considerations of raising entry standards for the particular Institution, maintaining a flow of new members and meeting the requirements for practice in each branch of engineering;

(c) employers, as the users of engineers, were only involved in Institutional qualification procedures, insofar as they happened themselves to be Institution members.

5.5 These weaknesses of the Institutions' qualifying activities became more critical in the 1960s, as an increasing proportion of engineers were academically qualifying through full-time higher education and employers and engineers themselves began to question what Institutional membership for which an engineering degree provided exemption from Institution examinations added to the degree award as a qualification. An early task for CEI was to establish common minimum standards for membership of its constituent Institutions and to set up a single register to denote recognition of those meeting the standards set. It introduced the new title of Chartered Engineer (C Eng) for engineers, to be based upon attainment of a degree in engineering (or the equivalent educational standard)—which became mandatory for registration in 1974—plus appropriate training and experience as an engineer plus membership of a member Institution. Registration was extended, through the Engineers' Registration Board (ERB) to embrace members of non-Chartered Institutions with the introduction of new qualifications bearing the titles Technician Engineer (T Eng (CEI)) and Technician (Tech (CEI)), based respectively upon the academic awards of HNC/HND and ONC/OND or the equivalents plus appropriate experience and training.

5.6 The CEI has achieved much in bringing order into the membership requirements of the numerous autonomous Institutions. It has established

127

acceptance among over 50 Institutions of three tiers of engineering qualifications, and has laid down minimum standards for each; it has established Registration Boards and protected titles for each tier, involving most of the qualifying Institutions in their administration; it has established a single set of examinations to replace member Institutions' own entrance examinations (although most candidates are exempted); and it has established a number of other related innovations and activities. It has not succeeded however in establishing C Eng and T Eng as generally recognised, respected or required qualifications in the eyes of the British public, nor—more importantly—in the eyes of employers. Neither has it established itself as a strong voice for engineers or as a force in national affairs. Some of the larger Institutions have expressed their disappointment and even disenchantment with CEI and are tending increasingly to go their own way with regard to their policies on qualification and other professional matters; for example, the Institutions of Civil, Mechanical and Electrical Engineers have each announced their intention unilaterally to impose stricter membership conditions than are required by the ERB.

5.7 The changes we have recommended, particularly those concerning the formation and qualification of engineers, will have important implications for the Institutions and the CEI, and will require them to review their functions and policies in the organisation of engineers and in fostering the engineering dimension. Particular functions for consideration are:

    (a) the qualification and registration of engineers;

    (b) the regulation of engineering practice;

    (c) learned society and related information activities;

    (d) providing leadership and a 'voice' for engineers;

    (e) professional services and representation for engineers.

(b) Qualification and registration for engineers

The need for registration

5.8 There is in effect a voluntary system of registration for engineers, through acceptance onto the membership roll of a member Institution of the CEI and thence listing in the unified register of such rolls maintained by the ERB carrying with it the right to the title C Eng. Parallel registers exist within the ERB for Technician Engineers and Technicians. It would be churlish to denigrate the admirable efforts of those who have worked to establish and operate these Institution-based registers, but we have strong doubts whether the existing system is constituted in a manner which can adequately achieve the critical objectives of a national registration system for engineers. These objectives are

    (a) to ensure that all practising engineers have undergone a full and balanced formation relevant to the level and branch of engineering in which they are working;

    (b) to confer authoritative national recognition upon qualified engineers, and thereby to help raise the standing of engineers in industry and society; and (*c*) to encourage engineers to maintain their competence and 'fitness-to-practise' during their careers, and to assist them in doing so.

5.9 The ERB and most Institutions within it would argue that this is just what the current C Eng and T Eng registers provide. They were unable however to produce convincing evidence to support this assertion, whereas contrary evidence came from many directions. Serious weaknesses persist with regard to each of the objectives stated. Engineering formation is not meeting the needs of engineering practice, and in too many instances virtually ceases when the young engineer begins working; the Institutional qualifications of British engineers are not generally recognised by employers, nor by many authorities overseas; the standing of engineers in industry and in society is lower in Britain than in any other major industrial country; and many engineers have complained about the problems they face in obtaining the time and support to extend their expertise. Employers in particular—those we visited[1] and those who submitted evidence to us—almost unanimously expressed their indifference to the benefits of Institution membership for the engineers they employ and were openly sceptical of the ability or the authority of the Institutions to regulate the practice of engineering. They have come instead to apply their own judgments of whether an engineer is qualified to fill a particular vacancy, based mainly on his academic qualifications and his past employment record.

5.10 We do not condone employers' negative attitudes to the existing registration system, since very few have attempted to help in improving it or to establish viable alternatives to it. Nevertheless, it is our firm conclusion that a register based on the existing machinery cannot satisfactorily achieve the important and desirable objectives sought. What is required is a register of qualified engineers which meets the following conditions:

(*a*) it commands powerful national recognition, and has the authority to over-rule sectional interests;

(*b*) it enjoys the active participation of employers and engineers, in furtherance of their mutual interests;

(*c*) it is open to all engineers who can satisfy qualification criteria laid down by a national Authority, regardless of Institution membership;

(*d*) it has the flexibility to change with social, technological and economic circumstances; and

(*e*) it is recognised by engineering authorities and employers in other countries.

Registration in other countries

5.11 We had the opportunity to review efforts to these ends in several overseas countries:

(*a*) In the *USA* the Engineers' Council for Professional Development (ECPD), formed by the Professional Societies, offers guidance to all schools of engineering as to the most suitable form and content of degree courses and accredits those courses meeting these criteria. The National Council of Engineering Examiners (NCEE) recommends

---

[1] See Appendix D

parallel national guidelines for the non-academic training and experience required (beyond an accredited degree) for professional qualification. Each State has its own machinery to assess and test aspirant engineers, usually applying NCEE tests, and accords recognition and a title—Professional Engineer (PE)—valid in that State to those deemed qualified. State registration is required in order to practise as a consultant engineer and in a few other specified areas. It is not generally required for employment in industry, though moves are afoot in some States to require all engineers to be registered. Although registration is not generally mandatory, many engineers choose to register voluntarily for the recognition and status it gives.

(b) In *Canada*, a first degree in engineering is regarded as a good general foundation for a variety of careers in industry or commerce. Those entering engineering careers (as defined in law) are however obliged to register their qualifications under the relevant Provincial Act (except for Federal Government or Armed Forces service). Registration is controlled by the engineering profession under delegated authority from the Provincial governments; for example, the Ontario register is administered by the Association of Professional Engineers (Ontario) under authority from the Attorney General's office. Accreditation of courses and vetting of individuals is administered under similar principles to those used in the USA. A single register is maintained for each Province, membership of which is required before an engineer can practise; the register places an onus on the individual not to work in areas outside his competence.

(c) In *France*, professional status and a legally protected title are accorded to engineers on graduation from one of 150 'Grandes Ecoles'; the title, Diplome d'Ingenieure, is awarded (for life) by each Ecole under delegated authority from the Government Commission des Titres des Ingenieures. The convention among employers is to recognise that graduate engineers, although notionally qualified, require several years of structured training through experience on the job before they are considered fully qualified. There are no statutory controls over engineering practice, except in a few activities involving potential public hazard, but few employers would call on a non-registered engineer for important engineering decisions.

(d) In *Germany*, two distinctive statutory qualifications have traditionally been awarded by the engineering schools, the Ing Grad, awarded to 'mainstream' graduates from the Fachhochschule, and the Dipl Ing awarded to potential leaders graduating from the Technische Hochschule and the Technical Universities. Both types of engineering school aim to produce 'finished', albeit inexperienced, professional engineers on graduation. Under the German system the engineering schools are recognised as the sole qualifying agencies; though State institutions, they have traditionally had substantial autonomy but have sought as a matter of course to meet the needs of industry. State intervention at the 'Lande' level has increased in recent years, mainly in an attempt to control the cost of operating the bipartite formation system. There are no generalised legal controls over engineering employment.

130

(e) *South Africa* introduced a system of statutory registration in 1968. Registration is at present compulsory only for engineers in consultancy, although there are plans to extend controls to manufacturing industry. Many engineers working in manufacturing industry already register on a voluntary basis even though only 6 per cent of those on the register are legally bound to be registered. The system works through professional Institutions, the universities and employers and involves the accreditation of academic and practical formation. It is claimed that registration, linked to licensing of practice, has helped develop the engineering profession in South Africa both numerically and in qualitative terms. Training in industry in particular is said to have improved.

(f) Other countries tend to fall into one of the above patterns. Japan follows the French system though there are no protected titles and US influences are also strong. Holland, Denmark and Sweden are close to the German model. Australia and New Zealand have some features in common with South Africa.

5.12 We found that machinery existed in all the overseas countries we looked at, in varying degrees of elaboration, for regulating the qualification process; and that in contrast to the position in the UK this machinery had a State involvement and an element of public accountability and generally provided for an organised employers' input. The absence of an organised employer input in Britain and of a State interest in the qualifying process thus sets us apart from our main competitors.

5.13 In the US, France and Germany in particular, the machinery for accrediting and regulating engineering degree courses was highly valued by employers and was seen as providing a means whereby their own requirements could be fed into the formation process and for guaranteeing minimum standards of academic formation. It was coupled with an acceptance by employers of their own responsibilities for continuing engineers' formation in employment. Employers' involvement in the formation provided by the engineering schools had the effect of making them aware of the limitations of the formation so provided and of the consequent need for them to continue the formation process in employment; it did not lead them to assume that they had no further formation responsibilities, as tends to occur in too much of British industry.

5.14 We found it impossible to reach any firm conclusions as to the effect of the registration systems in operation in other countries on standards of engineering practice or upon the standing and status of engineers. In every overseas country at which we looked the status of engineers and engineering was high; it attracted high quality entrants and was accorded a priority in social and industrial affairs that is generally lacking in the UK. Representatives of the profession in some of those countries that have registration argued that registration had contributed significantly to the status of engineering as an activity and of engineers as a group. In other countries the view was expressed that state involvement in engineering qualifications reflected the recognition which already existed of the national importance of a high-calibre stock of engineers. On balance we take the view that the priority and status

131

given to engineering in other countries depends largely upon deep-seated cultural factors. Registration may serve to institutionalise and confirm these factors but it cannot of itself fundamentally alter them.

5.15 These thumbnail sketches are intended not to disguise the problems and difficulties faced in the operation of the systems used in each of these countries, but simply to illustrate that there are many ways of approaching the issues in question. There is one respect in which all differ from practice in Britain, and that is in none of them is registration the responsibility solely of the profession itself. While qualification is often (but not always) a requirement for membership of professional bodies overseas, only in Britain is membership of a professional Institution made a requirement for qualification. This reinforces our conclusion (arrived at on other grounds) that registration in the UK ought *not* to be based upon Institutional membership.

Benefits of a statutory register

5.16 We have recommended the establishment of a new statutory Engineering Authority to undertake a wide range of functions within a general remit to further the engineering dimension in Britain. Among these functions (described in previous chapters and later in Chapter VI) would be the responsibility placed upon the Authority to maintain the sole statutory register of engineers qualified to standards and criteria laid down in conjunction with employers, engineers and others with a direct interest in engineering formation and practice. The new register would in due course be based upon the new qualifications R Eng (Dip), R Eng and R Eng (Assoc) described earlier. Registration would then demonstrate an individual's fitness to begin practice as a qualified engineer, having satisfactorily completed an accredited formation package or an acceptable equivalent according to the criteria described in 4.63–4.67. It would also entail a commitment from the registered engineer to develop and maintain his 'fitness-to-practise' throughout his career.

5.17 Statutory registration on these lines must not be seen as an end in itself. What it provides is an ordered, structured and authoritative means towards implementing some of the changes recommended in the previous chapters. In particular it provides:

(a) machinery for employers, engineers (through their Institutions) and engineering teachers to work together in establishing and maintaining new models of engineering formation, more acceptable to industry than the current system has been;

(b) means for engineers to obtain an integrated formation, and a consequent qualification, recognised and valued by employers and (by dint of its statutory basis) society at large.

5.18 The new statutory register would establish statutorily-based machinery involving employers, engineering teachers and practising engineers in establishing and assessing qualification criteria related directly to the requirements of engineering practice and the engineering dimension. They would thereby avoid the various criticisms commonly made of the existing regime, either that standards for particular Institutions' membership have been arbitrarily raised in isolation from wider needs, or that ERB standards have been kept low to preserve unity among Institutions. Although this change would remove from the engineering Institutions authority and responsibility for engineering qualifications, they would still have an important role to play with the new Authority in the specification and day-to-day administration of the new regime. The experience and expertise of the Institutions in their particular disciplines will make them a key source of advice to the Authority and of members for accreditation and assessment teams. Our philosophy, and we hope that of the new Authority, has been that the status of engineers is best improved through greater recognition of the importance of engineering, and in particular through propagating improved understanding of the engineering dimension. The Institutions will have a crucial role to play with the new Authority in generating that understanding.

Future of the ERB

5.19 Once established, the registration machinery administered by the new Authority will supersede that of the current Engineers' Registration Board (ERB) (except for the Technician (CEI) Board). We recommend that, at that time, the ERB be wound up. Responsibility for the registration of Engineers and Associate Engineers would pass to the new Authority. We suggest that pending the outcome of the review of technicians which we recommended in Chapter III responsibility for Technicians should in future reside with the Technician Education Council, SCOTEC and the Industrial Training Boards.

5.20 We wish to make clear that, in recommending the abolition of the ERB, we do not criticize, still less denigrate, the efforts made by the ERB and its staff to establish a register of engineering qualifications which would meet the objectives described earlier. Within the constraints upon them, the ERB have achieved a great deal of which they can be proud. They have argued that they are still a young organisation, and that, while improvements are still required, it is unreasonable to expect them to have achieved more than they have in the time. We do not dissent from this; but *we do not believe that a register constituted only by engineering Institutions (and excluding some of them) and based upon Institution membership can ever achieve the authority, representativeness and flexibility of a statutory register.* The CEI have intimated that they might be willing to recommend to their members changes in the constitution and working of the ERB which would ameliorate some if its current difficulties—for example, by allowing lay representation on the administering Boards and devising means of registering individuals who do not belong to a member Institution. Even if the CEI were able to carry through such changes to the current ERB, this would not remove the fundamental features which militate against it being made the basis of a statutory register, and in particular its lack of appeal to employers.

Registering the existing stock of engineers

5.21 It is from the existing stock of engineers that the urgently needed immediate improvements to practise within the engineering dimension must come. It is moreover the current stock of engineers upon whom we must rely to establish the new statutory register of qualified engineers and to prepare future generations of young aspirants to meet its requirements. *We are unanimous in our view that the new statutory register must embrace the current stock of engineers.* While it is not possible to change the initial formation of those engineers currently practising, the new system of registration by the Engineering Authority can from its outset help employers and the existing stock of engineers to make an enhanced contribution. It will benefit all engineers by giving them statutory recognition of fitness to practise, a Code of Practice to guide their activities and active encouragement to them to maintain and develop their expertise. It also provides a means for them to demonstrate their commitment to improving current engineering practice and future engineers' formation.

5.22 *The criteria governing recognition of the current stock of engineers on the new register should be as follows:*

(*a*) there must be a single register identifying those who satisfy the standards to be applied for the new formation streams and those registered on the basis of current academic and Institutional qualifications;

(*b*) registration must in all cases be on the basis of personal application, to indicate a commitment from each individual on the register; and

(*c*) there must be an element of selectivity and individual assessment in the registration procedure, since blanket acceptance of all those currently registered with the ERB would add nothing to qualifications which many employers and others have hitherto disregarded.

5.23 *Within these criteria the Engineering Authority should specify routes to registration for the current stock of engineers.* We were all concerned that those engineers currently practising who became recognised on the new register should be clearly identified; but we differed over the particular procedure to be adopted and the titles to be awarded for this purpose. We considered three alternatives (although there are probably others).

Under the *first* alternative, there would be a strictly limited period, say five years, during which engineers currently registered as Chartered or Technician Engineers with the ERB would be able to apply through their Institution for listing on the new register. In assessing their applications the Authority would take into account membership of engineering Institutions and the actual engineering capability represented by each applicant's career training, experience and working responsibility. Successful applicants would be eligible to use the protected titles Registered Engineer (Chartered) or Registered Engineer (Technician) according to the level at which their qualifications were recognised by the Authority. The Authority would have to make arrangements for experienced engineers who demonstrate a high level of professional expertise even though they do not possess the academic qualifications currently required by the ERB. Engineers currently practising and who do not wish to join an Institution to become registered could apply under the 'external entry' route described in 4.76, undergoing an intensive interview and assessment procedure to satisfy the Authority that through achievement they met comparable standards of knowledge, understanding and experience to those qualifying for R Eng or R Eng (Dip) through the new formation packages; similar facilities would also be available to those registered under the interim

'Institution route'. Institution or ERB membership would no longer be recognised as qualifications by the Authority and admission to the register would only be through the routes specified in Chapter IV.

Under the *second* alternative the Authority would make arrangements whereby engineers currently practising could apply for registration in the new categories R Eng (Dip), R Eng and R Eng (Assoc) from the outset, within standards and criteria as near equivalent as possible to those for the new formation streams. The assessment procedure would be similar to that for the first approach, with especially rigorous standards applying to those seeking the title R Eng (Dip).

The *third* alternative would be similar to the first, with the difference that the new titles R Eng (Dip), R Eng and R Eng (Assoc) would be reserved only for those qualifying through the new formation streams and those registered on the basis of current qualifications would be distinguished by different titles. (A new title would have to be devised for those currently practising who did not wish to seek registration through the 'Institution route'.)

5.24 *We stress that our difference of view only concerns the mechanics of registering today's engineers on the new register; the need to do so is not in question, and neither is the need to have a single register for all engineers.*

It will be for the Engineering Authority, after consulting with all the interested parties (including the Institutions), to decide the particular procedure to be adopted within the criteria (*a*) to (*c*) listed in 5.22.

5.25 The statutory register of qualified engineers will show each registrand's name, address, current academic qualifications, registered formation qualifications and professional titles, with the appropriate dates against each.

(c) Controlling engineering practice

The need for controls

5.26 The great majority of practising engineers are employees in industry or of local and national government. Their relationship with their ultimate 'clients', the customers for the products and systems which they produce, is therefore an indirect one. Hence, although their products may be subject to detailed regulation, engineers themselves have not in general been subject to the stringent legal controls which apply to other professional services provided directly to members of the lay public; there are some exceptions, but these are few and highly specific. Control over engineering practice has instead largely been left to employers' own judgements of their best interests in the light of the market demands and legal constraints within which they operate.

5.27 These demands and constraints are onerous and place great pressures on employers to ensure that they employ well-qualified engineers in responsible positions. Some observers have argued that the national interests involved are too important to be left to employers' individual discretion, and have advocated a wide-reaching statutory requirement that only registered engineers should be employed in certain categories of critical or highly-responsible engineering work. Their arguments ride on three main counts:

(a) many employers manifestly do not accord engineering or engineers the importance and priority required and in the absence of compulsion will not insist that the engineers they employ are properly qualified;

(b) unless failure to register implies a serious loss of employment opportunities for engineers, the incentive for engineers to seek registration will be weakened and the power of the new machinery to influence engineering formation attenuated;

(c) unless registration is necessary for significant areas of engineering employment, and is withdrawable, no effective sanction will exist against professional misconduct or incompetence.

5.28 Controls which go some way towards licensing engineering practice in this way are already applied in some other countries, notably Canada, the United States and South Africa. Each country requires consultant engineers to be registered, while provincial laws in Canada require all those practising as professional engineers to be registered with the statutory authority. We were able to review the working of these regimes in Canada and the USA, and most of us came to the conclusion that licensing as applied in these countries offered no benefits in the UK context. While the linking of registration with licensing has arguably produced benefits for engineers in these countries, we were not persuaded that it had contributed to any material extent towards improved engineering practice. We consider it significant that, in countries where engineering is established and valued within the national culture, engineers have not felt the need to seek recourse to professional 'closed-shops' to improve their situation.

5.29 Engineering is by its nature a team activity and decisions within the engineering dimension reflect the interaction of many such teams. Attempts to draw lines around functions within the engineering dimension and to prescribe who should be allowed responsibility within them would ossify and compartmentalise even further the working relationships which we have argued should be opened up and made as flexible as possible. Engineers work in such a diversity of roles and circumstances, with concomitant varieties of personal and shared responsibilities, that no general licensing provision could hope to validate the competence of them all, although regulations seeking to establish general licensing have been attempted in the various Provinces of Canada. We looked in particular at the system in operation in Ontario, which seeks to cater for the breadth of specialist areas of practice by stipulating that no registered engineer should practise in an area beyond his competence. In practice it seemed to us that there was no effective means of enforcing this provision and the individual engineer himself was responsible for determining the boundaries within which he was competent to practise. This does not amount to effective licensing, although the responsibility it lays upon the individual engineer might usefully be extended in Britain. *We are thus on the whole dubious of the desirability and sceptical of the practicability of any system of generalised licensing of engineering practice in Britain and we recommend against any such regime.* There are however two areas of engineering in which the arguments for linking registration of qualifications with licensing of practice are stronger—those where public health and safety are at risk and consultancy.

Health and safety, and the public interest

5.30 Though we are firmly of the view that *generalised* licensing of engineering practice is not desirable, there are nonetheless some specific areas of engineering practice in which the attendant risk to employees or to the public is deemed such that statutory licensing of practice is required. In some such instances the onus of responsibility is placed directly on employers: for example, the procedure regarding nuclear installations is to license the site with a general condition of the licence that the licensee (ie the employer) appoint 'suitably qualified persons' to perform critical tasks (in some instances this requirement is in practice taken to mean Chartered Engineers); in aircraft construction it is the company which is licensed, which is a form of licensing whole teams of engineers. In a few other instances, circumstances are deemed to justify the licensing of individuals holding particular responsibility—for example, engineers on ships at sea, mining engineers and those supervising the construction of large dams.

5.31 Nowhere in the evidence to us did anyone demur from the desirability and importance of these and similar specific controls over engineering practice, and indeed some witnesses suggested that they should be extended further. Assessment of particular suggestions for extending licensing of engineering practice is the job of the Committee on Major Hazards which advises the Health and Safety Commission. It would certainly be surprising if the current set of licensing arrangements were sufficient to cover all areas of potential public hazard or liability and it would be incongruous if these and any future areas of statutory licensing of engineering were not to be linked to state registration of engineers. *We therefore recommend that statutory requirements concerning the levels of qualification or competence of those taking responsibility for areas of engineering involving public hazard should wherever appropriate be framed to insist on the appointment of 'suitably qualified persons who shall be registered engineers'.* The Health and Safety Executive and the Engineering Authority should maintain a continuing dialogue over possible amendments to existing regulations and potential extensions of licensing controls within this structure.

Consultants

5.32 Our arguments against the general licensing of engineers apply primarily to situations in which they are employed within companies or other organisations. There is a small but important minority of engineers who are self-employed or working in partnership as consultants, to whom our earlier reasoning may not apply. Consultant engineers are more akin to other professional groups inasmuch as they have a direct relationship, often of a fiduciary nature, with their client. A strong case can be made, therefore, for licensing engineering consultants, as happens in North America and most of the old

137

Commonwealth. This could be expected to benefit the consultants themselves, giving them an imprimatur of State accreditation, as well as protecting public interests. The potential benefits to those employing consultants would be that the State licence would provide a more specific assurance of competence in the area in which the consultant was active than the general indicator of statutory registration. Licensed consultants would be able to show that they had satisfied a rigorously enforced assessment of their expertise and standing, which would be of benefit to many in obtaining work, especially overseas. As happens in some other countries such a regime might well attract many other engineers not currently working as consultants to seek a consultant's licence for the professional cachet it carries. While we thus favour the principle of licensing engineering consultants, we are aware that such an innovation would raise many practical problems, some of them highly complex. *We recommend therefore that an early task for the Engineering Authority be to advise the Government on the terms and coverage of a scheme to license consultant engineers.*

Other controls over engineering practice

5.33 If the practice of engineering is not to be regulated by comprehensive statutory licensing, what sanction will the statutory register hold over employers and engineers? The short answer is that the register will have as much sanction as employers choose to give it. To the extent that employers require the engineers they recruit to be registered, then registration will *in effect* become a licence to practise. This happens already to some extent in civil engineering and in parts of chemical engineering. We would expect employers to make increasing use of the new register, as it becomes a list of engineers qualified to standards which they have helped to set and monitor. Registration would not seek to tell an employer about an engineer's potential competence for a particular job, nor about his personal character and flair, but would certify that the registrand had undergone a full and relevant formation and had demonstrated his fitness to begin practice as a registered engineer (in the appropriate category).

5.34 *We recommend in particular that the Government and all other public sector employers*—in which we would include nationalised corporations and other state agencies—*set an example in recruiting engineers on the register, and in preparing trainee engineers for registration.* We further urge that this example be extended to companies supplying public sector requirements through procurement orders or development contracts; the Government, its purchasing agencies and other public sector organisations should insist that supplying companies employ Registered Engineers and Associate Engineers wherever appropriate as a matter of policy. Engineering teaching departments should also seek to employ Registered Engineers to teach accredited courses or to undertake research work; encouragement in this will come from the Engineering Authority in its accrediting role and hopefully also from the bodies funding engineering education and academic research.

A Code of Professional Practice for engineers

5.35 The increasing pervasiveness of legal constraints upon employers, particularly through health and safety regulations and product liability legislation will strengthen the onus upon employers to make use of the register

138

as a source of highly-qualified engineers. The employment of registered engineers in key posts cannot constitute a defence for employers who have contravened such laws, but it will hopefully lessen the likelihood of their doing so. In particular, employers will benefit from the sanctions and responsibilities to which each registered engineer will have committed himself through the Authority's Code of Professional Conduct.

5.36 Each professional Institution already specifies a code of professional conduct to govern the behaviour of its members, breach of which renders them liable to censure or even expulsion from their Institution. The CEI has formulated its own Code, designed to provide a general model for the particular codes and rules of conduct applied by member Institutions. It states:

'The Chartered Engineer shall at all times so order his conduct as to uphold the dignity and reputation of his profession; and to safeguard the public interest in matters of safety and health and otherwise. He shall exercise his professional skill and judgement to the best of his ability and discharge his professional responsibilities with integrity.'

We questioned the CEI and a number of Institutions in an attempt to ascertain the efficacy of this and similar codes, and the rigour with which they were enforced. It is clear that very few disciplinary cases have been brought before individual Institutions, and none at all before CEI, in recent years; those that were quoted to us were all instances of 'professional misconduct' rather than incompetence. This rarity of cases may reflect the rarity of lapses among currently registered engineers from the highest standards of professional competence; or it may, as some have suggested, reflect the Institutions' unwillingness to become involved in judgements over an individual's technical competence (an unwillingness not shared, for example, by the architects). As the CEI told us, public disgrace or the Institutional equivalent is not necessarily needed 'pour encourager les autres'. Nonetheless, we were not persuaded that the codes of conduct incorporated into the current registration system carry much weight or sanction in practice.

5.37 *A Code of Professional Practice,* based upon registered engineers' 'fitness to practise' and personal competence (rather than moral conduct) could nevertheless give added confidence in the new register to employers and the public, provided it was rigorously and sensibly enforced. *The Engineering Authority should therefore draw up and administer such a code, building onto the CEI guidelines specific responsibilities upon registered engineers:*

(a) *not to undertake work for which they could not validly claim competence;*

(b) *to maintain and develop their competence through participation in continuing formation programmes;*

(c) *to maintain their knowledge of, and to observe wherever appropriate, technical standards, codes of technical practice, health and safety regulations, and other such requirements; and*

(d) *to participate in and to encourage the formation and professional development of other engineers.*

Engineers reported to the Authority for instances of professional incompetence or malpractice would be examined on the basis of this Code, and would be judged culpable—and liable to deregistration—if they could not satisfy the Authority that they had abided by its conditions. At the same time the Code—and behind it the Authority—could serve to back up engineers if, for example, they were under pressure to cut critical corners, or to work outside their field of competence, or who were refused opportunities to update their personal expertise.

(d) The role and organisation of the Institutions

Institution activities

5.38 A great many Institutions, including all those within or associated with the CEI, submitted evidence to us which described their activities, which we were able to discuss in some detail with a large number of them. Institution activities can conveniently be grouped within six main headings:

—registration and control of qualifications and practice
—learned society
—education
—promotion of engineering and engineers
—liaison with related bodies and organisations
—professional services and representation for engineers

All have some activities within each category, although the level of provision varies greatly between Institutions. All have been heavily involved in qualification and regulatory activities, and these have hitherto taken up a large proportion of most Institutions' staff time and resources. The establishment of new machinery to take over the main responsibility and burden of this function will free the resources and energies of the Institutions to concentrate on developing their other functions, and in particular their learned society activities in the broadest sense (not just academic activities), supporting and complementing the activities of the Engineering Authority.

Learned society and education functions

5.39 Most of the present Institutions grew up originally to provide a forum for those with an interest in a particular branch of engineering to exchange views and information and work together in developing the state of knowledge and understanding in that branch and all have retained this learned society role. *We believe that the Institutions are uniquely placed to promote awareness of developments in engineering practice and new technology among their members and outsiders and we recommend that they concentrate further efforts to this end.*

5.40 *In particular, we wish to see the Institutions concentrating more upon disseminating best engineering practices and new techniques.* Almost all operate in this area already and also work with the British Standards Institution (BSI) in establishing national technical standards. This area of activity could be expanded with great value to the economy and to the Institutions. In this respect we were impressed by the scale of the operations of the Verein Deutscher Ingenieure (VDI) in Germany, which assembles teams of experts to draw up and publish codes of practice and recommended techniques in a very wide range of engineering activities. These are published and regularly updated, and provide a profitable income. The extension of Institution activities in this direction, working individually or jointly as appropriate, would complement the technical information services and library services already supplied by some Institutions. It should be noted however that one of the major engineering Institutions translated some of the best of the VDI's codes, but few British companies showed any interest in them. We envisage the focus, and much of the initiative, for Institution activities in the propagation of best practices and new techniques coming from the Engineering Authority. Acting, for example, in response to a specific area of need identified through NEDC (as discussed in Chapter II), the Authority might encourage either the BSI or a particular Institution to develop a code of technical practice for that area. We would expect the Authority to be able to back such encouragement with financial or other assistance where necessary and to be involved in the publication and dissemination of the results.

5.41 *The Institutions could also with benefit expand their learned society function in the direction of continuing formation provision for engineers.* All Institutions run programmes of lectures, seminars and short courses, but we understand that only about 10 per cent of their members participate in these in any one year. It would clearly be beneficial to the Institutions themselves and, more importantly, to their members if greater numbers could be involved in such activities. The reasons we heard quoted most often by engineers for not attending Institution activities were that they were inconveniently timed or located, or that they were too expensive. The answer to this lies in part with greater use of the Institutions' regional branches for educational activities, using the services of the Regional Engineering Centres recommended in Chapter IV; in instances where a local Institution branch is too small to mount viable programmes on its own these Centres could provide a focus for co-operative efforts with other Institutions, local teaching establishments and companies. The pump-priming fund which we have already advocated for the Engineering Authority to sponsor continuing formation provision should be available towards the costs of approved Institution programmes.

5.42 An important corollary of the learned society function is the Institutions' valid interest in the content of the initial formation of engineers, to which they have an important and continuing contribution to offer. The Institutions can draw on the expertise and experience of members working both in engineering education and practice, and are thus well placed to advise on the formation needs of their branch of engineering and the best teaching and training vehicles for meeting them. The most recent exercises in this respect have been conducted by the Institutions of Civil, Electrical and Mechanical Engineers, and respectively through the Chilver, Merriman and Dawson Reports each has recommended models for the formation of engineering in their discipline. The Institution of Chemical Engineers has for some years maintained a recommended core curriculum for chemical engineers, and many other Institutions have comparable activities. Although we have argued against the unilateral imposition of the Institutions' conclusions on the appropriate model of formation for their branch of engineering, it will be important that the Engineering Authority be able to draw on those conclusions and on the expertise within the Institutions in framing the details of the new formation streams we have recommended.

5.43 A number of the larger Institutions have been active also in the accreditation of academic courses and of industrial training programmes, although resource constraints have limited the scale of such activities. All Institutions claim competence in the assessment of individual applications for corporate membership, in particular in evaluating candidates' experience and their professional responsibility. The quality of such assessment varies greatly between Institutions; the best of them are extremely thorough and rigorous. This existing machinery and expertise should be drawn upon to the full by the new Engineering Authority. However we are against the Authority delegating the accreditation and assessment of courses and individuals to particular Institutions.

Promotion of engineering and engineers

5.44 All the professional Institutions have developed roles in promoting the standing and attractions of engineering. Again, the extent of such activities varies greatly between Institutions. In recent years the larger Institutions have greatly expanded these aspects of their activities but many others still do very little to this end.

5.45 Activities aimed at promoting the standing and attractions of engineering have mostly been directed at the schools, particularly in schools-industry schemes such as those to bring young engineers into schools to talk about their work and others to provide teachers and senior pupils opportunities to spend a short time seeing how engineers work within industry. We commented on these schemes in Chapter IV, where we recommended that the SATROs be encouraged to develop their role as catalysts for extending schools-industry links. The Institutions have a key role to play in this development, and in parallel career promotion schemes such as the Engineering Careers Information Service.

5.46 Few Institutions are very active in promoting understanding of engineering and the work of engineers to employers or to the public at large, although one or two have initiated programmes of visits to companies to discuss with them their use and training of engineers and any related problems they are facing. We envisage the Engineering Authority taking the lead in promoting such 'awareness programmes' but doubtless it will continue to look to the Institutions for practical support. As we have shown throughout this report, it is the lack of a cultural understanding of the nature and importance of engineering and the engineering dimension which underlies many current problems. The Institutions should regard it as one of their primary functions, individually and collectively, to foster that understanding, directly and through the Engineering Authority.

Organisation of the Institutions

5.47 Each of the professional Institutions brings together engineers with an interest in a particular area, which in some instances is very broad (eg mechanical engineering) and in others very specific (eg welding or non-destructive testing). Issues of common interest to the members of *all* the

Institutions are accordingly few, but issues of mutual interest to *some* Institutions are more numerous and have given rise to a number of specific ad hoc groupings of Institutions within and outside the CEI. Hence the efforts of the CEI to establish 'one voice and one ear' for a unified engineering profession have been fraught with difficulties, compounded by the limited budget which the Institutions were prepared to allow it.

5.48 The original constitution of the Council gave it no power to over-rule sectional interests among its member Institutions, a constraint which has not been removed by recent revisions to the CEI's Royal Charter providing for individual membership of the CEI and for a number of directly-elected members (chosen by Chartered Engineers) to sit on its Council. It is too early to assess the impact of this change, which has not been extended to the section Boards of the ERB. The limited budget is still a major constraint upon the CEI's scope and effectiveness; in 1978 it had a total revenue slightly over £250,000, mostly granted by the Corporation Member Institutions on the basis of a little over £1 for each registered Chartered Engineer. The CEI raises very little money on its own behalf and receives no income from public funds.

5.49 Despite these difficulties, the achievements of the CEI since 1965 are not inconsiderable. Most of these achievements have been in the area of qualifications and registration, although it has in addition established a number of regional branches, some of them in areas where individual Institutions could not justify viable branches; it has introduced a biennial Professional Engineers Survey of salaries and deployment; it administers two prestigious prizes—the MacRobert Medal and the Smeaton Award; it maintains a number of specialist committees, many of them concerned with maintaining relationships with fraternal organisations in this country and overseas; and it has established the Fellowship of Engineering, which we discuss below.

5.50 Without doubting the value of these activities, it must be said that the CEI has not made a significant impact upon the fundamental problems of establishing greater understanding of the nature and role of engineering and in promoting the engineering dimension in national economic affairs. Moreover, it does not appear to visualise a role for itself in this respect, despite the object stated in its Charter: 'to promote and co-ordinate in the public interest the development of the science, art and practice of engineering'. Individual Institutions have from time to time expressed their frustration with CEI's limited role and with the cumbersome procedures of seeking changes through unanimous consent from all sixteen members, and some have threatened withdrawal. In 1974, the Presidents of the three largest Institutions (Civils, Mechanicals, Electricals) voiced their concern and proposed a new structure for the profession based upon new groupings of Institutions around a newly-constituted Institution of Engineers; their pressure led to revisions in the CEI Charter, allowing individual membership of the CEI and elected representatives on the Council, but little radical change.

5.51 Our recommendations for a statutory Engineering Authority, with responsibility for promoting the engineering dimension and ensuring a continuing supply of qualified people to it, clearly have major implications for the future of CEI and its members; in particular our recommendation that the qualification of engineers become the responsibility of the new Authority will entail the winding up of the ERB and the curtailment of a large part of CEI's activities. It might be however that the Institutions, which will themselves have an important continuing role, will wish the CEI to continue as a forum for them to come together as a focus for their relations with fraternal organisations in this country and overseas. This is a matter for discussion between the Institutions themselves and the CEI.

5.52 We envisage, however, that for most purposes the Institutions will find greater value in groupings based upon shared interests in an area of technology or of engineering activity. This would certainly apply to their relations with the new Authority, which we recommend should be on the basis of a small number of functional groupings—for example, 'manufacturing', 'process' and 'construction'. Such groupings could be in line with a number of previous recommendations which found much favour among some Institutions but never came into effect. They would have benefits both for the Engineering Authority and other national authorities in providing means to consult with all those Institutions with an interest in a particular field and also as a basis for joint action and co-operation between different Institutions. We have not sought to prescribe the membership of such groupings but a number of possible models exist.[1] Some large Institutions will have an interest in more than one grouping while others, divested of their qualifying function, may find themselves too small to make an impact in any of them. The Authority should take an active role in promoting co-operation and changes in the organisation of the engineering Institutions, extending in some instances to promoting mergers between them. It could play a useful role as a 'marriage broker' to encourage groupings and mergers where they would benefit the engineering dimension, or to find ways of sustaining the learned society activities of Institutions which cannot survive on their own. It should be empowered to provide limited financial assistance in furtherance of this function.

(e) Professional engineers and trades unions

5.53 A number of engineers have expressed frustration at the apparent reluctance of some of the professional Institutions to provide personal services to members and to participate in furthering their material interests especially in pressing for better salaries. The Institutions for their part claim to be precluded from such activities by their Charters and by their charitable status. Nonetheless, some of the larger Institutions have developed their activities in this direction, for example providing model terms of service for engineers, offering legal advice over such issues as health and safety regulations or the

---

[1] eg Three groups: Structural; Manufacture; Process;—Evidence to the Committee from Mr Ewen McEwen.
Four groups: Mechanical, Aeronautical, Marine and Production Engineering; Civil, Structural, Municipal and Mining Engineering; Electrical, Electronic and Control Engineering; Chemical, Fuel, Petroleum, Process, Metallurgy;—The Fellowship of Engineering's membership sub-committee engineering panels.
Six groups covering: Electrical and Electronic engineering; chemical, fuel and nuclear engineering; mechanical, aeronautical and production engineering; marine engineering; mining and metallurgical engineering; civil and structural engineering;—Groupings for representation on CEI's Executive Committee.

implications of strict liability, providing careers advisory and placement services (in liaison with private recruitment agencies) and conducting and publishing regular surveys of engineers' pay and deployment. Once the qualification and registration of engineers becomes the responsibility of the new Authority there may be added pressure upon the Institutions to extend the other services they offer to their members in return for their subscriptions. It is likely however that many engineers will look for support in seeking better material standing, not to the Institutions or even the new Authority, but to the trades unions.

5.54 Trades unions are becoming increasingly important as vehicles for organising and representing engineers, and as such have to be taken into account in the overall framework of their organisation. This was made very clear to us in the evidence, both oral and written, from a number of trades unions representing engineers, from the Engineering Employers Federation (EEF) and from the engineering Institutions and the CEI. The subject also arose from time to time in other submissions of evidence, especially at our regional meetings and during our visits to employing organisations. There is a wide range of views surrounding the issue of trade union membership for engineers and differing stances have been adopted by different employers, individual engineers, engineering Institutions and the trades unions themselves. The main issues are:

—is trade union organisation likely to further the interests of engineers?

—is union membership compatible with engineers' professional obligations?

—are some types of trades union more appropriate than others for engineers?

5.55 On the first issue (whether engineers ought to join unions at all) opinions varied along predictable lines. The EEF told us that whilst they did not overtly oppose it they saw no reason for engineers to seek union membership. The individual trades unions and the TUC, not surprisingly, favoured union organisation for engineers. Three main reasons were advanced for this: that it would materially benefit engineers individually and collectively; that it would be to the good of the trade union movement by extending its influence and increasing its understanding of engineers and technology; and that by raising the standing and bargaining power of engineers, it would strengthen the engineering dimension of industry and contribute to improving industrial performance and better prospects for all union members.

5.56 The CEI and most of the engineering Institutions accept in principle the notion of trade union membership for engineers and many have issued guidance to this effect to their members. The CEI issued its own guidance for individual engineers and their Institutions in 1976, which was extended and reissued in 1979. It states: 'A professional engineer has a legal right to join a union; he does not contravene his code of conduct by so doing. He should have an absolute right to join the union of his choice or none at all if he prefers'. As noted, the Institutions themselves feel precluded from engaging in trades union activities because of their Chartered status.

5.57 Many engineers already belong to a union, and the proportion in union membership has been increasing in recent years. According to the CEI's 1977 survey, 44 per cent of Chartered Engineers belong to a trade union, compared to 37 per cent in the 1975 survey; the proportion of registered Technician Engineers in a union, in 1977 was nearly 60 per cent. The increase in the number of Chartered Engineers joining a trade union has been concentrated in the private sector, although still only 20 per cent of C Engs and 32 per cent of T Engs in the private sector belonged to unions in 1977. This contrasts with the public sector, where in 1977 77 per cent of Chartered and 85 per cent of Technician Engineers were in a union.

5.58 The recent growth in union membership in private industry is generally attributed to two factors. First, engineers have observed their salary and status differentials diminishing relative to the skilled and unskilled workers with whom they are in daily contact and whose work they often supervise. The relative improvement in the position of non-professional workers has been attributed to their effective union organisation and contrasted with the low level of unionisation amongst engineers, which has made engineers look more closely at trades unions as a means of improving their own lot. The second factor is that the trades unions for their part, responding to the more sympathetic attitude of engineers towards union membership have begun to organise and to recruit more actively at this level.

5.59 In spite of the steady trend towards increasing unionisation among engineers, many, particularly those working at the higher levels of responsibility, remain concerned at the prospect of joining a union on two counts. There is concern that the particular interests of engineers might be subordinated to, or overridden by the numerically greater interests of non-professional union members; and there is a fear of a possible conflict between the engineer's professional obligations and his interests as a trade unionist which might demand resort to strike action or other conduct possibly at variance with his professional responsibilities. These two concerns apply with varying force to different trade unions; for instance, they are held to be less applicable to membership of those unions which organise at professional level only. To this extent the issue of whether an engineer ought to join a trade union is bound up in the eyes of some with the particular union in question. All the unions who gave evidence to us declared that they were organised to protect the particular interests of engineers and other senior managers and that their policies were to deal separately with such grades in negotiations or disputes. The steady increase in the level of unionisation of engineers suggests that most believe that their particular interests are adequately catered for, whilst their rare direct involvement in strike action suggests that their professional responsibilities are rarely if ever compromised.

5.60 Notwithstanding the genuine concern which many feel about engineers joining trades unions, it seems highly probable to us that the trend towards increasing unionisation of engineers will continue for the foreseeable future. Younger engineers currently joining the profession appear much more sympathetic towards the unions than are older engineers, many of whom still tend to regard the unions with suspicion. We believe that over time a majority of engineers in private industry will probably opt for trade union membership, as is already the case in the public sector. This trend should be recognised and accepted as inexorable by all those involved in the engineering dimension. The possible advantages to be gained from well-organised and representative systems of industrial relations within employing organisations arise not only in negotiations over pay and conditions, but extend to consultation and joint action over a wide range of issues of common concern to the company and its employees. We also believe that engineers have an important contribution to make within trade unions.

5.61 Like the CEI, we recognise that trade union organisation among engineers is now a fact of life and is likely to increase. Nonetheless, we believe it important that the professional responsibilities accepted by a registered engineer under the proposed new Code of Practice are not thereby compromised. This Code should be framed so far as possible to protect the individual engineer from having himself to resolve any conflict which may arise between his union loyalties and his professional responsibilities, especially in respect of public health and safety, with the appropriate sections drafted after consultation between the Authority, the TUC and other concerned parties. Registration—and the threat of deregistration—can thus serve to provide engineers with an essential safeguard if they become involved in industrial disputes, and can help create conditions in which engineers wishing to join a union (but concerned about a potential conflict of loyalties) can do so. All the trades unions to which we spoke stated that their policy was to respect the professional obligations of their members, so that the proposed Code would in principle simply formalise this understanding. The Authority should nonetheless stand ready to intervene when problems arise over the application of the Code in an industrial dispute, and should take the initiative in establishing early discussion and solution of such problems with the TUC and the unions involved.

5.62 The CEI and some Institutions have stated that they wish to see a single union for engineers, outside those areas where there are currently well-established unions (such as in local and central Government and in public utilities). There are however great difficulties in this. First, effective representation in many organisations requires that a single union represents all those employed at particular levels of seniority, be they engineers, accountants, administrators or whoever. Moreover, there is opposition from the established unions within the CSEU and from the EEF to any disturbance to existing negotiating arrangements. A further complication is that those unions which the EEF are prepared to recognise within its arrangement with CSEU are different from those which the CEI has backed.

5.63 These factors do not mean that some rationalisation is impossible. It is certainly desirable. This was acknowledged by the TUC, which drew our attention to the general progress which had been made over the years in rationalising trade union structure though conceding that much still remains to be done. The TUC also drew attention to the relatively recent innovation where all the unions in particular industries are brought together in Industry Committees under TUC auspices. However, the immediate benefits of these changes in the context of representation for engineers have been attenuated by the inter-union disputes which regrettably have broken out, not only between TUC-affiliated unions and those which are not, but also between TUC affiliates. We have been urged to express a view about these disputes, but regard it as no part of our function to do so. We can only observe that they are damaging and harmful to the image of the unions, and that the advice thus far given by the CEI does not identify all the factors to be taken into account by engineers when choosing a union which can represent their best interests effectively. We therefore hope that all those concerned will bear in mind the effects these present conflicts have on their potential membership and take early steps to resolve them.

(f) The Fellowship of Engineering

5.64 It is generally accepted that the public standing and prestige of scientists has been greatly enhanced over 300 years by the activities of the Royal Society and election to its fellowship has come to denote one of the highest distinctions in British society. In 1976, in an attempt to establish a comparable prestigious body with its own accolade for eminent engineers, the CEI set up the Fellowship of Engineering. The Fellowship comprises Senior Engineers who, in the view of their peers, have by their personal achievement as engineers justified membership of a cadre of engineering excellence and the right to the title 'F Eng'.

5.65 The objective in setting up the Fellowship was to establish a centre of authoritative expert opinion which the Government and other bodies might consult on engineering issues of the day. In this it would complement for engineering the role played by the Royal Society in respect of science. During our visits overseas, we visited two organisations with similar aims to the Fellowship—the American Academy of Engineering and the Royal Swedish Academy of Engineering Science—and were impressed by their range of activities and the authoritative voice they had in national affairs. The British Fellowship has as yet not had time to achieve either the range of activities or the impact of its American and Swedish counterparts, although we see no reason why in due course it should not do so.

5.66 The Fellowship has been inhibited in its development to date by its constitutional position as a 'subsidiary' of the CEI; its lack of funds; its limited membership; and the predominance among its members of engineers nearing the end of their careers. Each of these factors is changing. The Fellowship is currently seeking its own Royal Charter, which would give it independent status; it has raised substantial subscriptions from industry with the promise of matching sums from Government which will enable it to rent its own premises and employ its own secretariat; and an active policy of inviting younger practising engineers to join the Fellowship has been adopted, although clearly it is in the nature of a body like this that they will always form a minority of members.

5.67 Given these changes, and time, we see a role for the Fellowship of Engineering to complement the activities of the Engineering Authority, acting as a major force in promoting the engineering dimension at national level. It will be important however that it maintains a clear distinction between its functions and activities and those of the Engineering Authority and other related bodies. Our impression is that, as yet, the Fellowship has not fully decided its future role and objectives; *we would recommend that it considers concentrating on the identification and promotion of new directions for engineering research, development and innovation which have not yet been exploited.* Were the Fellowship established in such a role it could assemble multi-disciplinary teams of senior engineers and others (perhaps associating with the Royal Society) to consider the most promising areas for further study; it could commission, debate and disseminate the results of detailed studies; and it could specify directions from which further research and eventual commercial applications might stem.

5.68 Other functions which the Fellowship might with value develop include:

—advising Government on the membership of public bodies concerned with engineering, including the new Authority;

—undertaking studies of important issues in engineering, commissioned by the Authority or on its own initiative;

—identifying needs for new academic Chairs in new or under-provided areas of engineering, both in universities and polytechnics.

(g) Conclusions and main recommendations

5.69 (i) A register of qualified engineers is potentially a valuable tool in regenerating the engineering dimension, but the basis of the present system militates against the full realisation of the potential benefits. *We therefore recommend the establishment of a new statutory register of qualified engineers, within the control of a new statutory Engineering Authority and based upon the new formation streams proposed in Chapter IV.*

(ii) The new register would replace the existing ERB register of Institution members once the new integrated formation streams were established. Meanwhile, existing engineers would be accepted on the new register according to criteria specified by the Authority.

(iii) Despite the arguments in its favour, *we recommend* against the generalised restriction of engineering practice to registered engineers, on grounds both of principle and practicability. However, we hope that registration will nonetheless become *in effect* a licence to practise through the requirements imposed by employers. *We recommend that the Government and other public sector employers set a lead in this.*

(iv) Where special considerations justify statutory licensing of specific areas of engineering practice, the requirements of the appropriate regulations should be based upon the statutory register.

(v) Additional sanction over engineers' activities should be sought by requiring adherence to a Code of Professional Practice drawn up by the Engineering Authority as a condition of registration.

(vi) The Authority should be charged to examine and advise upon the introduction of statutory controls over consulting engineers, based upon the new register.

(vii) Once the new registration machinery is set up the rationale for a separate ERB disappears and it should be wound up. The Institutions, freed of their qualifying function, should concentrate upon their other services to engineers and the engineering dimension and in particular on their learned society functions. We anticipate that most Institutions will in future perceive greater value from 'functional' groupings than from the CEI as currently constituted and the Authority should promote and facilitate such groupings. However, we regard the future of the CEI as a matter to be resolved with its member Institutions.

(viii) Trade union organisation among professional engineers is rapidly becoming a fact of life in the private sector, as it has long been in the public sector. This is acceptable provided the unions concerned abide by their undertakings to respect the professional obligations of engineers, as laid down in their code of practice. We venture no opinion on the merits and problems of establishing a single trade union for all professional engineers in private industry, but urge the TUC and the unions involved to work towards removing the current acrimony between unions competing to recruit among engineers.

(ix) The Fellowship of Engineering has a potentially valuable national role to play once it has fully established itself. In developing a clearly identifiable role the Fellowship should seek to establish close working relationships with the Authority.

CHAPTER VI

The Engineering Authority

The need for a new body

6.1 This Report has been concerned with improving the effective contribution made by engineers to national welfare and wealth creation in Britain, and in particular with the harnessing of that contribution to enhance the market performance of British manufacturing companies. Much can be done to this end within individual organisations—in the way they approach world markets and interpret their requirements; in the way they organise and manage their activities to further their business objectives; and in the way they employ engineers within those activities. We made a number of recommendations, all based upon existing best practices, in respect of each of these in Chapters II and III and have no doubt that a substantial improvement in manufacturing performance could be achieved quickly by individual companies implementing those recommendations as appropriate to their particular circumstances.

6.2 However, there is little in what we have said about the changes required within manufacturing organisations which is entirely new or is not done already by some companies; the hindrance to improvement has therefore certainly not been any lack of previous good advice or successful precedent. Rather it has lain with the priorities adopted by those in management and on the shop floor whose decisions and actions have determined the direction and pace of changes in industry. These priorities have too often relegated the need for up-to-date engineering excellence in products and processes below other concerns and the requirements of the engineering dimension have been neglected or overruled. As a direct consequence the market performance of industry has suffered.

6.3 This attitude among those working within manufacturing organisations is a reflection of the national undervaluation of engineering which is repeated in all the other institutions and bodies whose policies affect the capability of industry to respond to technological and market changes—in Government and its agencies; among trade unions and their members; in financial institutions; in schools and higher education establishments; and among those in the media and elsewhere who help shape national opinions. *A fundamental shift is required in national priorities, at many levels and in a wide range of different settings which will reflect greater acknowledgement of the crucial need for competitive manufacturing industries and of the key role of the engineering dimension in that context to enhance national welfare and prosperity.*

6.4 The responses demanded are not once-for-all but must be sustained and adapted to meet the continuing process of technological and market changes. An *engine for change* is required to overcome the inertia and negativism of prevailing attitudes and to press for actions to advance the national economy through the engineering dimension. Previous efforts to secure radical changes in the engineering dimension have in our view often foundered for lack of such an authoritative and permanent champion, capable of marshalling the many diverse interests concerned and of overcoming the apathy, inertia and resistance to change which exists among them.

6.5 The task of ensuring a continuing supply of high calibre engineering manpower for industry has become compartmentalised into a variety of component activities—schools/industry links, school and higher education, training, qualification, regulation, organisation, etc. Responsibility for each component activity has in turn been assumed by a plethora of institutions and agencies with no effective means of ensuring that each works in the knowledge of what others are doing, let alone in concert with them. The principal agents with an interest in the whole process—the employers of engineers—have been insufficiently involved in each stage, although they are the ones who inherit the product others have produced. Inevitably each agency in the process has developed criteria and objectives of its own with no means of relating these to agreed ultimate objectives.

6.6 What is required is not some new body to take over from all the existing agents in the engineering dimension, but some means of orchestrating the activities of those agents to produce coherent themes instead of the current dissonance. We have looked at the potential for developing existing machinery to achieve this, but saw no prospect of any existing body, or any amalgamation or extension of existing bodies, meeting the need. *We therefore recommend the establishment of a new Engineering Authority to create an environment in which the engineering dimension can be given its due weight within efforts to stimulate a vigorous and dynamic national manufacturing capability and to ensure the availability of an adequate supply of properly qualified engineers to progress those efforts.*

6.7 The Engineering Authority would provide both a focus and an impetus for improvements in all the diverse aspects of the engineering dimension, at national and company level, considered in this Report. *A great many of our recommendations rest in some degree upon the establishment of the Authority and we cannot stress too strongly the importance we attach to this particular proposal.*

Remit and terms of reference of the Authority

6.8 Reflecting the diversity of factors within the engineering dimension, the Engineering Authority will have to operate in a number of areas, carrying appropriate executive, consultative and advisory authority and responsibility in respect of each. Its role will be to relate activities in each area to a common purpose and its remit should be drawn to emphasise this. We propose that the principal objectives and terms of reference of the Engineering Authority be framed on the following lines:

—to promote the engineering dimension in all areas of the UK economy in furtherance of national economic needs;

—to initiate, maintain and otherwise encourage activities directed at ensuring the continuing supply and best use of engineering manpower;

—to work with all the bodies and institutions whose activities affect national engineering capabilities in all sectors in order to enhance those capabilities.

6.9 To meet its strategic objective of correcting the historic neglect of the engineering dimension in the UK and creating a climate in which the engineering dimension can flourish, will call for the Authority to operate in many areas within this remit. The precise means to be adopted will depend upon prevailing circumstances, recognising that continuous change will characterise the future state of the economy and of industry. In current circumstances we see the Authority's primary role being to follow up the recommendations of this Report and to foster actions which translate these into practice. Contributions to the engineering dimension already come from many established sources, which vary in their influence by reason of their differing authority, resources, knowledge or expertise. The Engineering Authority will provide a focus for the activities of these agents, maintaining close working relationships through liaison and consultation with them and exercising strong strategic influence upon them to progress the engineering dimension. It should be the task of the Authority to establish machinery for the continuous review of engineering standards, qualifications, courses, research and continuing formation programmes to ensure that developments in each of these at least keep pace with developments in markets, technology and current best industrial and employment practices. In addition to these general responsibilities the Authority will have a number of specific responsibilities in respect of the recommendations made in this Report, most notably its statutory responsibility for the qualification and registration of engineers and its functions relating to the formation of engineers.

Main responsibilities and functions of the Engineering Authority

6.10 The Authority will need to extend its activities in several directions in order to exercise the *strategic* influence which will give weight to its formation and qualification functions and ensure that these are effective. A number of such activities are proposed in the Report, of which the most important are: encouraging the general adoption by employing organisations of active manpower audits and allied development programmes for engineers; maintaining a national manpower inventory of the numbers, distribution and deployment of the current stock of engineers to back up manpower audits and supporting activities in industry and outside; encouraging the use of registered engineers by Government and public sector employers as an example to the private sector; and attracting more women into engineering and the provision of conditions assisting women to maintain their careers in engineering.

6.11 The effective commission of its remit in the strategic and particular activities cited here will require close working relations between the Authority and the many other bodies and agencies active within the engineering dimension. Organisations with which the Authority must establish effective *consultation and liaison* include the professional and academic institutions; Departments of State, especially those for industry, education, employment and trade; national bodies administering Government policies in education, manpower policies, industrial sponsorship, etc; private organisations concerned with generating and directing industrial development; employing organisations; and representatives of employers and employees.

6.12 The extent and diversity of this organisational infrastructure of the engineering dimension emphasises the need to ensure that improvements are introduced and pursued on a basis of wide consensus and unity of purpose. The aim of the Authority in this is to play a co-ordinating and rationalising role, building on, pulling together and extending many existing activities to establish a more effective system overall. This role currently goes by default.

6.13 Activities of the Authority in establishing improved *formation* programmes for future engineers will embrace the setting of standards and criteria for academic courses; the accreditation of courses against these criteria; setting standards for the structured learning and experience to be provided by employers; and the accreditation of employing organisations providing approved initial formation opportunities. In addition the Authority will have a major role in promoting the provision and uptake of continuing education, including the establishment and support of Regional Engineering Centres.

6.14 Backing up the Authority's involvement in engineering formation, and providing a platform for its other responsibilities in ensuring high standards and best use of engineers, will be its role in the *qualification* of engineers and maintenance of a statutory register of those qualified. Within this responsibility will fall activities including provisional registration of applicants who have obtained academic qualifications through accredited engineering courses; registration of engineers meeting the criteria laid down for full qualification; consideration for registration of engineers currently practising and of future applicants who have not undertaken an accredited initial formation; and specification and enforcement of a Code of Practice to be observed by registered engineers.

6.15 While the Authority will have a central directing role in raising and maintaining the standards of initial formation and an influence over the numbers of engineers produced, much of its work will need to be closely related to wider manpower considerations, for instance manpower inventories and continuing formation including management development, areas in which the Manpower Services Commission has major statutory responsibilities, including oversight of the Industrial Training Boards. We expect the MSC and the Authority to work closely together, particularly in providing manpower information and in the encouragement and support for both initial and continuing formation.

6.16 The Authority will be concerned on an important scale with the provision of improved intelligence and awareness of market and technological opportunities, working with the enhanced NEDC machinery recommended in Chapter II. We considered the arguments in favour of placing the whole of this function on the new Authority but rejected it, principally because the NEDC framework is already in being with an established track record in its contributions to industrial and commercial policy. To place this function upon the Authority would inevitably have entailed a high degree of duplication or re-invention of the NEDC machinery. Instead, we propose that the Authority, representing the interests of engineering, should be directly associated with NEDC activities, working closely with the NEDO staff and the various SWPs. To this end we recommend that the leader of the Authority be a member of NEDC.

Structure, composition and mode of operation

6.17 The effective discharge of the functions described above calls for careful design of the Authority's structure, composition and mode of operation. In particular the Authority must be *broadly constituted* to span its wide remit and to embrace the various interests of all those active within the engineering dimension; it must be sufficiently *representative* of these agents to bring together all the activities related to its overall objectives, including the active participation of employers; and it must have the *independence* and *authority* necessary for it to command national and international respect and to overrule vested interests where these contradict the national interest. This requires that it has a *statutory* basis and *direct funding* of its own.

6.18 The quality of the executive leadership of the Authority will be of crucial national importance. The post will demand a full-time commitment and great energy from someone with detailed knowledge of engineering and industry. The appointee should be an engineer with substantial industrial experience and standing at a senior level. The appointment should be for a fixed term and be renewable. As already recommended, the leader of the Authority should sit on the NEDC to ensure that due weight is given to the engineering dimension within the Council's work.

6.19 The leader and members will constitute the Executive Board of the Authority, which must be compact enough to be effective, suggesting a body of some 15–20 members. Initially these should all be appointed under statute by the Secretary of State for Industry, who should be required to consult widely amongst bodies representing employers, education, engineers and employees. The various statutory agencies with a direct interest in the Authority would doubtless be consulted also in the natural course of events. Those appointed would be independent and not spokesmen of organisations with

155

which they might be associated, and the spread of appointees should broadly reflect the wide span of affected interests.[1] It should be a condition that a majority of the members should be qualified engineers and that at least three members should be non-engineers. There should be no other constraints upon the process of appointments, though the aim to secure an effective employer input ought to be a prime criterion. Appointments should be set on a basis which provides for continuity on the Authority while ensuring a continuing supply of new blood and ideas.

6.20 After the Authority has been established for a while and once its register is in operation and is deemed to be sufficiently representative of the profession, consideration should be given (and provision made) for a system of elections whereby a proportion of the members of the Authority should be elected from the register by registered engineers. The remainder should be appointed by the Secretary of State who we would expect to select his nominees so as to ensure a broad spectrum of representation. The provision that at least three members should be non-engineers should continue.

6.21 The Chairman and Members of the Authority will form its policy-making level, providing leadership and determining the Authority's overall strategy and priorities. Beneath this policy-making level we envisage a network of standing and task committees responsible for particular functions and assignments. These committees will constitute the Authority's executive branches, with their members appointed and their activities co-ordinated and supervised by the Board of the Authority. Since virtually all the Authority's activities would impact upon or through engineers we would expect the engineering Institutions to provide many of the key participants in the Authority's executive committees. In nearly all respects the Authority will have to achieve its goals by working through other agencies, and representatives from these too should be fully involved in the working committees. Thus we envisage, as well as industry-based representation, the major Institutions, the Industrial Training Boards and various educational bodies continuing to play major roles in respect of formation and qualification within guidelines and criteria set by the Authority. The principle of working through existing bodies and thereby ensuring that the resources which they offer are deployed in support of the engineering dimension ought to characterise the Authority's operations.

6.22 Whilst the contribution from existing bodies is critical, the Authority will nonetheless require its own staff. As with the Authority's working arrangements, this is a matter properly left for its Chairman and Members to settle. Our main comment is that the quality of staff as in all other organisations will be a vital factor for the Authority's success. We are attracted to the idea of some staff being drawn on secondment from industry in particular and would advise that all the staff should have had previous working experience within the engineering dimension. To avoid it becoming a remote bureaucracy it is essential that the Authority remains in continuous and close touch

---

[1] One of us advocates a special arrangement whereby the engineering Institutions would be able to nominate a list of candidates from which the Secretary of State would be required to appoint four members. For this purpose the Institutions should be grouped along the lines discussed in 5.52. These members, like all others, would sit as individuals and not as representatives of the Institutions.

with engineering practice and developments in firms, educational establishments and elsewhere around the country. This can be achieved as a by-product of its activities in respect of accreditation, working with NEDC, the RECs, etc.

Resources and powers

6.23 Because the Authority will in the main be working through existing bodies, statutory and non-statutory, the cost of its activities will be considerably less than if it were starting from scratch and aiming to work apart from existing agencies, but *to accomplish its remit the Authority must have recourse to adequate resources and powers of its own.*

6.24 Substantial resources are already devoted to activities which will fall within the Authority's interest, funded by Government and by private organisations. Since the Authority will seek to work through these organisations as much as possible it follows that existing financial responsibilities will remain dispersed among these bodies; for example, engineering education will continue under the financial oversight of the Departments of Education, with the Authority exercising strong advisory powers over the allocation of DES and SED funds through its accreditation mechanisms. The training expenses to meet the criteria for EA3 and EA4 should, in our view, remain the financial responsibility of the employing companies who will benefit from the immediate and subsequent contributions they obtain from better prepared engineers. Most of the expenditure associated with the Authority's responsibilities will thus remain dispersed, with the Authority itself providing a framework and criteria for overall planning and co-ordination of this spending to greater national effect.

6.25 Costs directly attributable to the Authority will arise in respect of its executive functions—notably the accreditation of courses and training programmes and the operation and maintenance of the register—and its discretionary powers to provide finance for special studies, priming experimental education or training schemes (sometimes through the RECs), and other initiatives such as special studies of aspects within the engineering dimension. Administrative costs will arise in running its office and the RECs and in servicing its various standing and executive committees as well as for computer services and operators to maintain and produce the Register.

6.26 We have made some attempt at costing these activities, taking account of the operating costs of comparable organisations and the costs of current activities in the areas mentioned. Our estimate, taking into account the functions outlined above and allowing initially for only a modest spend on discretionary activities, is that the annual total cost of running the Authority will work out at around £10m pa at current prices. The gross costs envisaged are minimal when considered against the potential national benefits from an enhanced engineering dimension but could be offset slightly by the Authority charging modest fees of individuals and of educational and employing establishments for accreditation and registration services. As the Authority's work develops it may become necessary to augment its funding, with some activities being undertaken on a shared-cost basis with industry.

6.27 The Authority should report annually to Parliament and to the taxpayer through the Secretary of State. The Government should require an annual report from the Authority on the exercise of its statutory powers, on the use of the money voted to it by Parliament and on its non-statutory activities. It is important that the Authority should be capable of acting promptly and flexibly according to prevailing requirements, and the legislation establishing the Authority must have built into it provisions for the Authority's subsequent evolution, enabling it to extend its activities as need arises and providing for additional funding as necessary. This might be provided by giving the Secretary of State an enabling power to extend by Statutory Instrument the Authority's terms of reference and powers. Such a provision would need to be carefully framed to ensure that it could not be applied to circumscribe the Authority's autonomy without Parliamentary approval. The funding available to the Authority should within limits be capable of being increased without resort to prior Parliamentary approval and the Authority should be able to apply to Government for additional funding for particular purposes.

6.28 We would expect close working relationships between the Authority and Government, but Government ought not to be able to issue strategic directives to the Authority on the lines of those issued from time to time to nationalised industries. To do this would be to destroy the independent standing of the Authority which we consider essential on three counts. First, while engineering must be brought more into the public eye and made an issue of far greater public concern than at present, it must at the same time be protected as far as possible from discontinuities in national policies and the exigencies of short-term constraints. Secondly, the functions proposed for the Authority call for a continuity of policies towards the engineering dimension which the prospect of direct Government intervention might jeopardise. Thirdly, the Authority will be dependent on the commitment and contribution of employers and those who earn their living in the engineering dimension as well as from Government and its agencies, and it must be free to judge for itself the balance of priorities it follows; power for Government to overrule that judgement could destroy the relationship between the Authority and other non-Government bodies.

Conclusions

6.29 The industrial society of the future has to adapt not just to the consequences of past changes but also to the enhanced rate of change which new technology and its adoption throughout the world are creating and will continue to create as long as can be foreseen; microprocessors are just one example of future shock. In the introduction and management of these changes the main thrust lies in the area of engineering. Without highly educated and trained engineers, continually updating their skills and given authority and influence in concert with other industrially-biased disciplines to implement the products of those skills, there can be no confident prospect of stemming the decline of the British economy relative to its international competitors.

6.30 In our deliberations we have from the start been concerned with the 'wider issue' of the future economic health of this country. We have argued that this economic future, and hence the welfare and standard of living of this nation, depends upon the degree of its success in achieving growth in the output of its manufacturing industries, in terms of marketable products and of systems of services based on their use and of the efficiency with which these are provided to customers throughout the world. The commissioning of these tasks depends upon a variety of contributions, some direct and some indirect, and also upon the extent to which the people concerned with the separate contributions perceive common aims and how well they relate together in progressing the national interest in their activities.

6.31 Within companies it requires those determining the strategy and direction of manufacturing enterprises to recognise the need to relate technical capability to market needs; to ensure that they employ sufficient people with the necessary expertise; and to use, develop and organise the contributions of those people to fullest effect. Among engineers it demands a wide perception of their role within the enterprise and in particular the willingness and capability to relate their technical knowledge to its commercial objectives and the demands of its customers. Within Government and other sectors determining the commitment and distribution of resources within the economy—be they financial or human—it requires a recognition of shared direct interest in the success of companies achieving their objectives and a whole-hearted support for their endeavours to do so; in the education sector it requires astute perception of the kinds of skills and understanding demanded of those who will lead and carry through engineering-based changes in industry and elsewhere and provision to cater for those demands; and in all the other bodies and institutions concerned with industry and/or engineers it demands concomitant positive support through their respective activities.

6.32 The necessary coherence of objectives and consistency of activities in pursuit of them among all these people can only come about if they share the same attitudes and philosophy towards industry within the economy and towards determining industrial success. We have coined the term 'engineering dimension' as a shorthand to describe this industrial philosophy—a philosophy accepted as the basis of the industrial culture within other industrial countries with stronger economies than the UK and one which we must develop in this country.

6.33 The philosophy of the engineering dimension, and the policies and actions which stem from it, involve many people other than practising engineers—managers, union leaders, financiers, teachers, public officials, Ministers and others. Among all these, the contribution made by engineers is, however, central and critical and constitutes the keystone for the changes needed in the performance of manufacturing industry.

6.34 Against this background of change the skills of the present generation of engineers must be deployed to greater effect than hitherto, not just at the technical operating levels, but in the decision-making processes of companies and industrial sectors, and they must be given the authority and encouragement to influence and implement policies at that level as well as at the higher levels of community and nation. In addition it is necessary to attract, recruit, educate and train sufficient new engineers. This requires changes in attitudes and practices throughout society: in schools, universities and polytechnics, in institutions (technical, professional or political), in the machinery of national and local Government and its agencies; but above all by industry in its deployment and development of engineering skills and engineers.

6.35 We have attempted in this Report to reflect some of the changes which would facilitate this cultural and attitudinal change, particularly but not only in the areas defined in our remit. We do not believe, however, that these changes can be achieved solely through the voluntary good will of those involved directly or indirectly in the conduct of manufacturing industry. To ensure that the basic tenets of the engineering dimension are not lost sight of, and that activities deriving from them move forward in concert, *it is essential that an Engineering Authority with statutory backing be created to oversee the implementation of our recommendations and to keep under review the further changes that the future might demand to maintain or improve upon the manufacturing and industrial strength of this country through the more creative deployments of its engineers and their talents.*

Summary of recommendations

Engineering in the UK economy

See paragraph

1. The regeneration of UK manufacturing competitiveness must be given overriding priority in national policies, with the emphasis on developing market-oriented engineering excellence in the products made by British industry and in the production of them ... ...

1.31

2. All those involved with manufacturing industry, whether directly or indirectly, should review their activities to ensure that they perceive.and present engineering and engineers as matters of vital national concern in their own right ... ...

2.6

3. Companies should examine how to strengthen their access directly or indirectly to engineering research developments from whatever source; large companies should use such capabilities not only to cater for their own innovative requirements but also to encourage innovation in smaller enterprises ... ...

2.12

4. Government should consider imposing requirements upon companies regarding the publication of information about their 'total technical efforts' similar to those required in the United States ... .

2.12

5. Government should examine how industrial enterprises might be encouraged to make better use of the resources and expertise of its several engineering Research Establishments and of publicly funded research work undertaken in universities and other institutions ... ...

2.13

6. The Advisory Council on Applied Research and Development should be asked to review and advise upon the potential role and mechanics of an Engineering Design and Development Council to sponsor and encourage engineering developments to the point of commercial viability; the Government should respond positively if the review endorses this proposal ... ...

2.13

7. The Government should review its mechanics for encouraging innovation in British industry in the light of our observations regarding the engineering dimension and taking account of the advice given by ACARD in their report, 'Industrial Innovation' ... ...

2.15

8. The Government should take every possible measure to foster a financial environment more conducive to investment in manufacturing industry, and especially to direct such investment towards the design, manufacture and sale of products for world markets ... ...

2.17

9. The trade union movement should adopt the positive policies towards participation in technology-based innovations in industry advocated in the TUC document, 'Technology and Employment' 2.23

10. Government, employers and trade unions must work together within a major national programme of training and re-training of employees of all ages and at all levels to develop the skills and support needed to implement and sustain new technologies 2.24

11. The machinery of the National Economic Development Council (NEDC) and that of the new Engineering Authority should be used to bring together the relevant official bodies, institutions and industrial sectors to develop a national policy for standards and quality, using the Warner Report as a starting point 2.26

12. The machinery of the NEDC should be re-oriented towards establishing greater interchange of information and views about the impact of technological and market changes and the appropriate responses to them from the level of companies to Government and back 2.30

13. In this role NEDC and its working levels should work closely with the new statutory Engineering Authority which we propose to lead and co-ordinate national policies concerned to strengthen the engineering dimension   ...   2.32

14. Companies should take appropriate measures to ensure their capability to respond to the demands of the engineering dimension by fostering and giving the necessary authority to technologically-knowledgeable 'Product Champions' within senior management and also ensuring the development of an adequate supporting 'Corporate Expertise' within their organisations 2.35

15. Companies should also take measures to ensure that the contribution of engineers and others in related functions are responsive to and co-ordinated around the need to adapt flexibly to changing market demands, paying attention in particular to the organisation and relationship of engineering and other functions and to the career experiences of engineers in the organisation   ...   .   2.39 ff

16. Engineers themselves must be prepared and equipped to take a broad view of their contribution, taking into account not only the technical implications of their work but also the human and organisational factors involved and the processes of consultation and change through which innovations are realised 2.43

162

The supply of Engineers

17. Future official censal surveys should be structured to collect the information necessary for the maintenance of a continuing national inventory on engineering manpower to be built up by the new 'Engineering Authority'   3.5

18. Every effort should be made in schools to ensure that as many young people as possible retain the option to enter engineering and that they are properly informed about the attractions of an engineering career 3.12

19. In particular, all pupils should be strongly encouraged to maintain the study of mathematics and physics at least until after 'O' level and careers advisers should ensure that children are aware of the growing intrinsic and material incentives to qualify as an engineer in the modern world 3.13

20. The various routes into engineering degree courses for students who do not have 'A' levels or Scottish higher in mathematics and physics should be expanded and publicised by engineering departments and teachers 3.14

21. Employers should recognise and act upon the fact that the only sure way to attract more able young people into an engineering career if they see such a career as more attractive in terms of likely rewards, job interest, and career prospects than the alternatives   ...   .   3.16 ff

22. Greater emphasis should be laid by all those advising young engineers of the incentives being offered by some employers to attract more good engineers into the production function, so that more talent can be employed in this vital area 3.27

23. The Government, working with other interested bodies including in due course the Engineering Authority, should initiate urgent actions to increase the supply of engineering technicians and to enhance their preparation for careers in industry 3.31

Employment of engineers

24. Employers must recognise and act upon the responsibilities on them to complete the formation of young graduate engineers by giving them further support, training and structured experience; at the same time the teachers of engineers and the graduates themselves must recognise the growing variety of work in which engineers must be prepared to contribute 3.24

25. The new Engineering Authority should be remitted to take the lead in a sustained national programme to stimulate more wide-spread understanding among employers of the nature and importance of the engineering dimension and of the potential benefits to them from employing able engineers in a wide range of activities ...   3.34

26. Employing organisations should review their salary and career structures for engineers to ensure that they adequately reflect a value of engineers' contributions within the engineering dimension; the Engineering Authority should become a source of information and stimulus to employers in this 3.44

27. Companies should institute regular 'engineering manpower audits', building upon best employment practices in this country and overseas to ensure that they are making the best use of engineers as their key assets within the engineering dimension; the Engineering Authority should act as a source of information and encouragement to companies in this 3.47

28. Efforts should be made within schools, engineering departments and employing organisations to encourage more women to enter careers in engineering through school/industry liaison schemes, special bridging programmes and arrangements to assist women engineers to return to engineering work after a break from full-time practice 3.60

29. Companies, especially small enterprises, should ensure that they are making sufficient use of available engineering consultancy services and of the various schemes to help them gain access to such services   ...   3.62

30. The activities and services of the Overseas Technical Information Unit should be given greater publicity to encourage companies to use their scarce resources to build upon the best of relevant technical developments from overseas; this service should be expanded if and as industrial interest subsequently justifies it 3.63

31. The Government, and in due course the Engineering Authority, should greatly extend current schemes for the two-way exchange of staff between industry and engineering teaching departments 3.64

32. The contribution of applied sciences and others with similar skills to the engineering dimension should be encouraged by the establishment of a number of six-month or one year conversion courses through which people whose initial formation was in applicable subjects can develop engineering skills 3.65

Changes required in schools

33. The Department of Education and Science should direct attention and resources towards the improvement and possible rationalisation of the teaching of mathematics and science in schools, building upon the eventual recommendations of the Cockcroft Committee and taking into account recent measures to this end in Scotland 4.4

34. The various 'O' and 'A' level Examining Boards should extend and maintain their efforts to ensure that the syllabi for relevant subjects are geared to developing pupils' awareness of the nature of the modern economy and the role of technology in its development 4.7

35. The many schools/industry schemes should be built upon with the aim that every school and every company is involved in at least one such scheme. The Departments of Industry and Education and Science should ensure the availability of funds for developing the activities of the Science and Technology Regional Organisation (SATRO) movement in this regard 4.8

36. Related measures should be introduced to encourage a more positive and informed presentation of engineering to pupils in schools, including improved careers advice, more short secondments to industry of teachers and senior pupils and more emphasis upon industry and technology within teacher training programmes 4.9

Formation of engineers

37. The formation of engineers should in future be through one of three principal routes:

   (*a*) a route leading to the qualification of Registered Engineering Diplomate (R Eng(Dip)), for those showing potential for leading the development of advanced technology and/or the management of engineering operations which would be based upon new degree programmes leading to an award of a Master of Engineering (M Eng) degree plus a programme of structured post-graduate training and experience;

   (*b*) a route leading to the qualification of Registered Engineer (R Eng) for the main body of engineers based upon new degree programmes leading to a Bachelor of Engineering (B Eng) degree plus a programme of structured post-graduate training and experience;

165

(*c*) a route leading to the qualification of Registered Associate Engineer (R Eng(Assoc)) for those engineers who will work mainly in support roles based upon enhanced higher national or TEC(Higher) programmes plus appropriate structured experience and practical training ... ...   4.42 ff

38. We propose a system of statutory registration of these formation qualifications based upon the accreditation and assessment of each phase of the formation package to be carried out by the new statutory Engineering Authority 4.43

39. Selection for the M Eng stream should come after a diagnostic first year on a common course with B Eng entrance; thereafter it would take another three years (while the B Eng course would take another two to two and a half years) to graduation ... ...   4.47 ff

40. The design and planning of B Eng and M Eng courses within the criteria set out in the Report should be a task for engineering teachers and employers working together through the Engineering Authority; 'teaching contracts' should be placed with selected university and polytechnic departments for the development of model courses... ... ...   4.59

41. The academic part of the Associate Engineer package should be based upon the new TEC qualifications of Higher Certificate and Higher Diploma in appropriate engineering subjects, equivalent SCOTEC qualifications, and a modified form of the current Higher National Diploma in engineering which should be designated Higher Engineering Diploma 4.60

42. Graduates from accredited B Eng and M Eng programmes must undergo a further period of structured training and experience in a working environment to complete their formation; this should be in two phases which we have described as Engineering Applications 3 and 4 culminating in a period during which the novice engineer demonstrates the ability to carry engineering responsibility in a substantive post ... ...   4.63 ff

43. The post-graduate experience EA 3 and EA 4 would be subject to accreditation by the Engineering Authority, in addition to which individual young engineers who had gone through accredited degree and post-graduate formation programmes would have to satisfy the Authority that they had met all the requirements for registration as R Eng(Dip), R Eng or R Eng (Assoc) 4.69

44. The method of accreditation for EA3 and EA 4 would in most cases be for the Authority to accredit particular employing organisations who demonstrably provided adequately for these phases; non-accredited employers would be able to submit individual programmes for acceptance by the Authority, while engineers who had not undergone an accredited formation would nonetheless be able to seek registration through achievement via an 'external' route designed to assess their attainments against criteria for the three accredited formation streams   ...   4.72 ff

45. The Engineering Authority should maintain a variety of ladders and bridges between the three registered categories for those engineers who wish to extend their qualifications during their careers 4.62

46. Every effort should be made to increase the inter-change of staff between industry and teaching establish-ments to improve the teaching of engineering practice within engineering departments, including the introduction of systems of recognition (with associated additional pay) for engineering teachers who maintain close links with industry, and part-time teaching appointments for engineers working in industry to teach part of the B Eng or M Eng programmes 4.82

47. Academic research in engineering departments should emphasise work done in a context of economic pur-pose; to this end many current taught MSc courses in engineering should be discontinued and absorbed into the latter stages of M Eng courses, while suitably remunerated engineering 'teaching fellowships' should be established to attract working engineers to undertake research work and some teaching in engineering departments 4.87

48. Since the minimum size for viable M Eng courses will be 25–30 students, regional consortium arrangements should be set up to link several academic departments in a region in order that between them they can sustain a range of M Eng courses for their students 4.88

49. We oppose the separation of engineering depart-ments from the rest of the higher education system. Specific and long-term additional funding should be earmarked by the University Grants Committee for the establishment and maintenance of accredited B Eng and M Eng courses; courses which failed to get or lost accreditation by the Engineering Authority should not be eligible for these ear-marked funds 4.91

50. Comparable earmarking arrangements should be made for the funding of accredited engineering courses in the maintained sector. If this cannot be established effectively within the current management arrangements for the polytechnics, then the Government should introduce appropriate reforms in their constitutional standing ... 4.92

51. The training expenses associated with EA3/EA4 provision should be the responsibility of companies who will benefit from the services of the engineers concerned. We welcome existing arrangements whereby some firms can obtain help with engineers' training costs through Industrial Training Boards, etc, and we envisage the Engineering Authority being in a position to back up this support with 'pump priming' funds to stimulate experimental schemes and to assist group training schemes in getting off the ground 4.93

52. To stimulate student demand for places on B Eng and M Eng courses, allowing greater selectivity in those admitted, all students accepted on to accredited courses should be assured a bursary of at least £250 (over and above their mandatory LEA award and any industrial sponsorship) for the duration of the course 4.96

Continuing formation of engineers

53. Support through the Training Opportunities Scheme for engineers to follow full-time courses in either technical or management subjects should be extended ..., ... 4.109

54. The Government should introduce a statutory right of paid study leave for all registered engineers, on criteria and lines to be advised by the Engineering Authority ... 4.111

55. All registered engineers should be required to commit themselves to maintaining their expertise as a condition of remaining on the register, and demonstrable failure to uphold this commitment should be grounds for de-registration 4.112

56. A number of sites should be designated Regional Engineering Centres, funded by the Engineering Authority, to encourage the development of continuing formation provision for engineers and to act as foci for such activities in their region 4.113

57. The Engineering Authority, working with engineering departments, companies and Institutions should evaluate, promote and where necessary fund the initial trial and expansion of 'distance learning' methods as vehicles for continuing formation for engineers 4.114

58. We recommend that the Department of Education and Science, Scottish Education Department, University Grants Committee, and Local Education Authorities, when reviewing the extra resources needed by engineering departments to undertake the extra demands of B Eng and M Eng courses, also take full account of the importance of allowing adequate senior staff time for building up their activities in continuing and post-experience formation for engineers 4.116

59. The Engineering Authority should consider the special additional formation needs of the groups identified in the Report, and should be provided with funds to support preparatory and 'start up' work for selected continuing formation initiatives in these and other areas 4.117

Registration and licensing of engineers

60. Responsibility for the qualification and registration of engineers should pass to the new statutory Engineering Authority, which should register engineers on the basis of the new formation packages proposed in Chapter IV with no Institution membership requirements 5.16

61. Until the new formation packages are established, the Authority should make arrangements whereby engineers currently practising could seek registration against the principles outlined in the Report 5.21

62. Once the new statutory register is established, the necessity for the Engineers' Registration Board disappears, and it should be wound up 5.19

63. We are opposed to any generalised reservation of engineering work to registered engineers, except in areas of activity where public health and safety considerations arise ... ...:. 5.29

64. Where such considerations justify the licensing of engineering practice, the relevant regulations should require the employment of 'suitably qualified people who are registered engineers'; the Engineering Authority should work closely with the Health and Safety Executive and other bodies in the framing and extension of such regulations 5.31

65. An early task for the Engineering Authority should be to advise the Government on the terms and coverage of legislation to license engineering consultants 5.32

66. The Government and other public sector employers should set the lead in recruiting engineers on the new register and in preparing trainee engineers for registration, and should encourage supplying and contracting companies to follow their example; engineering teaching departments should also seek to employ registered engineers wherever appropriate 5.34

67. The Authority should draw up a Code of Professional Practice based upon engineers' technical competence and continuing fitness to practise, to which registered engineers would be required to commit themselves and breach of which would render them liable to de-registration 5.37

The role of the Institutions

68. The Institutions should continue to play an important role in advising upon and assisting in the education, training and registration of engineers through their involvement in the activities of the Engineering Authority 5.38

69. We would hope that in addition they would expand their learned society functions, particularly in the direction of continuing education provision for engineers; the pump priming funds allocated to the Engineering Authority for it to sponsor approved initiatives should be available to support the Institutions in this role 5.41

70. We would also wish to see the Institutions concentrating more upon disseminating best engineering practices and new techniques, again working closely with the Engineering Authority within the priority areas identified through the NEDC framework recommended earlier ...   5.40

71. The Institutions should also seek to expand their activities in promoting the standing and attractions of engineering among young people, working in collaboration with SATROs and within schemes like the Engineering Careers Information Service 5.45

72. The future of the Council of Engineering Institutions is a matter for discussion between the Institutions in the light of the changes which will follow from our recommendations 5.51

73. The Engineering Authority should take an active role in promoting joint activities and functional groupings among the engineering Institutions, extending where appropriate to promoting mergers between them; it should be empowered to provide limited financial assistance in furtherance of this function 5.52

170

74. The Fellowship of Engineering has a potentially valuable role to play complementing that of the Engineering Authority and the activities of individual Institutions; in particular it should consider concentrating upon the identification and promotion of new directions for engineering research, developments and innovation which have not yet been exploited, among other functions suggested in the Report 5.67

Engineers and trades unions

75. The trades union organisation among engineers in private industry must be recognised as a fact of life as it has long been in the public sector; it is important that potential conflicts between engineers' professional responsibilities and their union loyalties are minimised by including clear guidelines to them within their Code of Professional Practice, which should be drawn up by the Authority in consultation with the TUC and Employers' Organisations 5.61

76. We express no view on the argument for and against the establishment of a single trade union to represent all engineers, but we urge the TUC and the unions concerned to recognise the damage being done by current inter-union disputes over the rights to represent engineers, and to take steps to end them 5.63

The Engineering Authority

77. We propose the establishment of a new Engineering Authority with a remit to promote and strengthen the engineering dimension within the British economy and with the particular responsibilities identified in Chapters II-V 6.6

78. This should be a statutory body, funded by the Government with 15–20 members appointed by the Secretary of State to reflect the balance of interests within the engineering dimension; members, the majority of whom should be engineers, would serve in an independent capacity   ...   .   6.19 ff

79. The Authority should maintain close working liaison with a wide range of organisations and institutions   6.21
including the NEDC; to this latter end the leader of the Authority should sit on the NEDC 6.18

80. The Authority should be accountable to the Government for its exercise of statutory powers (particularly with respect to the registration of engineers) and for its use of money voted to it by Parliament, but should not be subject to direction or strategic intervention from the Government.

Actions required of employers

To emphasise the importance we attach to initiatives lying with employing organisations, we draw attention to the following recommendations which apply to industrial companies: recommendations 2, 3, 10, 11, 14, 15, 20, 23, 25, 26, 27, 28, 34, 35, 43, 45, 50, 73. A number of our other recommendations will also entail action from employers although the initiative rests with other bodies, notably the Engineering Authority.

APPENDICES

Committee Secretary's Letter of 16 August 1977 to Selected Institutions, Organisations and Individuals inviting Submissions of Evidence

COMMITTEE OF INQUIRY INTO THE ENGINEERING PROFESSION

1. You will no doubt be aware that on 5 July the Secretary of State for Industry announced to Parliament the setting up of a Committee of Inquiry to review the deployment, education and other aspects of the engineering profession, with particular reference to the needs of manufacturing industry. The Committee will be chaired by Sir Monty Finniston. I attach a copy of the Press Notice which incorporates Mr Varley's announcement, including the terms of reference of the Inquiry.

2. It is hoped that the Committee will begin its work in September. In view of the Secretary of State's declared wish that the Inquiry should not be unduly prolonged, a tight and demanding schedule is implied thereafter.

3. Accordingly, my purpose in writing to you now, before the Committee is established, is to invite you informally to begin consideration of your organisation's response to the invitation the Committee can be expected to issue, for interested organisations and individuals to send them their written evidence and views on the matters the Committee will be looking at. I know that some organisations have already begun work to this end.

4. I would not wish, without having consulted the Committee, to dictate or constrain the form your evidence should take—save to make a plea for as much brevity as is consistent with the wide field of the Inquiry—but will write again should the Committee feel that a particular format would be useful to them.

5. It would clearly be most useful if the Committee could receive and consider written evidence in the early stages of their Inquiry. Accordingly, while no deadline is set, it would be helpful if you could aim to submit any written evidence by the end of this year, earlier if possible. Please do not hesitate to contact me, at the above address or telephone number, if there is any help or information I can give.

M V BOXALL

List of Persons and Organisations who gave Written or Oral Evidence to the Committee

1. Individuals

J M Adams
T S Addison
E Adkins
A Albu
T H Aldridge
G Alexander
R S Alford
A C Allen
W Allen
C Allies
Dr A F Anderson
J S Anderson
F J Anker
T H Appleby
K B Armstrong
M C Armstrong
Sir Ove Arup
K H G Ashbee
L E Ashby
J D Ayer
J A Baird
Lord Baker
R Balmer
K Banks
T E Barany
G Barclay
H P Barker
A Barks
P A Barlow
Sir William Barlow
N E Barnes
C Barnett
J W Baxter
N W Bean
C J Beavor
K J Bell
R A Bell
W R Bell
Professor M Beloff
T P Benjamin

J M Bennett
G M Beresford-Hartwell
H C Bertoya
D J Bevan
Professor G S Beveridge
C Bexon†
P Bhatt
J Bilborough
J F Birch
D G Birkett
Professor O Bjorke
M J Blamey
Professor M Blaug
Professor C Bodsworth
W T F Bond
Sir Herman Bondi
C Bone
Professor R T Booth
C L Bore
W E Bouch
G N Bowling
E L Boyd
J Boydle
F Bradbury
M O Braimah
R Branson
Dr J N Brittan
V H Brix
E N Bromhead
T Brook
Dr G Brosan
A G Brown
G Brown
Lord Wilfred Brown
W E Brunger
R G Bryant
G A Buck
Dr D W Budworth
A Burgess-Webb
B Butler

J A Cade
A Cagney
J Caird
Miss F Cairncross
T E Calverley
J W Campbell
R L Cannell
Sir Peter Carey
J H Carr
P E Carr
Professor Sir Charles Carter
I Catt
Professor D R Chick (deceased)
Professor A W J Chisholm*
P Clarke
T Clarke
Captain E W Clements
I Clements
Professor S Coke
R Coker
Lt Cdr R F D Colby RN
P Cole
R J Coleman
J Coles
L Collis
J L Coltman
J Constant
B Conway
F R Cook
R Cooper†
A Copisarow
B H Corbett
K G Corfield
Professor R J Cornish
T M Corson
G Costello

---

* Gave oral as well as written evidence

† Gave oral evidence only

Professor S F Cotgrove
G H L Cox
Mrs J G Cox
O H Critchley
R Cropper
Professor B Crossland
K L Cull
J Currie
Dr D S Davies*
Professor L E Davis
L G T Davy
F Dawson
T Derrick
Professor B Downs
Mrs M M Doyle
M J Duckenfield
W E Duckworth
Professor J F Duncan
H A Dyson
P B Edgar
L S J Edmonds
A W J Edwards
Dr R W Edwards
Sir Sam Edwards
G H Ella
A Elliott
P H Elliott
W A N Ellis
F J Elvy
J G Endersby
N J Essex
B W V Evans
J A Evans
J W Evans
C J Farr
W Fawcett
H Ferry
Dr G B R Feilden†
F Finch
M Fine
P C Firby
D Fishlock
B L Flower
T Floyd
M Fores
M Forest
M J Fothergill
Dr H W Fowler

P Fraenkel
Captain J E Franklin
D D Fraser
R Freer
Professor M French
C S Frost
H Frost
J D Fyvie
J C Gale
J F Gamlin
J R Gammon
M W George
R E George
J A C Gibb
G M Gibbs
R A Gibson
S Gibson
R Gifford and
    A N Spark
G D Gimson
I Glover
W A Goode
Dr D S Gordon
H J Gorman, M G
    Satow,
R Smalley, C A Voss and
L S Wilson
R F M Grant
K E Gregory
S A Gregory
A W Griffin
K W Groves
A R Grun
A P Hall
Professor J Halling
J W Hancock
D H A Hannay†
J Hansbury
J M Hardman
P E Harries
J Harrington
H G Harris
J T Harris
G B Harrison
P J Haslam
C Hatfield
D W Heightman
C Hemley

D G Henderson
A W Hendry
D L Herbertson
R J Herd
J L Herring
Professor P Herriott
J Hersee
R Hetherington
C I Hicks
J Hicks
J W Hill
R E Hill
Lord Hinton of
    Bankside*
R Hodkinson
Professor F A Holland
R G Holland
J R D Holmes
W D Holmes
L A Holt
R G Hooker
Major G Horne
M Hoskin
Professor W Hryniszak
Professor L Hudson
Dr G A Hunt
R N Hunter
Professor S P Hutton
A C James
B M James
D A Jenkins
Captain W S C Jenks
Professor D J Johns
A H Johnson
F G Johnson
H R Johnson
S M Johnson
A R Jones
Captain C W Jones
D D Jones
G Jones
W S Jones
Dr H P Jost*
J G Kapp
L L Katan
F X Kay
R W Kelly
M J Kemper

---

* Gave oral as well as written evidence

† Gave oral evidence only

Professor Kennaway
Professor J Kennerley
R L Kent
G A King
J G Knibb
A M Kruger
Professor N Kurti
L Landon-Goodman
J Laporta
K Latimer
T Lawley
P A Lawrence
M W Leonard†
Dr R Leonard
J H Lethbridge
Professor J C Levy
D L Lewis
Dr J S Lewis
M Lewis and
Dr K Tubman
Professor Lezier†
Dr C J Liddle
J A Lilley
K D Lilingstone-Hall
Professor K Lockyer
Dr M V Lowson
W K Lumsden
Sir George Macfarlane
M Maclean†
Professor I MacLeod
Professor R Macmillan
   and Professor G Brock
Sir Louis Matheson
G McCarthy
K McCormick
E McEwen
A McKay†
C McKay
D P McNicholl
Dr J McQuaid
Mrs M K McQuillan
P J McVey
Sir Ieuan Maddock*
Professor W A Mair
A Mant*
J Marren
J B Marsh
A S Martin

Sir Peter Masefield
C Mattingley
A M T Maxwell-Irving
Dr R F Mayo
W D Medcalf
R O Meek
Professor A Mercer
F Metcalfe*
D Midgeley
R M Mill
I T Millar
Dr G Miller
G Mills
Dr D L Mordell
R J Morey
J Morgan
R Morgan
R G Morrison
G F Moss
Dr A E Moulton
R T Moxon
N T Myall
L F Napper
F Nash
A H Naylor
G E H Newton
F Nixon
J Norton
M J Nostley
P Offord
S Oliver
L Orenstein
H M Padgett
Dr P J Palmer
H Parker
Professor J Parnaby
R D C Passey
K W A Patterson
I H Paxton
J A Pearson
E Pendleton
E P Peregrine
P H Perkins
R J Perrett
Professor H J Pick
J Pilditch
A Poncelet
F Porges

R A Powell
C J Power
S Prasan
Dr G L Price
S D G Pryce
Professor R Pryor
S Pugh
G J Purdue
E J Purkiss
H V Radcliffe
D Raffe
J S Raine
D N Rampley
Sir Jack Rampton†
J Rankine
J Raven*
Professor G H Rawcliffe
W J Reader
A B J Reece
B Reeves
A M Reid
S P Ralph
D Reyes-Guerra*
Professor E J Richards
J Rigg
D W Rimmer
Commander D N D
   Roberts
K A L Roberts
A Robertson
S W Robertson
J Robinson
B Rochester
C F Rose
H E Rose
R Roslender
J N Rowen
Dr E Rudd
B M Russell
R I Sandham
D F Sansom
Ing Jost Schneider
H Scholes
G T Schwartz
R Scrivens
W T Shaddock
F A Sharman
E H Shaw

* Gave oral as well as written evidence

† Gave oral evidence only

176

P Shears

J Sheldon

W T Shiers

B J Shiner

R J Shrive

Professor R Silver

D Simons

Dr V Simons

V Slowikowski

Sir Alex Smith

A G Smith

Dr E M Smith

J C Smith

Dr A Sorge

P South

P G South*

D H D Southall

E J Spain

A G Spencer

R C Steed

G M Stephens

B Steptoe

Sir Sigmund Sternberg

D T Stevens

Professor R Stevenson*

R I Stokes

Professor T Stonier

J Strachan

K L Stretch

A H Summers

D C Summerton

L Sumner

T Sumner

M A Sutcliffe

V Sutherland

P E Sutton

R J Tapsell

G Taylor

L J Taylor

V T Taylor

C N Thompson

R J Thompson

F Thomson

Professor M W Thring

Professor S A Tobias

L A Toft

L J Tolley

M F Tong

R Roone

Professor M Trebilcock

Cdr J C Turnbull

J L Turner

O Tynan

G J Usborne

J C Van der Schans

R R Verner-Jeffreys

E L Vernon

M A H Walford

W J Walker

C P Walsh

F Walsh

T D Walshaw

C Walton

J D Ward

D A Warner

P C Warner

H Wassell

D A Watkins

A W Watson

G Watson†

Dr H Watson

Professor S H Wearne

N Weatherley

G F Webb

J S Webb

M Webb-Bowen

D B Welbourn

J F B Welch

J L S Whalley

R J Wheeler

A N White

C D Widdowson

Professor R Wild

D H M Williams

A Wilson

A J Wilson

P J Wiltshire

A J H Winder

M F Winter

M J Wise

P H W Wolff

K G Woods

D K Woodward

J C Wright

K A Yeomans

J D Young

O C Zienkiewicz

and others who wish
to remain anonymous

---

* Gave oral as well as written evidence

† Gave oral evidence only

2. Professional bodies

Association of Consulting Engineers
Association of Cost Engineers
Association of Mining, Electrical and Mechanical Engineers
British Computer Society
British Institute of Management*
British Technician Group
Bureau of Engineer Surveyors
Chartered Institution of Building Services
Council of Engineering Institutions*
CEI Cornwall Branch
CEI Thames Valley Branch
Engineers Registration Board*
Highway and Traffic Technicians Association
Incorporated Practitioners in Radio and Electronics
Institute of Automotive Engineer Assessors
Institute of British Foundrymen
Institute of Careers Officers
Institute of Cost and Management Accountants
Institute of Engineers and Technicians
Institute of Food Science and Technology
Institute of Fuel
Institute of Hospital Engineering
Institute of Marine Engineers
Institute of Measurement and Control
Institute of Metallurgical Technicians
Institute of Petroleum
Institute of Physics
Institute of Plumbing
Institute of Production Control
Institute of Purchasing and Supply
Institute of Quality Assurance
Institute of Road Transport Engineers
Institute of Royal Engineers
Institute of Scientific and Technical Communicators
Institute of Sheet Metal Engineering
Institution of Agricultural Engineers
Institution of Chemical Engineers*
Institution of Civil Engineers*
  —Association of London Graduates and Students
Institution of Electrical and Electronics Technician Engineers*
Institution of Electrical Engineers*
Institution of Electronic and Radio Engineers
Institution of Engineering Designers*
Institution of Engineers and Shipbuilders in Scotland
Institution of Gas Engineers
Institution of Geologists
Institution of Highway Engineers

---

* Gave oral as well as written evidence

Institution of Mechanical Engineers*
—Automobile Division, North Western Centre
—East Midlands Branch, Graduates' and Students' Section
—North Midlands Branch, Graduates' and Students' Section
—North Western Branch
—Peterborough Joint Panel, with the Institution of Electrial Engineers and Institute of Marine Engineers
—Scottish Branch, Graduates' and Students' Section
—Southern Branch, Graduates' and Students' Section, Northern Panel
Institution of Mechanical and General Technician Engineers
Institution of Metallurgists
Institution of Mining and Metallurgy
Institution of Mining Engineers
Institution of Municipal Engineers
Institution of Nuclear Engineers
Institution of Plant Engineers*
Institution of Production Engineers*
Institution of Public Health Engineers
Institution of Railway Signal Engineers
Institution of Sales Engineers
Institution of Structural Engineers*
Institution of Water Engineers and Scientists
Institution of Works and Highways Technician Engineers
London Metallurgical Society
Metals Society
National Institute of Agricultural Engineering
Norfolk Surveyors Association
North East Coast Institution of Engineers and Shipbuilders
Plastics and Rubber Institute
Royal Aeronautical Society*
Royal Electrical and Mechanical Engineers Institution
Royal Institute of Chemistry
Royal Institution of Naval Architects
Royal Signals Institution
Royal Society/Fellowship of Engineering*
Society of Architectural and Associated Technicians
Society of Chemical Industry
Society of Civil Engineering Technicians
Society of Electronic and Radio Technicians
Society of Engineers*
Society of Industrial Artists and Designers
Society of Licensed Aircraft Engineers and Technologists
Society of Petroleum Engineers (UK Sections)
Society of Surveying Technicians
Society of X-Ray Technology
Welding Institute
Whitworth Society
Women's Engineering Society

---

* Gave oral as well as written evidence

3. Universities, Polytechnics etc

City University
Cranfield Institute of Technology
Farnborough College of Technology
Hatfield Polytechnic
Heriot-Watt University—Faculty of Engineering
Huddersfield Polytechnic—Faculty of Education
Imperial College of Science and Technology
Merton Technical College—School of Engineering
Napier College of Commerce and Technology
Open University
Scottish Business School
Sheffield City Polytechnic
Sussex University—Science Policy Research Unit
University of Bath—School of Engineering
University of Bradford—Board of Studies in Engineering
University of Bristol—Faculty of Engineering
University of Glasgow—Faculty of Engineering
University of Lancaster—Department of Engineering
University of Leeds—Faculty of Applied Science
 —Engineering and Applied Science Departments
 —Mechanical Engineering Department
University of London—Institute of Education
University of Manchester—Faculty of Science
 —Institute of Science and Technology
University of Newcastle-upon-Tyne—Faculty of Engineering
University of Reading
University of Sheffield
University of Southampton—Faculty of Engineering and Applied Science
University of Strathclyde
University of York

4. Educational bodies apart from teaching institutions

Association of Graduate Careers Services
Association of Heads of Departments of Civil Engineering
Association of Principals of Colleges
Association for Scientific Education
Business Graduates Association Ltd
Committee of Directors of Polytechnic*
Committee of the Engineering Professors' Conference*
Committee of Vice-Chancellors and Principals of the Universities of the UK*
Consortium of Heads of University and Polytechnic Departments of Production Engineering
Council for National Academic Award*
Council of Professors of Building
Council of Science and Technology Institutes
Cranfield Society
Educational Institute of Scotland

---

* Gave oral as well as written evidence

Engineering Departments offering CNAA Degrees†
H M Inspectorate of Schools†
Independent Schools Careers Organisation
International Association for Students of Economics and Management
Joint Committee for HND's in Mechanical, in Production and Aeronautical Engineering
Joint Committee for ONC's and Diplomas in Engineering
Joint Matriculation Board
National Centre for School Technology and School Technology Forum
Scottish Business Education Council
Scottish Technical Education Council
Southern Science and Technology Forum
Standing Conference of Heads of Departments offering CNAA Courses in Electrical and Electronic Engineering
Standing Conference of Heads of Mechanical and Production Engineering Departments
Standing Conference on School Science and Technology
Technician Education Council*
Unversities' Committee on Integrated Sandwich Courses
University Grants Committee*

5. **Unions and staff associations**

Amalgamated Union of Engineering Workers (Technical and Supervisory Staffs Section*)
Association of Professional Scientists and Technologists
Association of Public Service Professional Engineers
Association of Scientific, Technical and Managerial Staffs*
Association of Supervisory and Executive Engineers
Association of University Teachers
British Aerospace Staffs Association
Electrical and Engineering Staff Association of the Electrical, Electronic, Telecommunications and Plumbing Union
Engineers and Managers Association*
Greater London Council Staff Association
Institution of Professional Civil Servants*
Institution of Professional Civil Servants—Atomic Energy Branch
National Association of Head Teachers
National Association of Teachers in Further and Higher Education
Society of Post Office Executives
Steel Industry Management Association
Trades Union Congress*
United Kingdom Association of Professional Engineers*

* Gave oral as well as written evidence

† Gave oral evidence only

6. Organisations employing engineers

W S Atkins Group Ltd: HQ, Epsom‡
Austin and Pickersgill Ltd—a member of British Shipbuilders, Sunderland‡
Babcock and Wilcox Ltd Group: Huwood Ltd, Gateshead‡
Black and Decker Ltd, Maidenhead‡
Booker McConnell Ltd (General Engineering Division):
   Fletcher Sutcliff Wild Ltd, Wakefield‡
   Fletcher and Stewart Ltd, Derby‡
British Aerospace: HQ, Weybridge‡
   Aircraft Group, Kingston-upon-Thames‡
   Dynamics Group, Stevenage‡
British Nuclear Fuels Ltd, Warrington
British Steel Corporation. Sheffield Division:
   Steel Works Group, Rotherham‡
Central Electricity Generating Board: HQ, London‡
   Regional HQ, Birmingham‡
   Rugeley B Power Station‡
Chloride Group Ltd: HQ, London‡
Conoco Ltd: Humber Refinery, Grimsby
Digico Ltd, Stevenage‡
Dunlop Holdings Ltd: HQ Dunlop Ltd, London‡
   UK Tyre Group, Birmingham‡
Electrical and Industrial Securities Ltd: HQ, London‡
   Kontak Manufacturing Co Ltd, Grantham‡
Esso Petroleum Co Ltd, Fawley Refinery, Fawley
Eurotherm International Ltd: HQ, Worthing‡
   Chessell, Worthing‡
   Eurotherm Ltd, Worthing‡
Ewbank and Partners Ltd, Brighton‡
Ferranti Ltd, Scottish Group, Edinburgh‡
The General Electric Company Ltd: GEC-Marconi Electronics Ltd, Chelmsford‡
   GEC Power Engineering Ltd, Rugby‡
General Motors Scotland Ltd, Motherwell‡
Guest, Keen and Nettlefolds: GKN Sankey Ltd, Telford‡
Glaxo Holdings Ltd: Glaxo Operations Ltd, Greenford‡
Arthur Guinness Son and Co (Park Royal) Ltd, Park Royal‡
Hawker Siddeley Group: Hawker Siddeley Dynamics Engineering Ltd, Hatfield‡
IBM United Kingdom Ltd—part of International Business Machines Corporation USA:
   London Office, London‡
   Development Laboratories, Hursley‡
Imperial Chemical Industries Ltd: Petrochemicals Division HQ, Wilton‡
IDC Ltd, Stratford-upon-Avon
Industrial Market Research Ltd, London
Lotus Cars Ltd, Norwich‡
Mars Ltd Confectionery Division, Slough‡
National Coal Board, London

‡ Visited by members of the Committee (see Appendix D)

Nippon Seikko K Bearings Europe Ltd, Peterlee‡
Plessey Ltd, Ilford
Post Office Telecommunications, London‡
Ransome Hoffman Pollard Ltd: Ransome Hoffman Bearings Ltd, Annfield Plain‡
Rolls-Royce Ltd, Aero Division, Derby‡
The Scott Bader (Commonwealth) Co Ltd: Scott Bader Company Ltd, Wollaston‡
The 'Shell' Transport and Trading Co Ltd: Shell Centre, London‡
    Stanlow Refinery, Stanlow‡
Sinclair Radionics Ltd, St Ives‡
Taylor Woodrow Ltd: Taylor Woodrow Construction Ltd, Southall‡
United Kingdom Atomic Energy Authority, London
Westland Aircraft Ltd, Yeovil‡

7. Government Departments and Official Bodies

Civil Service Department
Committee for Industrial Technologies (DOI)
Department of Education and Science
Department of Employment
Design Council
Equal Opportunities Commission*
Health and Safety Executive
Manpower Services Commission
National Economic Development Council
National Research Development Corporation
Procurement Executive—MOD
Science Research Council

8. Employers Organisations, Trade Associations, Training Boards and others

The Bow Group
Brick Development Association
British Association for the Advancement of Science
British Constructional Steelwork Association
Chemical and Allied Products Industry Training Board
Chemical Industries Association
Confederation of British Industry*
Constructional Steel Research and Development Organisation
Defence Industries Quality Assurance Panel
Electrical and Electronic Manufacturers Training and Education Board*
Electronic Engineering Association
Engineering Employer's Federation*
Engineering Equipment Users Association
Engineering Industry Marketing Group
Engineering Industry Training Board
Federation of Civil Engineering Contractors
Food Manufacturers Federation Inc.

---

‡ Visited by members of the Committee (see Appendix D)
* Gave oral and written evidence

Glass Manufacturers Federation
National Electronics Council
National Water Council
Nevis Institute
Process Plant Association
Rubber and Plastics Processing Industry Training Board
Society of British Aerospace Companies Ltd
Southern Gas (consensus views of a meeting of engineer employees)
Textile Institute
West Sussex County Council (Engineers and Technicians of the County Surveyors Dept)
The Sir William White Society

Report by the Council of Engineering Institutions (CEI) on Regional Conferences arranged by CEI Branches to assist the Committee of Inquiry

1. Introduction

During the first half of 1978 all the Branches of CEI organised meetings at which engineers and others could meet to discuss matters germane to the Inquiry into the Engineering Profession for which the Government had, at that time, appointed a Committee under the Chairmanship of Sir Monty Finniston. CEI arranged for the meetings to be reported individually and this Summary Report has been prepared from a review of the individual reports.

Some statistical information relative to the meetings is given at the end of this report. The report itself consists of a number of commentaries on topics extensively discussed at the meetings.

2. The social context of engineering occupations

The status and earnings of professional engineers were generally seen as closely connected with one another and quite inadequate. The remedy was believed by many engineers to lie in greater political strength and this was to be found in a single body to represent all engineers. Dissatisfaction was expressed with the Engineering Institutions and with CEI because they had failed to meet this need; the position of engineers was compared unfavourably with that of doctors who had BMA to represent their interests. These views were expressed in persistent disregard of the fact, stated on several occasions, that the Institutions and CEI were prevented by the terms of their Charters from filling this role and that a fresh initiative would be needed to create a single professional association or trade union. Such an initiative had been a clear policy option for a long time but attempts to pursue it had never, so far, been able to mobilise sufficient support.

The weakness of engineers in manufacturing industry was blamed on individual employers and EEF whose industrial relations policy was centred on the big trade unions; the representation of the interests of professional engineers by such unions was said be be ineffective. There was some disagreement with this view, sometimes from engineers who had worked for separate, strong representation of professional engineers' interests but had come to accept that sufficient support for a single body to represent the whole profession could not be organised. These speakers and some others advocated engineers becoming active members of existing unions and establishing an effective voice. This view was also expressed by officials of large unions who spoke at some of the later meetings.

It was not expected that the Finniston Committee could make recommendations that could help engineers to resolve problems of pay and status; indeed, it was pointed out that certain basic problems of industrial relations and of the relationship between responsibilities and rewards needed to be dealt with before many of the special problems of engineers could be effectively tackled. Employment in industry was said to be unattractive to able graduates and promising school leavers because of (*a*) the unhealthy social climate, (*b*) its reputation for poor pay and career prospects and (*c*) the antipathy of teachers with no experience of industry.

There were many references to the need to ensure proper consideration, in secondary schools, of the career opportunities and qualification requirements of engineering. Appreciation was frequently expressed of the work being done by engineers and their institutions to improve the quality of the information available for careers advisers but it was felt that more resources should be devoted to:

(*a*) influencing curriculum development in subjects relevant to later engineering studies

(*b*) providing opportunities for teachers in secondary schools to gain first-hand experience of work in engineering industry.

It should, perhaps, be said that the views expressed at the meetings by engineers on their pay and social status did not differ materially from those generally heard from occupational groups in conclave, as may be judged from the resolutions of meetings of doctors, teachers or of any trade union annual congress. No assessment of the merits of engineers was heard from an independent observer. There were, however, many calls for engineers to help themselves by taking a more active part in public life, including standing for Parliament. They should also press their Institutions to secure better publicity for engineering and engineers, bringing home to the public their dependence on engineering and the extent of the contribution made by engineering to the economy.

3. Employment policies of private firms as they affect professional engineers

It was said that current production methods employed by a wide range of small and middle-size firms (as well as some large ones) called for little use of the special abilities of professional engineers though it was recognised that exceptions were to be found in some small firms producing special products of sophisticated design. Large firms often offered opportunities for engineers in research and development departments while still offering little on the production side. Engineers needed to go into management to further their careers. The conclusion drawn from this situation by some engineers was that there was a need for a relatively small group of highly-qualified engineers and for a much larger sub-professional group and that a structure of this type could be imposed on the profession by raising the standards of education and training to meet the needs of the highly-qualified group. Others regarded management skills, developed on the basis of a sound understanding of engineering practice, as the summit of professional engineers' activities. Much of industry was represented as bumbling along on a hand-to-mouth basis, directed by non-engineers motivated by short-term profit considerations, preferring to invest in aggressive selling of inferior products rather than in improvement in product quality and performance. Engineers were, therefore denied recognition of their qualifications, offered little scope for the exercise of their professional skills, provided with few opportunities for training (and poor quality training at that), paid less than accountants and salesmen and given fewer opportunities for advancement. Registration and licensing were seen as a possible means of opposing these practices; firms using engineering techniques could be required to employ registered engineers and pay them at least a prescribed minimum salary.

Some sectors of industry were dissociated from this indictment, eg, chemical engineering, some sectors of electrical engineering, gas engineering. It may be significant that all these sectors are subject to rapid technological advance; they were all said to have engineers occupying a high proportion of places in top management. Construction, also, was seen as different from manufacturing industry since it offered good career prospects for professional engineers in consulting practices.

4. Public sector employment of engineers

Earnings and conditions of employment of engineers in the public sector were said, by engineers in private sector enterprises, to be better than theirs; there was particular resentment at advantages said to be offered by service industries but there was little reference specifically to the manufacturing elements in the public sector. These advantages were attributed to strong unionisation of workers in the public sector, including professional and other white collar workers even though membership of a public sector union was likened, by one engineer, to being 'drowned in a sea of egalitarianism'. There was some recognition of the relatively large contribution of the public sector to training which encouraged belief in the possibility of government financing training generally.

5. Training

Training was the topic receiving most attention at the meetings and it was generally agreed that the provision of training was inadequate both in quantity and in quality. The difficulties of securing adequate provision were recognised as mainly financial and, although many suggestions for improving training provision were put forward, there were very few proposals as to how they were to be financed. There were vague suggestions of government support (including a suggestion that Local Authorities should be enabled to impose a training rate) but there was no discussion of current provisions of legislation relating to industrial training apart from oblique references to inadequate training grants. There was wide agreement that industry should be 'responsible' for training though the implications of such responsibility were not defined. The establishment of more training companies was recommended and it was suggested that a training obligation should be imposed on industry but there was evidently no confidence in the requisite finance being forthcoming from industry. Several facets of training requirements were discussed including mid-career training where there was said to be urgent need for developments to update technical skills and to improve management skills. Better co-ordination of practical training with basic courses of study was advocated and several speakers stressed the social value of shop floor training for professional engineers. There were allegations of trade union obstruction to professional trainees being given instruction in manual skills but it was also said that shop-floor work was now too fragmented and specialised to provide good training. The need to monitor training was recognised both for the purposes of professional qualification and for in-company purposes and there was a suggestion that CEI should set up a Part III Test of professional competence. The difficulties of devising and operating such a test or of any objective assessment of training quality were not seriously considered.

6. Courses of study and qualifications

These topics also attracted a great deal of attention and there were several related lines of dispute with teaching and industry represented on both sides. The principal contentions were:

(a) that there were too many engineering graduates being produced. including many of inferior quality. The result was too many aspirants to C Eng qualification and too few technicians; there were also many graduates and some Chartered engineers working as technicians.

(b) that undergraduate courses in engineering were too strongly oriented to engineering science to the neglect of the human and creative aspects of engineering. It was also advocated that undergraduate studies should include the elements of economics and other social sciences; the increasing need for competence in foreign languages was also stressed. This broadening of engineering courses was cited as one reason for seeking the extension of undergraduate courses to at least four years full-time but, against this, it was contended that much of this work would, like management studies, be more effective after the student had gained some industrial experience.

(c) that the academic requirements for C Eng should be set at good honours degree level. This view was advanced by those who held that there was need only for a relatively small number of fully-qualified professional engineers but there were many other engineers who took the view that there was already a tendency for engineers to be too academic and that what was needed was increased practical rather than academic experience.

(d) that the problems of British industry were problems of the control of men and of money and that the education and training of British engineers did not equip them to deal with the social and economic problems now inseparable from the technical problems of engineering.

The remedies prescribed for the resolution of these problems took the form of improved training and better co-ordination of practical training and courses of study. It was pointed out that a course of study was only one element (and not, necessarily, the most important element) in the development of a professional engineer. If the practical training given was inadequate, whether in quantity or quality, the outcome for an engineering graduate was likely to be disappointing. Engineers expressing these views derided what appeared to them to be a widespread belief that an engineering degree led inevitably to a professional qualification in engineering. This was not and, in their view, never had been the case, a fact that should be made widely known. The real difficulty was the low standard of the provision of practical training; until that was corrected, sound discrimination between graduates who qualified and those who did not was impossible and graduates who failed to qualify would inevitably feel that they were the victims of mischance. The standard of practical training was unlikely to be raised significantly until an acceptable means of financing training was arrived at.

There were many suggestions for improving the effectiveness of courses of study and facilitating their co-ordination with practical training. Sandwich courses were widely advocated; teachers in undergraduate courses should have experience of working in industry and, also, should have continued involvement with industry through research or consultancy; training provision should be continued throughout a working life so that students could bring, to their studies, appropriate experience of engineering practice. Part-time courses were advocated as fitting in with work in industry and it was said that it would be an incentive to post graduate studies if qualifications were obtainable on a modular basis.

7. The supply of technicians

The numbers of students in engineering degree courses and in National Certificate and Diploma courses respectively were used as measures of numbers in training for C Eng and Technicians. The result was seen as a massive imbalance of training provision leading to large numbers of graduates doing technicians' work. This representation of the situation was attacked on the following grounds:

(a) The majority of firms in manufacturing industry provided no training in technicians' work and gave no recognition to technician qualifications.

(b) In industry generally, no career structure was provided for technicians. In particular, there was a complete lack of mid-career training for technicians and a consequent lack of opportunity for technicians to up-grade their academic qualifications with a view to qualifying as C Eng.

(c) In some branches, at least, of manufacturing industry (eg, parts of electrical engineering) graduates other than those holding good honours degrees had an academic background appropriate to working as a technician.

The academic requirement of a first degree for qualification as C Eng was said to be excluding many able engineers who had come up by the technicians' route and many pleas were made for a more flexible assessment of academic attainment. It was also pointed out, however, that many young technicians, holders of HNC or HND, would like to proceed to degree courses (for which they would be acceptable) if they could afford to do so. It was, in fact, generally realised that insistence on a degree was at least as much a financial as an intellectual barrier to advancement. The prescriptions for correcting the imbalance of production of C Eng and technicians were, predictably:

(a) Define training objectives and career structures for technical workers at all levels and provide training programmes and places according to needs.

(b) Provide well-designed opportunities for advancement of people whose potential as engineers is late in appearing. Such opportunities should include financial provision to enable them to undertake any necessary further study and practical training.

189

8. Engineering Institutions and CEI

The weakness of CEI was seen to lie in its federal structure and in the deep divisions of opinion and policy between the various constituent Institutions. There seemed to be little appreciation of any possible effects of the new Charter. CEI was criticised for having failed to unify the profession and for not being accountable to individual engineers. The engineering Institutions, generally were criticised for ineffective protection of the salaries and conditions of service of their members; the critics were quite impervious to explanations of Charter restrictions to which they replied with demands such as 'Get the Charters altered' and 'Get rid of the Charters'. The essential need, in their view, was for the bodies representing Chartered engineers to get more political power and, to this end, they urged a reduction in the number of Institutions in order to promote unity in the profession. Some realism was brought into the debate by engineers who had been disillusioned through working for a single strong body of engineers and by active supporters of UKAPE. The option of a single body was clearly open though attracting only limited support.

But the contributions of the Institutions and CEI to the engineering profession and to engineering generally were also widely recognised. The monitoring of the training of entrants to the profession was generally seen as not capable of being provided by any other body. The extensive mobilisation of services of very able engineers for a variety of work (eg, examining, moderating, production of standards, codes of practice, technical reports on current developments) at no cost to public funds was cited as a great contribution to the economy which was largely unrecognised by the general public. On financial grounds alone, it was said to be desirable to resist the transfer of qualifying functions from the Institutions and CEI to a government controlled body.

Recommendations for action by the Institutions and CEI include:

(a) keep open alternative routes to CEng; the all-graduate entry was not proving satisfactory.

(b) employ expert assistance to improve publicity for engineers and engineering.

(c) concern themselves more with the provision of training places.

(d) put more resources into careers advice work in secondary schools and encourage development of engineering studies there.

(e) initiate more co-operation between CEng and technician grades within Institutions.

(f) raise the standards of Fellowship of Institutions in order to increase prestige of engineers.

(g) monitor the content and standard of engineering degree courses.

9. Registration and Licensing

There was a conflict of opinion between those who wanted a Registration Board developed out of the existing ERB, possibly with additional independent members appointed by Government and, possibly, established as a statutory authority; and those who wanted a completely fresh start, on a statutory basis, with all the members of the Board appointed by Government, completely independent of existing Institutions. It was contended on several occasions that the difference between the two systems, when it came actually to operating the registration system, would not be very great because the establishment and monitoring of qualifying standards would have to be performed by the same people in either case; in fact, not very different from those who did it now. This view was not contested but the supporters of an independent statutory body contended, for their part, that their system would carry more weight with the general public at home and with interested parties abroad and would, therefore, be more effective in raising the status of the profession. Against this, opponents of the independent board contended that it would involve a substantial increase in expenditure which would, in the end, have to be paid for out of the pockets of individual engineers. Whichever method was adopted, the supporters of registration (particularly of statutory registration) hoped that, besides leading to improved status of engineers, it would speed up improvements in training and, in the long term, improve the capability of the average engineer; it would improve the chances of the engineering profession being consulted in high-level negotiations on public policy; it would stimulate recruitment among school-leavers of high ability; and it would promote unity in the profession. Pecuniary advantages for engineers might, of course, be expected to follow from many of these developments. The point was made that admittance to the Register should not depend on payment of a subscription to a CEI Institution.

As regards licensing, the general view was that limited licensing, as practised at present, where considerations of public safety were concerned, was all that was needed. There was some advocacy of more extensive systems of licensing as practised abroad and, among other advantages claimed for these systems, it was contended that the standards of engineering competence in small firms could be regulated by these means. Objections to general licensing on the grounds of administrative difficulty and expense and of fragmentation of the profession seemed, on balance, to carry more weight with the engineers in attendance at the meetings.

TABLE 1: Locations and Dates of Meetings: Numbers in Attendance: Contributions to Discussion.

Location	Date 1978	Number in Attendance	Number* of Contributions to Discussion
Manchester	Jan. 18	400	47
Bristol	Jan. 25	630	52
Plymouth	Feb. 14	290	36
Cardiff	Feb. 24	275	32
Leeds	Mar. 8	250	67
Glasgow	Mar. 28	450	41
Cambridge	April 4	200	25
Southampton	April 13	400	43
Liverpool	April 24	220	58
Belfast	April 25	220	29
Newcastle	May 3	550	34
Birmingham	May 4	700	45
Nottingham	May 18	200	38
Tunbridge Wells	May 25	350	47
London	June 1	342	47
Reading	June 7	200	45

* At some meetings the same speaker made two or more contributions to the discussion. In these cases each contribution has been counted separately.

TABLE 2: Proportion of Discussions Devoted to Various Topics

Location of Meeting	Percentage of Contributions* Dealing with Specified Topics.				
	Training & Education	Registration & Licensing	Institutions & CEI	Engineers & Industry	General social context of engineering occupations
Manchester	75	19	13	49	13
Bristol	48	25	46	69	27
Plymouth	50	39	28	31	24
Cardiff	81	25	25	53	41
Leeds	39	27	19	40	24
Glasgow	51	20	17	47	29
Cambridge	68	60	16	36	20
Southampton	58	21	26	47	5
Liverpool	28	22	26	12	26
Belfast	41	24	17	52	31
Newcastle	38	15	26	65	32
Birmingham	20	33	22	33	44
Nottingham	53	21	26	37	32
Tunbridge Wells	38	19	23	32	23
London	38	19	28	45	23
Reading	23	28	18	28	18
Average	48	26	24	43	26

* Nearly all contributions dealt with more than one topic.

Visits to Organisations Employing Engineers

1. In order to discuss aspects of our remit with some employers of engineers, members of the Committee visited 46 employing organisations in the UK during the course of the Inquiry, in addition to those visited overseas. The 46 organisations (identified in Appendix B) were not chosen to form a statistically valid sample of all employers but to provide a wide range of experience and opinion to guide the Committee's thinking. Care was taken to include large and small companies, some nationalised organisations, and multinational and other employers in the private sector. Organisations visited were not confined to those in the engineering industry. Discussions were held with top executives and senior engineers and we deliberately sought personal rather than corporate views. For convenience we refer below to those to whom we spoke as 'employers', even though most of them were themselves employees. Employing organisations were invited to submit evidence independently of our visits and some did so. They were briefed by a member of the Committee's staff in advance of the formal visit. In some cases visits occupied two days in order to encompass operating units as well as head offices. We are most grateful for the co-operation, hospitality and considerable amount of time given to us by the people we visited.

2. The main purpose of the visits was to inform Committee members about various aspects of the engineering dimension at the level of the individual organisation. This is reflected in the report itself. Industry is so diverse that it is difficult to generalise from such a limited survey but this appendix has been included in order to provide a brief summary of some of the most pertinent points emerging from our visits.

Deployment of engineers

3. Information on the current deployment of engineers was generally available in employing organisations, although we observed that many did not look upon engineers as a separate resource distinct from their overall professional and management strength. Forward projections of the demand for engineers were not generally available, or else available only in the broadest terms; employers clearly recognised the need for a spectrum of engineering ability but did not define this need in terms of discrete numbers of Chartered Engineers, Technician Engineers or Technicians. Some mentioned a dislike of the title Technician Engineer.

4. In the majority of organisations with a high engineering content we usually found engineers strongly represented in senior technical roles and also often in such other functions as marketing, though not in financial control. At general management level we found some cases where the Chief Executive and the majority of Board members were engineers but this was not generally the case. In organisations where engineering was mainly concerned with the

193

installation, maintenance and operation of plant used in making non-engineering products, engineers were generally seen as providers of a service and, with some exceptions, did not rate highly in the hierarchy. The point was made that in these organisations it was often hard to recruit engineers of high ability because the engineering challenge was necessarily limited.

5. Employers frequently described deficiences of their engineering staff in terms of personal qualities rather than specific engineering skills, though a few instances were cited of lack of innovative or problem solving skills. A more general lack of capacity for man management, and of flexibility and communication skills was also mentioned, as was the need for flair and enthusiasm. Cases were reported of reluctance on the part of engineers to move out of research, design and development departments and mention was made of a lack of motivation, of confidence and of cost consciousness. Particularly in the private sector, there were reports of a shortage of able middle managers with the potential to rise to the top and some derogatory comments were made about non-promotable engineers in middle management who could not be sacked.

6. Those employers who recognised that the morale of engineers might be low attributed this variously to restrictive practices on the shop floor; to the time taken up by industrial relations problems; to the feeling among some engineers that they were employed below their capabilities—though it was suggested that some engineers had inflated ideas of their ability and, in very large organisations, to bureaucracy.

Availability of engineers

7. We got a clear impression that most employers had difficulty in filling all their engineering vacancies. Shortages were mentioned of mechanical and production engineers, and particularly of system and control engineers, electronic engineers, design draughtsmen and computer software specialists. Individual firms reported difficulty in recruiting men willing to go overseas, or those trained in disciplines specific to their industry.

8. Frequent remarks were made about the lack of engineers with the personal attributes essential for management and vital if technically able engineers were to make their full contribution to wealth creation. Criticism was also voiced of the poor intellectual quality of some of those recruited and some manufacturing companies emphasised the difficulties they experienced in attracting graduates to work in production; many new graduates appeared to prefer to work in research and development rather than production which was seen to entail shift work and the hassle of shop floor industrial relations.

9. A shortage of technicians was generally reported and occasionally employers stated that they had to deploy professional engineers on sub-professional work in order to meet contractual commitments. Others reported that work was held up or business lost because of lack of support for professional engineers. In addition to the shortage of technicians, shortages of draughtsmen and skilled craftsmen were also mentioned, this again militating against the engineer's ability to work effectively and efficiently.

Recruitment

10. Recruitment policies in the organisations visited varied widely according to the age and size of the organisation and the nature of its business. We distinguished three main patterns of recruitment for professional engineers which were widely used:

(a) Recruitment, from the labour market, of experienced engineers with proven technical and personal qualities, ie with good track records. Such recruitment was typical of small organisations and consultants; these made little claim to provide training, eg to Institution requirements. They were generally able to recruit by bidding as high as they needed in order to secure the man they wanted and/or were able to attract good material because of the interest of the work offered.

(b) Recruitment of new graduates either into formal graduate training schemes or directly into jobs. This represented the major flow of recruits to large organisations who generally recognised the need to refresh their management and technical streams with new blood. While most employers appeared to be satisfied with the numbers they could recruit, many expressed doubts about their quality.

(c) Recruitment at either age 16 or 18 into training schemes, often with sponsorship of a small proportion of the intake through university or polytechnic. Organisations which were largely dependent on this type of recruitment tended to recruit only a limited number of graduates. This was a feature of older established industries, including some in the public sector. Such organisations were effectively creating their own engineering culture with clearly some risk of in-breeding the weaknesses and strengths of their own organisation. This type of recruitment, and the resulting progression pattern through the organisation, was in some cases built into union agreements on recruitment and promotion. Employers using this method were broadly satisified with the numbers they took in but not always with the quality of those they classified as engineers.

11. To meet the shortage of technicians many organisations were trying to forge stronger links with local schools and further education establishments and some offered lower level education and training opportunities to drop-outs from degree courses. With a few notable exceptions, employers who had themselves come up by the part-time route favoured part-time or sandwich graduates while those who had been full-time degree students looked for recruits with a similar background.

12. To overcome some of the difficulties they were experiencing, organisations occasionally recruited graduates from disciplines other than engineering and had found some success in so doing and appeared satisfied with the results. Some employers were chary about taking on engineers with first class honours or post graduate degrees, commenting that these people sometimes lacked the ability to understand what industry was all about. A general criticism of many new graduates was their lack of appreciation of industry and of business 'nous' in that they did not recognise the importance of marketing and supplying customer needs and had little understanding of the economics of production. We heard comments such as 'poor engineering sense'

195

which led to 'over engineering in tooling and tolerancing and the building in of wasteful margins resulting from too much theory and too little appreciation of cost.' Some graduates were thought to be too intellectual in their approach and to have had insufficient drawing office and practical training.

Views on education

13. Employers frequently asserted that the education system in the UK was not meeting the needs of industry in turning out people who were numerate, could communicate and were prepared to face the world of work. It seemed to us that there was a real need for industry to be better informed about the education system as well as for teachers to be more aware of the needs of industry. In particular employers mentioned the inadequacy of the careers advice available to young people at various stages in their education. And there was a general consensus on the need for a change of emphasis in an engineer's academic education with greater stress being put on the exploitation of knowledge rather than its pursuit.

14. Employers did not favour the inclusion of management as a subject in undergraduate engineering courses, since this was felt best left until after the graduate had obtained some industrial experience. There was some support for an MIT type of establishment and particular praise for Cranfield, especially for its MBA Course. We noted that a number of employing organisations had 'preferred' engineering schools from which they expected to recruit most of their new graduates. In addition many had forged close links with certain universities (and in some cases polytechnics) for collaborative research, consultancy and the development of courses suitable for the education of particular types of engineer. A number of examples were quoted of excellent links between industry and universities though there was also some bitter criticism of the apparent isolation from the needs of industry of some university and polytechnic staff. The comments we received in this respect did not fall into any clear pattern; some big companies and some small ones have excellent links with certain universities. Geography does not seem important; one of the smallest companies we visited appeared to have an excellent relationship with a university 300 miles away. We gained the impression that co-operation between universities and industry was possible over a wide range of disciplines and establishments and that success appears to depend mainly on the personal commitment of those directly involved on both sides.

15. The sandwich course was widely favoured for producing good practical engineers. This view, as might be expected, was particularly strong amongst organisations sponsoring students on degree courses; they appeared to be stressing the students' greater knowledge of the employing organisation rather than the academic levels achieved.

Career development

16. The larger organisations aimed to develop managers in-house and many had formal review and career development schemes. We found that in a number of cases new schemes were being set up or existing ones augmented,

reflecting an increasing awareness on the part of employers that professional staff were an asset to be nurtured. A number of employers stressed the necessity for close involvement at Board level in career development for professional staff. Management development 'on-line' was usually preferred but we felt that in some cases the organisational culture and management systems had not been adequately developed to facilitate the engineer's easy transition into the broader responsibilities of business management. There was wide recognition of the need for continuing education and training but occasionally a reluctance to release key employees for such career training; it was reported moreover that some engineers declined to go on courses.

17. Among the factors mentioned as militating against the satisfactory development of engineers were:

(a) the reluctance of some engineers to move because of the financial burdens of rehousing, or the disruption of their children's education or of a wife's career and interests;

(b) the unwillingness of some unions to accept graduates in, for instance, foreman positions, though there were notable exceptions to this;

(c) the unwillingness of young graduates to become embroiled in union/ management confrontation;

(d) the reluctance of able ex-apprentices or technicians to accept sponsorship for degree courses, for a variety of social and financial reasons.

18. We were told, almost universally, that an engineer with good qualifications and a proven track record, with determination and ambition, could win through successfully at all levels of the organisation and nowhere did we find any bias against the engineer in this respect.

Professional Institutions and C Eng qualification

19. Membership of an Institution was seldom specified in the conditions of employment in the organisations we visited. It was held to be desirable by some of those we saw, particularly for engineers engaged upon overseas contracts, although even here some felt it unnecessary provided the engineer had academic qualifications and the appropriate experience. Concern was expressed about the fragmented structure of the Institutions and a number of employers advocated some streamlining. Employers, when pressed, praised the learned society role of the Institutions and some gave considerable support to local activities.

20. If employees expressed a wish to join an Institution and to work towards Chartered Engineer status, they would generally find employers supportive. In some cases membership fees would be paid and individuals encouraged to attend meetings. Some personnel managers in the private sector commented upon the increasing demand for training to meet Institution requirements on the part of young graduates and attributed this to encouragement by university teachers. They remarked that the young graduate's enthusiasm often

197

waned once he was in employment. However, active encouragement by employers to join Institutions was not common and we were told that membership was not considered to have any impact on career progression and was rarely recognised or rewarded.

Registration and licensing

21. When invited to express views on registration and licensing, employers agreed that the existing licensing regulations associated with health and safety were necessary and valuable but they found little of value in ERB registration. In considering possible alternatives, they were fearful of possible rigidity, if a statutory register were instituted, which incorporated arrangements involving licensing to practice. Some respondents said that statutory registration might enhance the status of engineers but others expressed fears that a new system might exclude non-graduates and thereby cause problems for many good practising engineers and also that it could produce a closed shop situation 'crying out to be taken over by a union'.

Future prospects

22. On our visits we asked about the ability of the organisation to raise the necessary finance for development and we were usually told that this presented no problem. Some employers emphasised that their ability to compete depended upon the quality and reliability of materials, components and plant and on delivery dates; in many cases we were told that UK suppliers fell far short of the required standards in these respects, necessary to meet world competition. A number of organisations planning further development or even continuing on their existing sites, stressed the importance of breaking down large manufacturing units into small cost-centre based, semi-autonomous organisations. Some employers were moving to green field sites as a means of breaking the restrictive practices ingrained in some of the older industrial areas of the country.

Visits Overseas

1. Our terms of reference required us to review the arrangement relating to the engineering profession in other major industrial countries, particularly in the EEC. For this purpose during 1978 members of the Committee visited Canada, the United States, Japan, France, West Germany, Denmark, Sweden, and the European Commission in Brussels. A member of the Committee also attended the 1978 conference of SEFI (European Association for Engineering Formation) held in Pavia, Italy. We also visited the Netherlands in 1979 for a detailed examination of engineering education in that country. The principal findings and impressions emerging from those visits are given below, with lists of our main meetings. Besides the organisations listed, we saw informally countless individuals, including emigré British engineers, and representatives of various other bodies. These contacts contributed significantly to the impressions we formed during our visits.

2. This report provides a resumé of our main findings from overseas, mixing factual material and impressions. The findings are based on what we were told at meetings and what we observed during various tours around factories and educational establishments. We did considerable research to prepare for our visits, including consulting numerous studies of the engineering profession overseas and talking to various experts and people with experience of engineering overseas. We also benefited from briefing provided by the staff of UK diplomatic posts in the various countries. We are especially grateful to them for their considerable assistance in arranging and advising on our programmes. In addition many of the submissions of evidence to us referred to the position of engineers and engineering overseas and we benefited from these.

3. From all of this effort we have reached important conclusions from overseas and we have drawn upon them substantially in the body of our Report. We have tried to check points of fact where possible but it is inevitable in a subject of this nature, from which the influence of opinion cannot be excluded, that some of our findings might be subject to challenge. Further, we include in this Appendix the points that came to our notice which we feel are worth reporting. The Appendix does not aim to provide a comprehensive account of engineering overseas.

CANADA

4. Programme: Ministry of Science and Technology, Ottawa
Canadian Council of Professional Engineers, Ottawa
Carleton University Engineering Professors, Ottawa
Association of Professional Engineers of Ontario, Toronto
Professional Organisations Committee, Toronto
Federation of Engineering and Scientific Associates, Toronto
Ontario Hydro, Toronto

Manpower

5. There are between 80–100,000 professional (ie graduate) engineers in Canada, most but not all of whom are registered under various provincial statutes which make registration compulsory in order to practise. We were told that less than one-third of all registered engineers were working as practising engineers. Conversely not all of those practising were registered or necessarily had formal engineering qualifications, in spite of the legal requirement for registration. The Ministry of Science and Technology estimated that 10 per cent of practising professional engineers had no degree qualifications while another 25 per cent had degree qualifications in a non-engineering subject.

6. An engineering degree is generally considered by young people in Canada to be a ticket into management positions. Of 4,000 new graduates emerging from engineering degree courses each year, about one-half go straight into management trainee positions or into MBA courses; after about seven years from graduation only around 30 per cent of Canadian engineering graduates are still in 'hard' engineering positions, and we were told they tended to be the less able ones. Industry's requirements for practising engineers are then topped up by immigration, with some 2,000 engineers coming into Canada each year from abroad, mainly from the UK and Europe. Although immigration is strictly controlled, industry seems to have no difficulty in attracting engineers from outside Canada. It was suggested that immigrant engineers, although well paid by their own national standards, were considered by Canadian industry as cheap labour and were also seen by some as thereby depressing the relative salary levels for native engineers. Conversely it was said that most of the pressure for union organisation and organised wage bargaining came from immigrant engineers, particularly British ones. British Chartered Engineers who apply for Canadian registration generally qualify automatically. British engineering graduates, who are not Chartered, have to demonstrate their experience and, provided this is adequate, usually qualify.

7. We were told that there had been considerable difficulties in matching manpower supply with the demand for professional engineers. This was due partly to fluctuations in industrial demand—reflecting the cyclical nature of Canada's primary industry base—which fed back to the supply side with a four to seven year lag, by which time the demand picture was usually quite different. Quantitative mismatch arose also from changes in the demand for engineers from the USA, to which many of the best Canadian engineers were attracted. Immigration was thus viewed as a sluice gate, to be turned on or off as domestic requirements dictated. The Ministry of Science and Technology were developing a manpower forecasting model, in conjunction with the Canadian Council of Professional Engineers (CCPE) and the main employing organisations, which it was hoped would produce better informed market decisions and reactions but not to intervene in the manpower market.

Pay and status

8. Salaries of engineers in Canada are undoubtedly high, both absolutely and relative to those in the UK. Pay negotiations tend to be carried out within individual organisations rather than nationally and the CCPE publish

indicative salary scales which, we were told, had helped in keeping engineers' salaries on a par with those of other professional groups. The standing of engineers we found to be high both in society and within the place of work. Also there was a strong sense of identity and fraternity between engineers, brought about in part through their involvement in professional bodies.

Formation

9. Engineering degree courses are normally single discipline in approach, usually four years in length, and are accredited—for acceptability for professional registration—by the Canadian Accreditation Board (CAB). We got a strong impression that the CAB seeks to ensure balance rather than academic depth in its accreditation criteria, laying heavy emphasis on synthesis and design. While this is criticised by some academics as leading to a sacrifice of depth for breadth, it seems to be appreciated by employers as encouraging the production of graduates with a broader perception of the totality of their subject and of its application in industry.

10. We heard of no industrial sponsorship of students through university, and little evidence of firms sending their better technicians or apprentices to university for a degree course. An interesting new development is the co-op scheme being developed at the University of Waterloo and three other centres, which is directly akin to our thin sandwich courses with industrial placements. These new courses are able to attract a very high calibre of student, and the graduates are apparently keenly sought after by industry. An important feature of the Waterloo programme is its large scale. Overall there are around 2,800 students, half of whom will be on industrial placements at any one time. To arrange this there are 12 full-time placement officers.

11. Very few Canadian students stay on to do post-graduate research in engineering, partly because they can earn far more by entering industry than by taking up research studentships, and partly because the majority of them intend to enter management rather than engineering. The most common second degree for an engineer, we were told, is an MBA, usually after a few years in employment.

12. The Canadians have an equivalent problem to ours with the rapid expansion of university education and the consequent reduction in numbers training as engineers on an employed basis to fill junior engineering posts. Another consequence has been the emergence of many small engineering departments without the staff or resources to provide top level education. Control over minimum standards is emphasised by the CAB, and the Ministry of Science and Technology is seeking to restrict the number of smaller courses through their control of the Federal purse strings. We heard no complaints that Canadian engineering courses were not attracting the highest quality of entrants—on the contrary—but there did seem to be some concern about this 'tail' of graduates from the smaller, more out-of-the-way universities.

Registration and the profession

13. The institutional structure of the engineering profession in Canada is based on a clear division between various functional bodies and between provincial and national authorities. Registration (which in the Canadian context really means licensing to practise) and professional supervision are looked after by the provincial associations, such as the Association of Professional Engineers of Ontario (APEO); learned society functions are undertaken by about 12 national institutions, which unlike the associations are discipline-based; accreditation of courses is again done nationally by the CAB; and the material interests of engineers are looked after by company or organisation based staff associations—there are no national trade unions for engineers. The whole is grouped together under the umbrella of the CCPE, which seeks to co-ordinate and inform the activities of the various constituent bodies and to act as a lobby group for the engineering profession *vis-a-vis* Federal Government and others.

14. On registration, we were told it worked well in maintaining standards of professional competence among engineers without unduly restricting or rigidifying engineering practice in industry. We were told that the sanction of being brought to task by their peers was a real factor in ensuring a 'professional' attitude among engineers, supplementing the legislative framework of health and safety regulations and other controls. Public liability considerations were also important and the concept of protecting the engineer from being pressured by his employer into acting in a non-professional manner, say by endangering safety, was cited as one of the functions of registration.

15. It was our impression that pressure from the engineering profession itself led to the introduction of registration. The impact of registration within industry did not seem to us to be great but the only specific complaint we heard was that it was very hard for a technologist (akin to our technician engineer) to gain the further qualifications necessary for professional registration—for which he would have to return to full-time education for at least two years—and that this could sometimes be a hindrance to promotion, but only in purely technical functions.

Industry

16. We were told that, despite their high standing within organisations and despite registration, there were some complaints from Canadian engineers that they were underemployed and were not given a wide enough role in company decision-making. On the other hand, British engineers working in Canada generally said that they had more responsibility and a greater role than they would have had at home. It is normal in Canadian firms for there to be a two year training programme for all direct entry graduate engineering recruits, and also a positive policy of moving them around the organisation during their careers.

17. A very high proportion of Canadian manufacturing industry is US-owned, and the technology employed is thus—with one or two areas of exception—primarily of US origin. While the Canadian Government funds a heavy

202

R & D programme, mainly for the primary, extractive and power generation industries, Canadian industry does very little research or product or process development. The Federal Government, we found, was concerned at the long-term implications of this, and was considering measures to encourage Canadian industry to undertake more research. For example, an agreement with US car manufacturers that they produce within Canada a certain proportion of the output to the Canadian market was to be renegotiated to extend to placing a similar proportion of the R & D work in their Canadian subsidiaries.

Impressions

18. Our general impression was that a number of people in Canada were becoming aware of various problems in relation to engineering, and that many of these paralleled British problems: the lack of practical, junior-engineers (technologists); difficulties of transfer from technologist to professional qualification; the matching of university output to the requirements of industry; and the organisation of the profession, a subject currently under official investigation in Ontario. On the other hand, a good many of the problems facing engineering in the UK do not exist in Canada. Engineers enjoy high status and are frequently found in positions of responsibility in industry and in the economy generally. University engineering departments have no difficulty attracting good recruits, and engineering graduates are sought after and considered well prepared for employment in industry and in other areas.

UNITED STATES

19. Programme: National Academy of Engineering (NAE), Washington
American Society for Engineering Education (ASEE), Washington
Engineers' Council for Professional Development (ECPD), New York
American Societies for Civil, Mechanical, and Electrical and Electronic Engineers, New York
Polytechnic Institute of New York
General Motors Research Labs and General Motors Institute (GMI), Detroit
Georgia Institute of Technology, Atlanta
Southern Institute of Technology, Atlanta
West Coast University, Los Angeles
California Institute of Technology (CALTECH), Los Angeles
University of Southern California, Los Angeles
Jacobs Engineering Company, Los Angeles
Lockheed Aircraft Corporation, Los Angeles
Hughes Aircraft Company, Los Angeles
Northrup University, Los Angeles
University of California at Los Angeles
California Polytechnic Institution, Pomona
General Motors, Los Angeles
Litton Industries, San Fernando

The popularity of engineering

20. There is less specialisation in secondary school in the States than in the UK and in consequence the level of attainment in individual subjects tends to be lower. This affects admissions to higher education in engineering. Compared with the UK, a relatively larger share of secondary school leavers apply for and secure admission to undergraduate engineering courses, but they enter these courses with a lower base of attainment in mathematics and science subjects. Engineering is highly attractive to young people and many engineering students have no intention of practising. There are several factors behind this popularity:

(a) a first degree in engineering is a very useful qualification, providing options either to enter industry with a clear and quick route into management, or to move into another discipline (by taking a master's degree in business administration, law, accountancy, or even medicine), or to lead to a career as a practising engineer;

(b) there is great demand from industry for engineering graduates, and starting salaries are around $20,000 and rising fast;

(c) it is one of the few undergraduate courses which leads to professional status immediately or very soon after graduation;

(d) it is seen as a demanding and intellectually satisfying course of study for bright students (despite the fairly heavy work load);

(e) for all these reasons, it is the course most frequently recommended by teachers to bright students with good mathematics and an aptitude for science and by the large number of careers advisers and counsellors in American high schools.

21. We were impressed by the extent to which engineering is viewed as a good preparation and general education for the modern world. American attitudes in this respect are markedly different from those prevailing in Britain. There is an enormous throughput of engineering graduates. Exact figures are difficult to obtain but in 1975 there were 81,000 graduates produced—including both BS (Bachelor of Science) and BET (Bachelor of Engineering Technology) graduates—and the number has gone up since. With this large throughput the ability level spans the full range from the very brightest students to those comprising the 'tail'. In spite of the substantial supply of engineers, several people told us that it was still below the level of effective demand from employers. The labour market for engineers was becoming increasingly tight all round; there was a rapid turnover of staff, particularly among junior engineers, and a shortage of fully qualified professionals with 5–10 years' experience. There is also mounting concern that after 1985, when the US college population is expected to decline, there will be major shortages of engineers unless engineering is able to attract students from other subjects or to attract more women and minority students. Considerable effort is already being devoted by the engineering colleges and professional bodies to attract women and students from ethnic minorities, with evident success in some instances.

Academic formation

22. The standards and general content of engineering courses are set by the ASEE. The accreditation of individual courses against these criteria is conducted by the ECPD, which brings together academics, industrialists and professional societies. The objective of the accreditation process is to maintain standards, to gear the content of courses to the needs of professional practice and to reconcile this with the objective of providing a satisfactory general education. We found that in spite of the accreditation system there was still enormous variety and flexibility in the provision of undergraduate engineering courses, more so than in the UK. While some schools oriented their teaching in the direction of engineering science/research others, probably the majority, had a highly practical approach and sought to produce graduates ready to enter manufacturing industry and make an early contribution. The same variation applies at post graduate level and it is increasingly common for aspiring professional engineers to proceed to graduate school either directly from their first degree or, quite commonly, on a part-time basis after having entered employment.

23. Within this overall picture of considerable variation in approach, and probably in standards too, we found at most schools a strong emphasis on analysis, synthesis, design and problem solving, providing a mixture found in few other disciplines. The activities of the ECPD accreditation machinery were thought to have been helpful in encouraging this approach, and also in ensuring that time was devoted to the humanities (but not to any great extent to business management or accountancy). Employers saw this as providing the right initial preparation both for engineering and for management functions, perhaps because a large proportion of senior managers were themselves engineers by origin.

24. We found that there was scope for individual students to work at the level and pace which best suited their abilities and circumstances, facilitated by the modular course structure, to study part-time or full-time, or through a combination of day and evening study, and to transfer between different types of institution and course (eg from community college to the junior year of university). American higher education is based on the accumulation of credits and on the credit transfer principle and this undoubtedly makes the system highly flexible and responsive to the needs of individual students.

Employment-based formation

25. Also impressive was the level of continuing formation activity, with a wide range of programmes being provided within educational institutions, by training organisations and in-house within firms. The high level of continuing formation activity reflects the strong achievement orientation prevalent in the United States. Continuing formation is also actively encouraged by employers who commonly provide time off, assistance with fees and in-house programmes. It is clear that education and personal development are viewed by individual engineers and their employers alike as a continuing process beginning, rather than culminating, with the first degree. This is much more widely recognised than in the UK.

26. Although we heard some complaints that graduates were entering employment with little idea of what they were coming into, in general employers seemed content with the quality of the engineering graduates they were able to recruit. Employers did not expect more of them than the fundamentals of engineering knowledge and a minimum level of intelligence and motivation. They saw it as their function, and indeed preferred, to develop 'their kind of engineer' from this foundation, by instilling in their recruits a clear understanding of the company's philosophy both in respect of its products and its operating methods. American companies tend to take this task of generating a culture throughout the firm far more seriously than do UK firms. It is exemplified in extreme form by General Motors Institute, which we visited. This serves as General Motors' own in-house university. It provides mainly undergraduate courses, turning out around 500 engineering graduates each year (of the 1200 recruited by the company). The Institute also provides mid-career and short specialist courses, and this branch of its activities is expanding. Students coming into the Institute are recruited directly from the firm's operating divisions, which nominate their best young people. Competition for entry is keen, with only one in twelve applicants accepted. The Institute's objectives are to provide a sound technical and industrial training and to identify the company's future senior managers. It is also concerned with grooming people so that they are able to fit into the organisation and to work as part of the team. It is to these latter objectives that General Motors as a whole and American firms in general devote such high priority. In our view this is inseparable from the successful record of US engineering.

The role of engineers in industry

27. Training in industry is primarily 'on the job', through structured experience and close monitoring of progress, with the aim of placing the new recruit into a position of responsibility as soon as possible. Some firms combine this with further, part-time, formal education either in-house, or outside. We were told that many companies deal with the US equivalent of the 'technician gap' by employing young engineers in first line supervisory positions as part of their training. The general approach of employers is that the bachelor's degree provides a foundation, and that it is in employment that the engineer develops his vocational skills and abilities. Employers seemed to recognise and accept this responsibility as a matter of course. Thus US employers are increasingly seeking graduate recruits with an engineering background which provides them with a sound technical base from which to develop the financial, management and other skills necessary as their careers develop. American manufacturing companies see engineering, and engineers, as being at the heart of their businesses. Thus, they look to engineers as a main source of leadership across the firm's various activities. It was put to us on several occasions that UK engineers, whilst they were technically as able as their US counterparts, tended to be rather narrow and specialised in outlook. A comparison between General Motors' British and American engineers was drawn along these lines. It was also suggested that the relative narrowness of British engineers was in large part due to the prevailing attitude within British management that engineers were 'people to do a job, rather than to run a company', and also to the failure of British employers to take steps to develop the full potential of their engineers in non-technical areas.

28. While companies usually provide separate career ladders for technical and managerial staff, most engineers are recruited with a view to becoming managers sooner or later in their careers. With the exception of those in research labs, we got the impression that any graduate still in a purely technical position after about 35 had missed the promotion boat; one personnel director spoke of these people reaching a 'flat spot, career and reward-wise'. Engineering development, in whatever function, is thus very much the province of younger people. We found everywhere a strong stress on bringing the best out of people by putting them into small groups with specific tasks, giving each individual considerable freedom of expression within the group, and providing real incentives for new ideas in the form of open recognition, financial rewards, and promotion. Creativity was encouraged, facilitated, recognised and rewarded. Conversely there was considerably less security of employment or position than is generally expected in the UK. Thus the engineer's career depended largely upon the results he produced. At the same time the atmosphere within firms was informal and relaxed. These two features of a high level of achievement orientation and informality at the places of work probably apply generally to the US and not just to engineering. But they are, nonetheless, key ingredients in the successful record of American engineering.

29. American firms, including the big corporations, consciously apply a system of challenges and opportunities coupled with a pattern of rewards and incentives to get the most out of their professional engineers and other staff. Their approach to this is more far-sighted and imaginative than in the typical UK firm. In some respects it can be a ruthless system in that American firms are in general far less reluctant than UK companies to identify and penalise individuals associated with failure; but equally successful achievement is openly recognised and rewarded. This serves to make American business and those whom it employs highly sensitive to the firm's performance in the market place, which is seen as the ultimate arbiter of the company's fortunes; and this applies to engineering as much as to other functions.

The engineering dimension

30. Within US firms we detected a different approach to engineering as compared to British practice, which can be encapsulated in the term 'concurrency'. This denotes the process of constant interplay and feedback between marketing, design and manufacturing functions so that the product reflects customer requirements, is adaptable to changes in those requirements, and can be provided in the time scale required. In our discussions this American approach was contrasted with the British approach of designing a new product, building it, and then going out to sell it. The characteristics of the British approach were that high quality, sophisticated products were offered, but our engineers were felt to be inflexible and unresponsive to customer requirements which differed from the specification offered. The typical American approach of tying manufacture closely to customer requirements applies even to items of mass production. We witnessed it, for instance, at the General Motors assembly plant in California, where each car assembled was at the request of an individual dealer and was 'customised' according to the dealer's

specifications. Thus output was customer rather than manufacturer regulated. Because this made for considerable variation in the cars following one another down the line, the entire production operation had to be computer controlled.

31. Just as manufacturing operations are closely geared to sales requirements, so, we were told, American companies typically organise their R and D functions and the process of engineering innovation in such a way that it serves marketing needs. We did not have the opportunity to go into this in detail, though we saw an example of it at Litton Industries in the defence field, where the project approach was used, with development work subject to continuous scrutiny to ensure that it conformed to the budgetary guidelines for the project and met the requirements of the customer. We understand that this approach of delegating R and D as far as possible down the line close to the point of customer contact and integrated into day-to-day project management is becoming increasingly common in US firms; the centralisation of R and D into large laboratories and other remote establishments is becoming relatively less popular. Everywhere we went—firms, academic establishments and professional bodies—there was a keen interest in the process of innovation and in the conditions in which it flourishes. Again we got the impression that the level of awareness on this subject—regarding both the constraints and the opportunities in relation to innovation—was markedly higher than in the UK.

Registration and the profession

32. Turning to the organisations and regulation of the profession in the States, the discipline-based Societies (equivalent to British Institutions) are almost solely learned societies, although they have also been active in the area of promoting the image of engineering and engineers. Their constitutions generally preclude them from activity in the area of their members' material interests, though some of them engage in lobbying. The major lobby group for engineers is the National Association of Professional Engineers, which represents those engineers registered under the various State Acts, and seeks to protect and extend their interests. Under these Acts, State registration is generally required to practise as a consultant and in other specified spheres. It is not currently needed for employment in manufacturing though the extension of mandatory registration is widely debated. A pass from an accredited ECPD course is necessary for State registration, but it is not sufficient and has to be topped up by a pass in a State examination designed to test the applicant's actual ability to practise, the guidelines for which are mostly set by the National Council for Engineering Examiners. Administration of the State Acts is undertaken by separate authorities in each State, with a rigour and standard which seem to vary widely from State to State. At the pinnacle of the profession is the National Academy of Engineering, an offshoot of the National Academy of Science, and closely akin to our Fellowship of Engineering.

33. We tried to ascertain the impact of this structure on the standards and practice of engineering. It was commonly claimed by US engineers that the system had ensured minimum standards of competence and professional

integrity but this could not be proved. Accreditation was valued by employers as providing a check, which they would otherwise have to undertake themselves, and by some academic institutions who were able to use the threat of not getting, or losing, accreditation as a lever to extract funds from their authorities. It also served to protect students from sub-standard courses, an important factor given the number of courses available.

JAPAN

34. Programme: University of Tokyo
Ministry of Education, Science and Culture
Agency for Industrial Science and Technology
Ministry of International Trade and Industry
NSK Bearings
Science and Technology Agency
Sony Corporation
Fujitsu Company
Nippon Telegraph and Telephones
Mitsibushi Research Institute
Fujitsu Fanuc Company

Manpower

35. Japan is an homogenous, classless society with a high general standard of education, especially in mathematics. This has two effects of relevance to Japanese engineering. First, the level of education of the average Japanese worker is markedly higher than that of his UK counterpart; this applies at all levels of the firm, especially on the shopfloor. We saw evidence of this in the ability of operatives to stand up and give technical presentations of their work and in the extent to which they were able to cope with high levels of automation and other sophisticated production methods. The strength of Japanese engineering is in our view partly due to the standard of education of those involved in the engineering dimension at working level.

36. The other effect of the highly developed educational base of Japanese society is in the level of participation in higher education. Currently there are around 1·5 million undergraduates at university in Japan (from a total population approximately double the UK's), with nearly 30 per cent of school leavers entering higher education. Engineering accounts for between one-fifth to one-quarter of these. The result is that Japan produces many more graduate engineers than the UK. The supply of trained technicians from Higher Technical Schools is similarly well in excess of the UK supply. This large numerical supply of engineers and technicians provides the foundation for the striking strength of Japanese engineering.

37. This level of output of qualified technical manpower is due to two main factors. First, it reflects the intrinsic popularity to the school leaver of technical subjects compared with other areas of study. Engineering is much more popular than pure science and is the largest subject within higher education. Secondly, it has been brought about by the deliberate Government policy of expanding the number of places at university engineering schools. Given

the competition for university places this has been sufficient to increase the supply of qualified engineers. The main expansion of engineering education occurred during the 1960s, during which period the proportion of the workforce employed in technical and engineering areas rose by 160 per cent, a significant shift in the pattern of employment. We were told that around half of all engineering graduates entered manufacturing to work as engineers. The current level of supply was sufficient to meet industry's demand and was not likely to be expanded further.

Formation

38. The Japanese engineering course is normally four years in length. The initial two years provide a general education, biased towards engineering science but including humanities and foreign languages. The final two years of so called 'professional education' aim to build up the student's knowledge of a particular subject area, so that a specific engineering discipline is studied in some depth. In the final year there is often a project to provide an appreciation of applications but the emphasis is on theory and principles. We were told that some criticism had been voiced by industry that courses were too basic and did not provide enough detailed knowledge which could be put to use directly the graduate entered industry. To this the universities' response was that they provided their graduates with a firm foundation on which they could build for maximum flexibility and responsiveness to changing technology in the future. However, in recognition of the need for a more practical, applications-based formation, two new technical universities were being set up to offer programmes along these lines. We were told that in general employers expected their graduate recruits to have a sound basic technical knowledge and a certain breadth of perspective; commercial ability, leadership and specialist skills were generally seen as being the responsibility of the employer to develop through training and structured experience.

39. The relationship between Government, the universities and industry we found difficult to define. The official position is that they work quite independently of one another and we discovered no formal machinery for consultation and planning in relation to the supply of engineers. However, considerable informal influence and contact behind the scenes undoubtedly occurs and this works effectively. Moreover, Government exercises direct financial control over much of the higher education system and private industry also funds a large part of it. The declared position is that courses are designed without regard to industry's needs and simply reflect advances in engineering science. However, we observed courses in manufacturing methods, for example, which were directly applicable to industrial requirements. Moreover, a good proportion of engineering teachers have practical industrial experience and many of them are part-time teachers with full-time jobs in industry. Another pointer to the strong informal links between the engineering schools and industry is the importance which is attached by employers when recruiting to the references given by Professors. We understand that it is common for Professors to have the final say on industry's recruitment of engineering graduates. Whilst there is no system for universities to do contract research for industry, the universities do a considerable amount of research which is eventually used by industry.

The culture of Japanese industry

40. The relationship between the Japanese employee and his firm is quite different from that which exists in the UK and probably unique in the world. The Japanese employee identifies totally with his firm and is personally committed and involved in its fortunes. A range of factors are behind this including the extent of employee participation and consultation in decision making; the taking of decisions on the basis of consensus throughout the firm; the prevalence of life-long employment, and the importance of seniority; the existence of company-wide unions covering all workers below management; and the absence of rigid job specifications and the high level of job flexibility. Each firm generates its own culture which affects all aspects of its operations. In our view the successful record of Japanese engineering cannot be dissociated from the Japanese ability to develop a cultural system at the level of the firm commanding universal loyalty throughout the workforce.

41. It was apparent that what motivates the Japanese employee, including the engineer, is not so much self-aggrandisement as the success of the team or group in which he plays a part. We formed the view that this motivation was central to the general unity of purpose with which the Japanese pursue their chosen goals. The process of selecting these goals and the agreed means towards achieving them often appears cumbersome and ponderous, but once consensus is achieved all concerned feel involved and committed, which has a tremendous impact on the effectiveness of what they do. This applies at different levels, from the agreement of national technological objectives to the agreement of maintenance procedures for a production line.

42. As far as the engineer specifically is concerned, he is directly affected by the concept of employment for life, which is virtually a contract between the employer and the individual whereby both will work to develop the employee's abilities for their mutual benefit. The engineering recruit after a short induction programme commonly spends a period on the shop floor or in sales, where he is generally under fairly close supervision and encouraged to make suggestions for improvement. He is then given specific responsibilities of a more advanced nature and his performance is carefully assessed. Career planning and development are given considerable attention. Most training is provided on the job. We were told that 'training on the battlefield' was more effective than training in a classroom. Formal off-the-job training, though it occurs, is much less important than continuous self-development through private study—at the individual's own initiative. We did not have the opportunity to explore the extent of this private study, but we got the strong impression that a considerable effort in this direction was expected and made. Individual motivation for self improvement is strong, but the philosophy seems to be that, by improving his own abilities and contribution, the individual engineer is improving the effectiveness of the group within which he works, and also his reputation within that group, both of which will redound to his long-term advantage. Thus, a long-term view of self-interest operates.

Industrial development and planning

43. The central importance of technology to economic welfare and progress is universally recognised at all levels in Japan; this is reflected in the fact

211

that around half of the senior civil service hold degree qualifications in engineering or related subjects, half of these having postgraduate qualifications. Also within industry about half of all Directors have engineering qualifications. The Japanese economic miracle is well known. For example, between 1965 and 1974 manufacturing output grew by 15 per cent per annum on average. We found a widespread realisation that considerable industrial adaptation would be needed if this record were to be maintained. It was widely accepted that declining world trade, more expensive raw materials and energy, increasing competition and the prospects of protectionism all meant that existing industries would have to modernise substantially and new ones be created. These problems of industrial restructuring are seen in Japan in mainly technical terms, and the technological requirements for achieving objectives are identified—they are not regarded as political problems.

44. There is a growing concern that Japan should develop a greater capacity to develop original technological innovations herself, rather than relying on imported ideas and technologies as has been the case hitherto. Considerable efforts are going into this, for example through the creation of a Science City on the north side of Tokyo to group together as much as possible of the national basic research effort. By this year there are to be 43 research institutes located at Science City, constituting the biggest R and D effort in the world. The planning of Japanese R and D rests with various Government agencies. We were impressed by the coherence and scale of their programmes; they are co-ordinated under the National Council for Science and Technology, chaired by the Prime Minister. A central feature is to involve private industry in the planning and execution of R and D policies. This reflects the preponderance of total Japanese R and D in private industry, with 65 per cent of all activity occuring in this sector, over 20 per cent higher than in the UK. We were told that Japanese firms contracted out R and D work to academic establishments and other outside agencies even less frequently than occurs in the UK. Thus R and D is regarded as mainly an in-house function. In the manufacturing sector considerable attention is now being devoted to automating production methods and it was our impression from what we were told and from what we observed that the level of automation and use of robotics in Japanese factories is markedly higher than in the UK. We understand that this is going ahead at plant level on the basis of full consultation throughout the workforce and with employee co-operation.

45. The Japanese Government is seeking to reorient the economy away from what are regarded as declining industries, such as steel, shipbuilding and chemicals, towards low energy using, high value added industries and towards the service sector. To achieve this a mechanism of indicative planning has been adopted. The Ministry of International Trade and Industry (MITI) together with other government agencies, draw up 5-year forecasts in the shape of an input/output model, and these are discussed and ratified by an Industrial Structure Council, chaired by the Minister for International Trade and Industry and constituted on a similar basis to our NEDC. It is then left to individual companies and organisations to make use of these forecasts; MITI saw their role as creating the appropriate environment, encouraging changes and initiatives which were in accord with the plan, and discouraging

212

those which were not. A range of policy instruments were used for this. But also important were the extensive informal contacts between the Government machine and private industry, the high level of staff interchange, especially at senior level, being an important factor here. There is no doubt that the combined efforts of government and industry have in this way effectively mobilised technological resources to realise industrial and market objectives.

The engineering dimension

46. The Japanese approach to engineering appeared to us to be totally market-orientated. Even basic research work is undertaken to achieve explicit marketing goals and is frequently on a contract basis either in-house or with an outside agency, so that the potential application and pay-off are always kept in mind. The philosophy with regard to product development tends to work backwards from the identification of a market need or gap, and the appropriate price, to the design of a product to meet the identified specification; this specification is entirely in terms of market requirements for minimum costs, maximum reliability and required performance. This philosophy is a function of corporate objectives which are geared to market share rather than profit maximisation, and a financial regime in which companies do not have to keep one eye on their share price (lest they be bought out on the verge of success) and the other on their creditors. Engineering is perceived by engineers and management alike as the lynchpin of a commercial enterprise, where the aim is to produce the product demanded by the market at the price the market is willing to pay, with constant stress on raising quality and lowering costs.

47. Thus there is a ruthless logic to the Japanese approach to engineering. Clearly defined market goals are set both for the immediate and the longer term. The various engineering resources available to the firm are then carefully and systematically deployed to realise the market objectives. Throughout the exercise continuous attention is devoted to lowering costs, either through introducing new technology or by improving operations. Similar attention is devoted to the related requirement of improving quality. Here the QC Circle method is frequently employed, with groups of employees from all levels of the firm getting together on a regular basis to agree and hammer out methods of improving quality. Informing all this is the general realisation that the company stands or falls according to its ability to satisfy the demands of the international market; a willingness on the part of all employees to identify their own success with the prosperity of the firm for which they work; and an appreciation that high levels of engineering skill and performance are inseparable from market success.

48. During our visit we frequently asked why Japanese engineering performance outstripped the UK's. Four factors were commonly cited. First, Japanese management was said to be more deeply involved in the organisation of the shopfloor and in production generally. Secondly, the production function itself was claimed to be more integrated within Japanese factories, with the setting up, operating and maintenance of a machine generally being carried out by a single worker, whereas in the UK they were usually split between different

workers leading to delay. Thirdly, it was reckoned that work in Japanese factories was organised more on a team or co-operative basis. Finally, it was held that man for man the level of skill and education of Japanese factory workers was higher than in the UK, it being reckoned that 80 per cent of operatives in many factories in Japan were graduates of Technical High Schools.

FRANCE

49. Programme: Comite d'Etudes sur les Formations des Ingenieurs (CEFI), Paris
Electricite et Gaz, de France, Paris
Union des Industries Metallurgiques et Minieres, Paris
Commission des Titres d'Ingenieurs, Paris
Ecole Nationale des Telecommunications, Paris
Conseil National des Ingenieurs Francais, Paris
Thomson C S F, Paris
Institut National des Sciences Appliques, Rennes
Thompson's, Rennes
Ecole Nationale d'Ingenieurs de Metz
Dept de Sciences et Techniques, University of Metz
Institute des Sciences de l'Ingenieur de Nancy
Ecole Nationale Superieure de Mecanique, Nantes
Union Regionale des Groupments d'Ingenieurs, Nantes
Institut de Technology, Nantes
Union Regionale des Groupements d'Ingenieurs de Lorraine, Nancy
Ecole des Mines, Nancy
Ecole Nationale des Ponts et Chaussees, Paris
Ministry of Universities, Paris

The appeal of engineering

50. The French engineering schools are able to attract the very best talent. Even those schools ranking lowest in the tacit but real hierarchy of the 150 designated schools of engineering have 10–20 applicants for every available place. The most prestigious engineering schools of all are the dozen or so 'General Ecoles', though the term 'Grande Ecole' tends to be applied loosely to all engineering schools. This competition arises not because young Frenchmen have a vocation for engineering. What is prized and sought is the State awarded title of Diplome d'Ingenieur. Holders of this award are identified as the intellectual cream of their generation, chosen through a fiercely competitive entrance procedure and trained to a high level of analytical ability. As such their future careers and prosperity are assured. They are in great demand from industry and the public sector, they can command higher starting salaries and steeper incremental scales than contemporaries with other qualifications, and they are automatically recruited into the higher echelons of employing organisations. It is not surprising therefore that the competition to enter the Grandes Ecoles begins in effect at age 13 when the first streaming of school children by their abilities in maths is made. Students must study two years of advanced mathematics and physics beyond their 'baccalaureate'

at special 'cramming' schools to prepare for the examinations for entry to the Grandes Ecoles. The attractiveness of engineering is reinforced by the unattractiveness of the alternatives. A 'maitrisse' degree from an ordinary university, even in a science or technological subject, is regarded as a very poor second to a Dip Ing and by no means the same passport to success. Also, there is a large gulf between the value of a high level technician award and a Dip Ing.

Formation

51. The French do not make the British distinction between education and training. Instead they used the one word, 'formation', to cover both, implying an integrated, coherent approach to the preparation of engineers for employment. In theory the engineering schools provide the total formation package. However, in reality, the first few years of an engineering graduate's employment are devoted to training to supplement the formation provided by the engineering schools.

52. The formal education period concentrates on developing general skills of analysis, mathematics, and engineering science, on the premise that the function of the engineering schools is to provide their graduates with the conceptual foundation and tools which they can then learn to apply in the particular tasks for which they gain employment. Thus the French engineering schools do not aim to produce finished engineers to the same extent as do engineering schools in most of the rest of the continent. On the other hand, a French engineering graduate is deemed qualified. Also the practical aspects of formation are not neglected completely; a good many schools have workshop facilities, and virtually all of them require their students to spend one or more periods or 'stages' in industry. These last a few months at a time and vary from no more than factory visits to real industrial projects. There is a general trend towards a more applications orientation even in the more theoretical schools, though this is a change of emphasis rather than in philosophy.

53. The aim of all the Grandes Ecoles, including the more vocational ones, is primarily to produce technical administrators, capable of managing a wide range of activities in industry and Government. With one or two exceptions, they make little attempt to prepare their graduates to practise as professional engineers immediately on graduation, even though graduates will often be 25 or 26 by the time they leave the Ecole. While practice varies greatly, we were told that most new Dip Ing's entering industry were required to spend their first two to three years in technician posts, learning practical skills and 'man management' on the job. After this period they could expect to rise quickly into administrative positions—the level depending to a large degree on the type of school attended, at least in the early years—in which posts they would have the advantage of having an intimate knowledge of the work done by those in their charge.

54. French engineering courses are generally both longer (four to six years) and more intensively taught than their British counterparts. This enables them

to cover a wider field of study in greater depth, and to develop a higher level of mathematical ability than British courses. The emphasis is upon engineering science and analysis. We saw little evidence that the 'extra' time was used to develop abilities in synthesis, design, systems approaches, originality, cross disciplinary studies or any other wider perspectives. On the other hand, the final year is generally devoted to specialised study in a branch of engineering, which may encompass project work in engineering applications. The full-time teaching staff rarely have any industrial experience or undertake much research, but the content of the formation is kept up-to-date by the use of outside lecturers to teach courses or topics in the fields in which they work. Relevance is also ensured by the use of the industrial 'stages' during the course and through the presence of local industrialists on the governing bodies of each school. Although the length and intensiveness of Dip Ing courses in France are greater than British degree courses, so that a broader field is covered in greater depth, the programmes we saw appeared to differ little in academic content from a good British degree course. The main difference is attributable to the greater breadth of study (sometimes crossing the boundaries between disciplines) and to the emphasis on project work in the later stages of the course.

Careers

55. The Grandes Ecoles do not prepare engineers solely of the type emerging from our own engineering schools, and many of their graduates would not be viewed as engineers in Britain. The French Dip Ing may well find work as an agronomist, or an industrial chemist, or a textile technologist; if he does, he will do so from a formation almost exactly the same as his colleagues from the same school who enter work as agricultural engineers, chemical engineers, textile machinery designers—the only difference in the course, if any, would be in the elective options chosen in the final year. It is commonly claimed that the 'debutant' Dip Ing is a skilled analytical generalist. We were unable to assess the extent to which this is so, though some of our party felt that the versatility of the Dip Ing is exaggerated. Either way it is widely accepted that he requires several years of experience and training before he can fill an engineering post.

56. Dip Ing's are in very heavy demand from employers and have no difficulty at all in finding work. The notion that most of them enter public service is something of a myth, based upon a generalisation from the special case of the Ecole Polytechnique, whose graduates are bound to enter public service for a period after graduation, but who account for only 300 of the 10,000 Dip Ing's graduating each year. The majority enter the private sector, usually into large organisations where salaries and opportunities are greater. A common early posting is to research which is considered a good training position, in view of the close contacts it entails with the commercial, production and marketing functions in the firm. Within a few years most Dip Ing's will be in positions which would be labelled 'management' in British companies (the term is used in France, but does not have the same non-technical connotations), but they continue to take a close and direct interest in the technical details of operations.

216

57. On recruitment to an organisation, an engineer immediately enters the 'cadre', or officer corps. The concept of the 'cadre', explicity recognised as the senior level of administration and authority, reflects the systematised, codified and hierarchical nature of French organisations. The 'cadre' of French organisations, including Government Departments, has historically been dominated by engineers—this explains the predilection to recruit engineers as the new life blood—and still admits only a relatively small proportion of accountants, lawyers, MBAs and others. Not all the engineers in the 'cadre' will be Dip Ing's, since many will be 'ingenieurs maisons', promoted internally from 'the ranks'. Another route into the 'cadre' is for a technician to be sponsored by his firm to study for the Dip Ing on a part-time or block release basis.

58. The young engineer undergoing his period of technical training and experience will be recognised and rewarded as a member of the 'cadre', even though this may result in his earning more than those under whom he is working at that stage; this system apparently causes no conflict. As he rises to his career level, so he will do much less applied engineering work, delegating these tasks to technicians while he concentrates on policy and strategy matters. We were told that only in the State-run research institutes were large numbers of engineers involved in high level practical engineering work. Thus a distinction is commonly drawn between engineers, who think, and technicians, who do.

Organisation

59. The legislative requirement, that firms spend the equivalent of at least 2 per cent of their annual payroll on continuing formation, seems to have encouraged widespread updating and retraining programmes, with a high level of participation. We were told that it was common for engineers to return to their original school for one or two weeks every few years to update themselves. Thus initial formation provides only a foundation for subsequent professional development and continuing education features prominently in the system.

60. There are no organisations in France which seek to supervise or control entry to the engineering profession. The nearest thing to control over entry is the Commission des Titre's exercise of delegated powers to maintain the standards of Dip Ing awards. The bodies which bring engineers together are either the 'old boys clubs' of their Ecoles, or specialised learned societies, or trades unions (representing engineers, but as members of 'cadres' and not as a professional group). We gained the impression that engineers saw themselves much less as members of a profession than as members of an administrative elite.

61. There is enormous complexity and diversity in the arrangements for engineering formation and employment, and the difficulties of marshalling all these disparate and autonomous interests to even consider changes has led to the establishment of the Comite d'Etudes sur les Formations d'Ingenieurs (CEFI). This body provides a neutral forum for the discussion

of topics relating to the education or utilisation of engineers, for undertaking special studies which cut across the aegis of more than one interest group, and for stimulating and pressing for changes without being identified with vested interests.

Changes

62. The most apparent change under way is towards making the teaching in the Grandes Ecoles more 'applications' oriented and practical, usually by extending the amount of time spent in industrial 'stages'. This trend was described as a swinging back of the pendulum in engineering education, from its current highly theoretical extreme towards the more practical orientation which prevailed in the immediate post-war years. This swing back was attributed to industry's need for more high-level 'doers' and fewer abstruse 'thinkers', indicating the sensitivity of the engineering schools to the needs of industry. Feedback is achieved through the external teaching staff, through industrialists on school boards, and through the Commission des Titres (acting for the Ministry of Industry).

63. Other changes we noted included the changing nature and composition of the 'cadres' in industry, with more non-engineers being recruited to the 'cadres', and also with the lower demarcation of the 'cadres' moving down towards the technician levels (under pressure from the unions). It may be that engineers see a need to consolidate their position in the face of these potential challenges, and that this is part of the reason for the more specialised, more vocational pattern of formation which is emerging.

64. We were told of the concern felt that France was not devoting enough attention to engineering research. Some felt that the Grande Ecoles' model of formation did not encourage a creative and innovative approach among its graduates. Many of the schools are finding difficulty in attracting as many external teachers as formerly, and are thus having to look for ways of keeping their full-time teaching staff in touch with the latest developments in engineering. For these reasons the amount of research done in the Grandes Ecoles, often on a contractual basis for industry, is increasing and can be expected to grow significantly. In time this trend may well come to affect the model of undergraduate teaching in the Ecoles.

65. French engineers are prepared for work in different roles and in a different environment from their British counterparts. They are trained to manage technical activities—and all functions in industry are seen as technical activities of one sort or another—from the basis of high intellect plus detailed practical knowledge of the work of their subordinate staff. This latter aspect of engineers' formation is clearly important to understanding their role and contribution to their organisations; the fact that around one-third of 'cadre' engineers are *not* products of the Grandes Ecoles, but are 'ingenieurs maisons', supports this view. The role of the Dip Ing's is less to push forward new technology, than it is to be a technically competent administrator with his feet firmly grounded in practical experience.

218

WEST GERMANY

66. Programme: Federal Ministry of Education and Science, Bonn
West German Rectors' Conference, Bonn
VUBI (Federation of Consulting Engineers), Bonn
Technische Hochschule, Aachen
Wissenschaftsrat (Science Council), Cologne
Verein Deutsche Ingenieure, Dusseldorf
Messer Griesheim, Frankfurt
Bureau for the Rationalisation of German Industry
(RKW), Frankfurt
Optische Werke Rodenstock, Munich
Fachhochschule, Munich
Siemens, ,Munich

Entry into engineering

67. The German secondary schools provide a broadly based education culminating for the abler students in the Abitur examination. For this the pupil specialises either in classics, mathematics or modern languages, but he is able to go on from any of these to engineering in higher education. A student specialising in classics or modern languages at school can cope with an engineering degree course because he will have kept up his mathematics and science throughout his period at school. We formed the impression that German engineers were more rounded than their British counterparts and in part this may be due to their broader education at school.

68. The German education system has changed substantially over recent years under various reform measures. There are complaints that this has led to a slipping of standards. There are also complaints that the schools are indifferent or even hostile to industry and that they are out of date. We were unable to pursue these points but we gained the impression that German expectations of the schools are very high.

69. Most entrants to the engineering profession in Germany follow the conventional route from secondary school straight into higher education. But there is still a strong industrial apprenticeship system in Germany and some who have served apprenticeships choose to re-enter full-time education by attending special schools and then proceed to engineering degree courses. In effect then there is an employment based route into the engineering profession and a minority come up this way.

The traditional system of formation

70. Under the traditional German formation system two distinctive types of engineers have been produced: the Ing Grad, who followed a practically oriented three to four year course at a Fachhochschule, and the Dipl Ing, who took a course nominally lasting five to six years but capable of being much longer, at a Technische Universitat or a Technische Hochschule (TH), where he received advanced training in both engineering theory and applications.

219

71. Under this system the first three years of the Dipl Ing course are largely devoted to engineering science, although the student is required to spend at least six months working in industry during this period. To this extent the early years are not dissimilar to a good UK sandwich course, although the best courses achieve a better synthesis of theory and application—but it is in the subsequent years that differences emerge. The last two (nominal) years of the course are devoted to professional engineering practice in particular disciplines. The instruction is given mostly in the TH itself, relying heavily upon the close integration between those institutions and industry and on the substantial industrial experience (required by law) of engineering professors. This extra phase is a vital difference between the 'German' and UK models.

72. In the final two years of the course the emphasis is upon developing skills of synthesis and the integration of knowledge and techniques. This can be illustrated by the example of 'Verfahrenstechnik' which translates roughly to 'process technology'. Verfahrenstechnik is one of the options commonly available to mechanical engineering students in the final two years of the course once they have completed their initial studies in engineering science. The range of options available to mechanical engineering students naturally varies from institution to institution. Those available at the Technical University of Munich include, in addition to Verfahrenstechnik: Mechanical Engineering with emphasis on design and development; with emphasis on theory and research; with emphasis on manufacture and operations; with emphasis on energy and power engineering; and Aeronautical and Space engineering. So far as Verfahrenstechnik is concerned it aims to cover the fundamental principles involved in the planning, design and operation of process plant and equipment. To illustrate the fundamental principles students are given real design problems to investigate and other projects requiring the application of theory to real or simulated industrial problems. The course aims to equip the student for work in any of the process engineering industries either in a specialised capacity or as an all-rounder.

73. The potential 'graduated' engineer (aspiring to the Ing Grad award) generally enters industry from a 'lower' secondary school, and progresses to full-time study in a Fachhochschule (FH) after a period of craft experience. In the FH he follows a shorter (three or four year) course, with a strong practical orientation which prepares him well to begin working as a mainstream engineer. Many 'graduated' engineers proceed, either immediately upon graduating or after a few years' experience, to topping-up courses leading to a Dipl Ing award, although the career prospects and rewards for Ing Grads are good enough to keep the majority in this stream.

74. We were much impressed with the thoroughness of the education and training, and with the quality of staffing and equipment, in the FHs and THs which we visited in Germany, and their equivalents in Holland. It is important to stress that both qualifications, denoting very different types of engineering formation, are respected and valued by employers in the countries concerned. Both 'graduated' and 'diploma' engineers find their way to the top in industry, although the path is generally easier and faster for the Dipl

Ing. In a sense this model is analogous to the old UK two-tier system—degree plus graduate apprenticeship or HNC/D plus apprenticeship—with the crucial difference in each case that both phases in the German system are centred in the teaching institution.

Ing Grad and Dipl Ing

75. Under this traditional system of formation the Ing Grad and the Dipl Ing used to be produced in the approximate ratio of 4:1 and, whilst performance on the job was an important factor determining career progress, the rationale of the system was that the Dipl Ing was trained to lead engineering innovation and development and the Ing Grad managed day-to-day engineering operation and provided development support. The Ing Grad was therefore roughly equivalent to the UK HNC engineer except that he followed a full-time pattern of education. He often had substantial shop floor or drawing office experience before he started studying for the Ing Grad; the course he followed was strictly practical in emphasis, the theory being restricted to that which was necessary for practice; and the position he occupied was in mainline engineering, working to a Dipl Ing on development work, or serving as a middle manager in production.

76. Recently this system of formation has undergone substantial changes. The expansion of higher education (student numbers have jumped from 240,000 in the mid-1960s to their present 930,000) has brought about a relative decline in the numbers seeking the Ing Grad qualification compared to the Dipl Ing. On current trends, we were told, the ratio looked like switching from 4:1 to 1:2. Students have opted for the Dipl Ing, the higher qualification, for status reasons and because it is a more secure ticket to the better engineering jobs. Also large numbers of Ing Grads have not entered employment as junior engineers. Instead they have stayed on to do another degree, say economics or business studies, or have upgraded their qualifications to Dipl Ing. The latter course has been especially prevalent amongst engineers entering the public sector where academic qualifications are important in salary and career terms.

77. This switch in the supply of engineers has meant that industry has found it increasingly difficult to recruit the right mix of people; in particular it has found itself short of people with the practical skills associated with the Ing Grad. Also the schools training Dipl Ings have been overloaded, have had high drop out rates and have been unable to provide as much training in advanced applications as previously.

Changes in the formation system

78. To correct these trends various new measures are currently being considered. First, in an attempt to shift students back into the Fachhochschulen, the Ing Grad title which they have awarded in the past may be phased out and the Fachhochschulen will henceforth award the Dipl Ing, although their courses will remain basically unaltered. The intention here is to divert more of the brighter students back into the Fachhochschulen. The German engineer-

221

ing profession have pressed for this change, though employers seemed opposed or indifferent to it. It is accepted that the change in titles will not automatically bring about the desired shift and that it will probably lead to a position where employers have to look carefully at the institution which the student attended rather than just at nominal qualifications. Another related change concerning the Fachhochschulen is the proposal that their courses take a minimum of four years to bring them closer to the Universities.

79. The second area of change is the growing interest being shown in schemes for strengthening the teaching of engineering practice, particularly by using sandwich courses; several institutions are developing along these lines. A third change is the new planning machinery being set up at Lande level under Federal co-ordination. This machinery involves so called 'curriculum commissions', which will formulate curricula for specific subjects for institutions of higher education to follow. The object of this new system is to allow labour market considerations to have a greater influence than hitherto upon higher education programmes and, for this purpose, employers will sit on the commissions. The new planning framework provides a potentially powerful means of ensuring that engineering education keeps in step with industry's requirements.

The role of engineers

80. Although under these proposals all future engineers in Germany may be awarded the title Dipl Ing, it is clear that there will still be two underlying formation streams corresponding to the current distinction between the Dipl Ing course and that for Ing Grad. The distinction works well so far as German industry is concerned and it is not intended to alter this fundamentally. The basis of the distinction is that the Dipl Ing is educated to be able eventually to occupy positions of senior engineering and management responsibility; and the Ing Grad is educated to make an immediate contribution to engineering practice, to provide support to the Dipl Ing and to manage day-to-day operations. The chief advantage of the system to employers is that it provides a reliable framework from which to recruit.

81. Both the Dipl Ing and the Ing Grad receive an education well-founded in both theory and practice, with the Ing Grad sacrificing some theory to secure a broad exposure to practice and the Dipl Ing receiving a good grounding in both theory and applications. Thus all engineering graduates in Germany are intended to be practice-oriented. Until recently most students did a considerable amount of training in industry as a requirement for their degree. The amount of such training has generally been reduced—except in the case of sandwich courses—and most students therefore receive their practical training within the academic institution. The institutions are geared to provide this because of their strong links with industry, the substantial industrial experience of their teaching staff, and their up-to-date and extensive equipment. Because the degree course is relatively long, there is enough time to devote the final two years to practical applications and project work, material for which is commonly provided by industry. Thus the student generally graduates more fully formed than his UK equivalent and needs less practical postgraduate training in industry.

82. The Dipl Ing is educated to a higher level than the Ing Grad but, as far as we could tell, employers use the two types of engineer flexibly. On first appointment the Dipl Ing enjoys a marginally higher salary than the Ing Grad but this is no more than might be expected since he is generally two years older. Thereafter the Dipl Ing is expected to proceed further and faster than the Ing Grad. However, there is no guarantee that this will be the case, since progress depends more upon performance on the job than upon initial qualification. We were told that the Dipl Ing's education, because of its heightened theoretical and analytical content, provided the background and perspective enabling him to tackle a wide range of engineering problems. He is equipped to anticipate problems and solve them more quickly than the Ing Grad. The Ing Grad's education does not give him the same perspective. However, the Dipl Ing's superior ability is merely a potential one; it requires motivation and commitment for it to be converted into a real advantage. Not all Dipl Ings are able to convert their higher potential into superior performance on the job and for this reason many Ing Grads do better in career terms than some Dipl Ings. Moreover, whilst the Ing Grad's formation does not give him the initial breadth of vision of the Dipl Ing, he is often of more immediate value to his employer because of his ability to make an immediate contribution to practice.

83. We formed the impression that the Ing Grad/Dipl Ing system is well understood by employers and provides a firm basis upon which employers can recruit according to their particular requirements. The system seems to be operated flexibly so that performance on the job outweighs initial qualification. Further, the system provides a choice of routes into the profession for the student: a shorter route for those who prefer their education confined to the essentials, so that they can make an immediate contribution to engineering practice and the chance to advance according to performance; and, a longer route for those seeking a more rigorous education and who are prepared to defer entering employment.

84. The formation of the German engineer is intended to prepare for a career as a practising engineer. German engineers are not expected to become administrators or technical generalists as in France. However, the public sector is now a major recruiter of engineers and currently employs one-third of the total stock. Moreover many engineers, whilst they may start their careers practising engineering, soon move out of engineering into commercial functions and some go straight from higher education into commercial work. Around 20 per cent of qualified engineers are working in sales and commercial functions. We heard that a current issue was whether the pattern of engineering education should be adapted to reflect the type of work which German engineers are increasingly entering.

Engineering in Germany

85. Although German engineers are to be found in increasing numbers outside engineering functions, this is not because engineering offers less attractive career prospects. On the contrary, we formed the impression that engineering is regarded as an attractive career both in status and in more tangible

terms. The senior managers of German industry tend to emerge through the engineering function and about 60 per cent of board members of German companies have engineering backgrounds. Furthermore, the engineer does not have to move out of engineering in order to reach senior level but can stay within the engineering function and still reach the top. This reflects the central position which engineering is accorded within the firms. Other functions tend to be viewed as providing specialist services to engineering, rather than the other way round. Moreover, the Engineering Director of a German firm typically outranks the Commercial Director.

86. The various engineering functions of the firm tend to be carried out in accordance with this concept of giving prominence to engineering considerations. Thus much of the contact with customers is through the firm's R and D Department, which deals directly with customer requirements. In this way R and D tends to be less of a reactive and problem solving activity and is more concerned with marketing policy and with forming overall corporate strategy. Engineers are also found in marketing and after-sales functions and it is they rather than other specialists who man the various interfaces between the firm and its customers. Technical considerations relating to the reliability, serviceability and use of manufactured products are viewed as vital to sales and marketing and engineers are expected to provide the expertise here.

87. Similarly, engineers generally dominate the production function which is seen as central to the manufacturing firm's overall operations. We are told that there was no shortage of competent and well qualified production engineers and that, because of the importance attached to the production function, it was viewed as providing a challenging and rewarding function to work in. The production engineer is expected to draw upon the expertise residing in the various engineering resources of the firm and is generally given a free hand to improve productivity; he is expected to succeed in this respect and to keep production going within fixed parameters of cost, quality and time. We were impressed in the firms we visited by their thoroughness and general efficiency, rather than by the level of technology employed.

Continuing formation

88. Training and continuing formation tend to be provided in-house by the large German companies. We formed the impression that substantial resources were devoted to this. Siemens, for example, told us that they spent just under £100 million per annum on organised in-house training within Germany, amounting to roughly 5 per cent of their payroll. In addition they estimated they spent a similar amount on on-the-job and other types of informal training. Small and medium sized firms make more use of outside agencies to provide continuing formation, some of which are publicly supported. There is a legal framework to encourage continuing formation activities. The various Lander have passed legislation providing the employee with the right to paid education leave and the institutions of higher education are also under an obligation to provide adult education courses of a professional type. There is a general feeling that in spite of these legal provisions more needs to be

done to encourage continuing formation for technical staff, particularly for those in small and medium sized firms.

VDI

89. German engineers qualify through the institutions of higher education. There are no separate professional qualifying bodies as in the UK. However, there are professional Institutions with non-qualifying activities. The largest of these is the Verein Deutscher Ingenieure (VDI). With some 70,000 individual members, VDI represent about one-seventh of all German engineers and one-half of those in professional Institutions. It covers almost all engineering disciplines, except electrical and metallurgy. In addition to individual members, VDI have some 2,000 corporate members, mostly industrial companies.

90. VDI make a clear distinction between their activities for the engineering profession and their activities for engineering practice. In the former area these are primarily learned society activities. The VDI have no qualifying role, accepting all holders of the State-protected title 'Ingenieure' to membership. Neither do they undertake trade union activities. They must therefore appeal to their members on the services they offer. Much of their effort in this direction has been in the area of post-experience and continuing education. There is a wholly-owned company within VDI to provide facilities for continuing education. These include large scale technical conferences; short (one to three days) courses and seminar groups, attended by some 10,000 engineers per annum; and regional programmes of lectures and special discussion sessions, often held in the evening, which were attended by some 50,000 engineers last year. They also collaborate with the Hochschulen and universities in providing longer, more specialised technical courses, and intend expanding in this area. Microprocessor applications and programming are the most sought-after courses and lectures at present, followed in popularity by environmental control, system applications, and sales and marketing for engineers.

91. VDI seek to influence the development of engineering education and have been involved in the recent changes affecting the Fachhochschulen discussed above. One of their current concerns is to ensure that engineering education gives a broader awareness than at present to the 'wider issues' of technical decisions and develops a greater sense of social responsibility in engineers whom, it is felt, are vulnerable to public criticism on this count.

92. We were particularly impressed by the role played by the VDI in the area of professional engineering practice. They have a highly developed committee system, with up to 500 specialist technical committees covering a whole range of disciplines and cross-disciplinary issues, manned by VDI members, representatives of member companies, and co-opted specialists. These committees issue codes of practice for their particular remit, which are adopted and widely used by German industry. In some areas, especially air pollution and noise abatement, the VDI have delegated power from the Federal Government to specify the technical parameters and requirements within 'framework' legislation. In other areas the committees seek primarily to rationalise and disseminate best practice in particular activities, to which end they frame their

225

recommendations in discussion or 'exposure' drafts for wider debate, and then revise them into published codes. These codes are published in a loose-leaf format and are bought mainly by companies as reference sources for their engineers. The up-dating cycle is around two to three years. The VDI codes have come to have great standing, and have been used as national standards of practice, eg in contract or liability disputes. Their potential value for technology transfer and for the dissemination of new applications seems enormous.

93. The VDI is also active in encouraging the application of research findings into current engineering practice. They are particularly active in the dissemination of modern technology and applications to small and medium sized companies, and have set up a new Technology Centre to this end with Government funding and encouragement. This Centre provides an advisory service, and will put companies in touch with consultants if necessary.

Economic development

94. Although the economic framework in West Germany depends upon market forces there are various schemes of intervention and support designed to improve engineering performance, especially through the encouragement of new enterprises and new technology ventures. For instance the Ministry of Research and Technology support research and training programmes directed at small and medium sized companies; currently microprocessor applications are being supported on a sizeable scale. The RKW, which we visited, is a Government-funded agency concerned with raising the efficiency and profitability of small and medium sized enterprises through various consultancy and continuing formation activities. The various Lander offer incentives of different kinds to encourage industrial development in their territories. We were told that these, and other, support agencies considered the medium and long term effects upon industrial efficiency and performance as the prime criteria rather than short term employment effects. In other words, assistance was channelled to those firms with the potential to grow.

95. We were unable to go into the financing of German engineering, though it is generally accepted that the close relationship existing between German financial institutions and German industry has substantially helped industrial performance. The important contribution made by the Trade Unions' own bank in this respect was drawn to our attention.

96. As to the performance of the German engineering industry, it was suggested to us that its success was due in large part to the high standards of engineering practice of the leading companies in Germany who had had a major influence in improving standards in smaller firms, by imposing rigorous standards upon their sub-contractors and suppliers, and because their excellent reputation meant that newcomers to the market had to do even better in engineering terms to compete. The leading companies thus played a key role in stimulating high quality engineering right through the economy.

97. A final point concerns salaries. At the time of our visit in October 1978, the German engineering graduate's starting salary was around £10,000

and the good engineer could earn around £20,000 by his early thirties. We met several young UK engineers who had been attracted to work in Germany by these high salaries. It was put to us that, with the greater mobility of professionals in Europe, Britain was in danger of losing an increasing number of qualified engineers to the continent because of the better career prospects available there.

SWEDEN

98. Programme: Royal Academy of Engineering Sciences (IVA), Stockholm
The Swedish Committee for Technical Development (STU), Stockholm
L M Ericsson, Stockholm
Decca Navigator A B, Stockholm
Swedish Authority for Universities and Technical Colleges, Stockholm
Chalmers Technical University, Gothenburg
Volvo, Torslanda
ASEA, Vasteras
Royal Technical University (KTH), Stockholm
Saab-Scania, Sodertalje
Incentive Group, Stockholm
Confederation of Swedish Employers (SAF), Stockholm

99. In recent years there has been a widespread reform of the Swedish education system, widening opportunities at all levels. New subjects and teaching methods have also been introduced. We were told that the system was still in a state of flux and that many did not understand the details of the new system. Compulsory education lasts until around the age of 16 and is on a comprehensive basis. Streaming has been abolished and this has given rise to considerable criticism, especially from employers. At the age of 16 the student can enter the gymnasium and, if his school record is adequate, he can take a four-year course in technology. The graduate of such a course is know as a 'Gymnasium Engineer'.

Gymnasium Engineers

100. Gymnasium Engineers form the main body of Swedish engineers. The system for their formation has undergone considerable change in recent years with the general reform of the education system. The typical pattern now is a four-year programme, with six months to one year spent in industry. We equated the Gymnasium Engineer with HNC level. We found considerable uncertainty as to the role and standards expected of the Gymnasium Engineer. We did not have the opportunity to pursue this but the general impression was that the category of Gymnasium Engineer covered a wide range of abilities and that there was no reliable standard. Gymnasium Engineers are found at all levels of industry, from the shop floor to the board room.

101. Some Gymnasium Engineers proceed to a Technical University in order to gain the superior qualification of 'Civil Engineer'. However, they form a minority of the entrants to the Technical Universities, the majority of whose students are graduates of three-year gymnasium courses in science.

Entry to engineering

102. There are two notable aspects about admissions to higher education. First, there are a large number of mature students, arising from recent reforms giving adults legal entitlements to higher education provided they show minimum basic standards. The universities have become concerned at the large influx of mature students with minimal qualifications. The second unusual feature of admissions is that they are determined by a central authority in Stockholm and not by individual institutions. We were told that this authority gave particular weight to attainment in non-academic fields; for instance, a student with a good record in voluntary service would be favoured. The central authority, known as the Office of the Chancellor of the Swedish Universities, sets numerical targets for each undergraduate discipline both on a national basis and by institution. It also exercises some control over the standards and content of degree courses. For engineering there is a national planning commission with substantial employer representation.

103. Engineering has become relatively less popular with school leavers compared with other subjects than it used to be, reflecting current attitudes, questioning the social purpose of industry, and the widespread concern in Sweden about environmental and nuclear issues. We were told that the relative drift away from engineering had probably been halted but it still worries employers and educationalists. Although engineering is relatively less popular than it used to be compared with other subjects, the significant expansion of higher education in recent years has nonetheless led to an increase in the supply of qualified engineers. This is generally reckoned to have brought about a decline in mean quality at both Civil Engineer and Gymnasium Engineer level. We found considerable concern over this drop in quality and also an interest in ways of reconciling greater educational opportunity with the identification and encouragement of excellence.

Manpower

104. We were told that overall supply and demand were broadly in balance at both Civil Engineer and Gymnasium Engineer level, the ratio between the two being around 1:2. The figures for 1970 show that there were some 22,000 Civil Engineers in employment and about 50,000 Gymnasium Engineers, out of a total Swedish population of 8 million. With the expansion of the universities the total number of Civil Engineers is expected to reach 38,000 by 1980. This means that relative to her total population Sweden is currently producing engineers at a markedly faster rate than the UK.

Formation

105. The formation of Civil Engineers is provided by six institutions only. The two most prestigious are the Royal Technical High School in Stockholm and Chalmers Institute of Technology at Gothenburg. Entry to these two

schools is more competitive than to the other newer ones. Engineering formation is organised on the continental pattern. The engineering schools are relatively separate from the rest of higher education. They are State institutions specifically designed to provide for industrial needs, and they, rather than professional bodies, are the main qualifying agencies. There are no professional registers.

106. All engineering schools have a $4\frac{1}{2}$ year course. However, this is a minimum period and on average the student graduates after $5\frac{1}{2}$ years, and there is also a high drop-out rate. The first two years consist mainly of basic science and engineering science. From the third year onwards the subjects are of a more applied character. It is a requirement of the degree that the student gains 4 months industrial experience and completes an independent project during the course. This is often carried out in conjunction with industry. The student specialises in a specific discipline, though various interdisciplinary centres have been established to promote interdisciplinary courses and research. Industry does not generally regard the graduate as a 'finished product' and therefore usually provides further training after recruitment.

107. Although the objectives of engineering education in Sweden seemed to us to be similar to those in the UK, we were impressed by the extent to which the environment and framework of the Swedish technical universities differed from that in the UK. First, the links between teachers and industry are stronger than in the UK. The impression was that more engineering teachers in Sweden have had substantial industrial experience than their counterparts in the UK. Also, they keep their experience up to date through consultancy and research for industry. Secondly, there is more industrial involvement in the planning and assessment of courses through the structure of course committees within the universities, and at national level within the Office of the Chancellor of the Swedish Universities.

Engineers and the engineering dimension

108. The real differences between the Swedish and the UK formation systems appear after the graduation stage. The firms we visited recognized that the continuous development and formation of their engineers was crucial for their business performance, and that the engineer's potential is developed through the provision of formation opportunities and carefully planned experience and responsibility. Developing the talent of the engineer was seen to be the key.

109. Closely related to this is Swedish industry's general recognition of the crucial importance of the engineering dimension. We expected to find that engineering is awarded greater priority within Swedish manufacturing than it is in the UK. These expectations were fulfilled. In particular, we found that Swedish companies were looking to their engineers to pull them through the tougher world trading conditions they expect to meet during the rest of the century. We found a general awareness of the need for the Swedish economy to move up market through greater application of technology and engineering skills. The expectation was that engineers would be in the forefront of this.

110. This reflects the dominant position which engineers play in Swedish industry. Around 80 per cent of industrial management have technical qualifications. Furthermore the rapid development of the Swedish economy this century from being a relatively backward one, founded on mining and agriculture, to a highly successful modern industrial economy has been built substantially upon engineering-based industries. This has made Sweden a highly successful country in economic terms with a per capita income twice that of the UK's and amongst the highest in the world. Her economic success has been interrupted in recent years by inflation, mounting energy costs, currency problems, culminating in a two-fold devaluation in 1977, and by growing unemployment, some of it concealed by Government measures. For these and other reasons many of the certainties of the Swedish scene are now being questioned and successful industrial performance is no longer taken for granted.

111. We found that there was a general feeling that Sweden was at a crossroads. Either she could sit back and lose her leading industrial position or else she had to adapt to new conditions to maintain her competitive position. As a contribution to the current debate on Sweden's future, the Royal Swedish Academy of Engineering Science has conducted a major Inquiry into Sweden's industrial capability and competitive position. The major conclusions of this Inquiry are that the centre of gravity of Swedish industry should move up market into new technology bases products and systems; that engineering R and D should be substantially stimulated through Government support and planned procurement; that the current policy of Swedish industry of identifying and supplying carefully selected world markets should be continued; and that the supply of technical manpower for Swedish industry should be strengthened.

112. We were impressed by the scope and approach of the Academy's study which, it is claimed, is one of the most comprehensive investigations ever conducted by any country into its industrial failure. In carrying out the study the Academy, which is the top body of the Swedish engineering profession, have drawn substantially on the advice of their membership in industry and elsewhere. We understand that the Inquiry has been able to win the commitment of employers and trade unionists and that the various actions recommended—which add up to a further strengthening of Sweden's highly effective engineering dimension—will soon be put into effect.

Industrial performance.
113. We formed the conclusion that the successful record of Swedish industry was in large part due to the weight accorded to engineering considerations. Product design and development, and production planning and control stood out as particular strengths. Swedish industry is well known for having pioneered new group production methods and for its high productivity levels, and we were impressed with what we observed in these respects.

114. However, the effectiveness of Swedish engineering cannot be entirely divorced from aspects of the Swedish social system as a whole. In part this is a matter of size. Sweden is a relatively small country with an homogeneous

population of around 8 million. One result of this is that communication is relatively easy, say between industry and the education sector. The same goes for communication between employers and employees, with there being a strong central employers' confederation, the SAF, and a strong trade union confederation, the LO, both of which are able to speak authoritatively on behalf of those they represent.

115. Another factor is the existence in Sweden of a high degree of social consensus, albeit under strain in recent years. The consensus shows itself particularly in relations within industry. There is general agreement within industry about the need to conserve and make the most of Sweden's limited natural resources. This is rooted in the fact that until recently Sweden was a relatively poor agricultural country. But the consensus is not simply a matter of heritage. It is worked at consciously through the extensive system of worker participation that permeates Swedish industry. Swedish companies have at least two 'representatives of labour' on the board. At national level employers and employees work together, for instance in the joint Rationalization Council, whose purpose is to facilitate communication with respect to improving productivity and other matters. The highly developed system of employee participation has provided a basis upon which Swedish industry has been able to introduce advanced technology with the consent, and to the benefit, of the workforce and it provides a platform for this to be taken further in future years.

Professional organisation

116. We formed the impression that Swedish engineers are less concerned with professional issues than are UK engineers. Their orientation tends to be more functional, but this may reflect the fact that they have successfully achieved a position where they enjoy high status and salaries and dominate industry. The professional institution to which Civil Engineers may belong is Svenska Teknologforeningen (STF, the Swedish Association of Engineers and Architects). This body, some 100 years old, comprises nine societies based on branches of technology, and an association of teachers at technical colleges. Its membership, now over 20,000 is restricted to graduates of recognised institutes of technology. STF is not a qualifying body. It collaborates with the union for professional engineers Sveriges Civilingenjorsforbund (CF, the Swedish Union of Graduate Engineers), in organising numerous educational courses and seminars for practising engineers. STF also works with central and local government bodies on technical aspects of policy.

117. Swedish engineers are highly unionised. Thus CF has some 30,000 members which represents between 80 and 90 per cent of those eligible. It is split into three groups representing those working in the State, private industry and community services. Its other main activity is the provision of short courses which are open to members and non-members. CF is a member of the trade union grouping for professional workers and as such partakes in the trade union consortium that negotiates with the employers' confederation. There is a separate white collar union (SIF) to which Gymnasium Engineers belong.

DENMARK

118. Programme: Federation of Danish Mechanical and Metal Working
Industries, Copenhagen
Dansk Ingeniorforening, Copenhagen
Ingeniorsammenslutningen, Copenhagen

119. Our programme in Denmark was restricted to one day, during which
we visited the above three organisations and held general discussions with
a wider cross-section of people connected with Danish engineering. Thus we
were able to form some general impressions but not to explore matters in
depth.

Formation

120. There are three streams of formation for professional engineers in
Denmark. Two of these are well established: the university stream where the
student takes a $4\frac{1}{2}$ to $5\frac{1}{2}$ year course with half a year industrial/practical training and is awarded the title of 'Civilingenior'; and the Technical College
stream where the student takes a three year practice-oriented course following a period in industry and is awarded the title of 'Technicumingenior'. A
third new stream had been introduced intermediate between the two established ones: the Engineering Academy stream where the student follows a
$3\frac{1}{2}$ year course at the Danish Engineering Academy with similar standards
to the university course but run on a more intensive basis, and upon graduation receives the title of 'Academiingenior'.

121. This third stream has been created to cope with the growing number
of students applying for admission to the university stream, for whom there
are not enough places. In fact there is only one established institution teaching
engineering to university level, the Danish Technical High School (DTH) in
Copenhagen; though a new one has recently been opened at Aalborg, but
has yet to produce its first graduates. The numbers of engineering students
in 1976 were as follows: DTH 3,300; Aalborg 850; Danish Engineering Academy 1,200; Technical Colleges 2,200.

122. The two main streams of professional engineer, the Civilingenior and
the Technicumingenior, differ from one another in terms of the breadth of
their initial formation. However, in terms of employment and salaries there
is no sharp distinction. Many Technicumingeniors hold more senior positions
than Civilingeniors. We were told, for instance that the head of Danfoss,
one of the largest Danish companies, was a Technicumingenior. The main
difference between the two types of engineer is that the Civilingenior is
expected to provide innovation in technology. We were told that the public
did not generally recognise the distinction between the two streams of engineer,
who were thought of as being on a par. The titles 'Civilingenior', 'Academiingenior' and 'Technicumingenior' are all protected by law and are for life.
They are awarded upon graduation and there are no experience requirements
or tests of competence.

123. The Technicumingenior stream provides a practice based route into the profession. Ten to twenty years ago, this route picked up people who had served a four-year industrial apprenticeship and then sent them on a three-year practice oriented course at technical college, sometimes following a foundation year in basic science. With the growing number of school pupils staying on at school it is no longer feasible to rely upon apprentices alone to fill this channel and the majority of technical college students are not now ex-apprentices, but are school leavers, who have two years of training before entry to the technical college, the first year of which involves attendance at a workshop school and the second year practical experience in industry. Employers are involved in the selection of students for technical college to strengthen the industrial relevance of this route into the profession. The Technicumingenior qualification is reckoned to be an excellent career ticket for engineering and other fields. Some 25 per cent of Technicumingeniors go on to top up with a business studies qualification.

Careers

124. On the general standing of engineering as a career, we were told it ranked highly and was on a par with medicine, architecture and dentistry. Engineering is generally regarded as an attractive career offering good prospects. However, it became less popular some five or six years ago when young people turned away from technology on ideological and environmental grounds; but there has been no lasting effect. On the other hand, there has been an expansion of educational opportunities in recent years, including in engineering, which, it was felt, had led to some slight slippage in overall standards. But engineering still has a good image as a career. A Civilingenior starts (in 1978 values) on a salary of around £10,000 on graduation, can expect almost £20,000 by the time he is thirty and over £25,000 by thirty-five, though the high cost of living in Denmark has to be taken into account. Around eighty per cent of all managing directors in Danish industry are qualified engineers reflecting the excellent career opportunities open to the engineer.

Manpower

125. We were told that the current supply of engineers was broadly in balance with industry's requirements, both overall and by discipline. Any imbalances by discipline were lessened at the Civilingenior level by virtue of the breadth of the curriculum followed by intending Civilingeniors, enabling graduates in a specific discipline to adapt easily to employment in another one. The Civilingenior programme is modular in structure and highly flexible, around fifty per cent of the course being made up of electives. This has produced a situation where some employers complain that the course fails to provide a reliable grounding in fundamentals.

126. The two professional institutions Dansk Ingeniorforening (DIF), representing Civilingeniors, and Ingeniorsammenslutningen (IS), representing Technicumingeniors, told us about their joint study of Denmark's engineering manpower requirements. The study took account of likely technological developments and attempted to compare the projected supply against the expected

demand. It was reckoned that on current trends there would be a shortfall in supply by 1985. To overcome this the study recommended that the idle teaching capacity of the technical colleges should be used. The optimum supply rate was felt to be around 2,000 engineers per annum split equally into Civilingeniors and Technicumingeniors, whereas the current rate of supply was around 500 Civilingeniors and 600 Technicumingeniors. Survey data had shown that Denmark had a low density of engineers for a modern industrial country with only 35,000 qualified engineers. This, it was felt, needed tackling. On the other hand, there was no perceived 'technician gap'.

Profession organisation

127. The Danish professional institutions like most bodies of their kind on the continent have no qualifying functions, this task falling to the State and the education sector. Because they have no qualifying functions, the Danish institutions have to attract members by providing a range of services capable of appealing to practising engineers. Their success in this regard is shown by the fact that they have as members between 70–90 per cent of all qualified engineers, and a higher proportion still if only those practising are considered. Thus, there is a high membership ratio.

128. The two Danish institutions are active like their UK counterparts in the learned society and information areas. An area of growing activity for them is continuing education. Together the two institutions run a range of short courses to provide technical up-dating and management training. Currently we were told that 100 programmes were available, amounting to '100,000 participant hours a year, corresponding to a turnover in excess of ten million Danish Kroner' (around £1 million). Employers and academic institutions were involved in various ways in these courses. Apart from this activity, larger employers, particularly multi-nationals provide in-house training. The general level of post experience training is reckoned to be very high and the institutions see themselves as major contributors to this.

129. Other functions of the institutions include large information and publishing operations and the setting of codes of practice. The latter amount to engineering practice norms and the institutions' work involves them in the technology transfer process, disseminating best current practice throughout Danish engineering. Related to this is the work of the institutions in providing technical advice to Government and other public agencies. Another important interface is with the education sector and here a range of informal and formal channels are used both with the Ministry of Education and with individual academic institutions.

130. The Danish institutions differ from their UK counterparts in that they work actively to promote the general economic and social interests of their members, acting as quasi-trades unions. The institutions have a long track record of trade union activity in the public sector where they negotiate on behalf of their members for salary and other conditions of employment. They have also, historically, conducted salary surveys of their members in the private sector. Now they are moving from simply collecting information in respect of the private sector to carrying out trade union functions for professional engineers. The institutions are mainly concerned with fixing a global

sum for the remuneration of their members in a given company, leaving it to employers to settle differentials. This trade union activity, which is expected to expand, emerged as a result of pressure from members because of the high level of unemployment amongst engineers four to five years ago, and because professional engineers had felt squeezed by blue collar workers.

131. The Danish institutions provide other services, including acting as employment agencies and as counselling services for members and they also fulfil certain social security functions under State delegation. For instance, they provide pension and unemployment benefit schemes and an employment advisory service which investigates cases of alleged unfair dismissal and unfair working conditions. The two institutions—who have exceptionally close links with each other—produce jointly a weekly newspaper which carries around 95 per cent of all engineering vacancies in Denmark and is regarded as an important publication for Danish engineers.

EEC COMMISSION

132. A party of the Committee visited Brussels in December 1978 to discuss with officials in the European Commission the interest of the European Community in matters relating to the engineering profession.

133. The main objective of the Community in this respect is to remove hindrances to free movement and the right to practise. This objective has been achieved in the case of some professions, including doctors, nurses and dentists, with the agreement of Directives covering these professions. Directives relating to vets and architects were in the pipeline at the time of our visit. So far as engineers are concerned, the Commission drew up in 1969 a draft Directive to facilitate their full mobility and right of establishment. This Directive is still on the table. It has not yet been considered by the Council of Ministers and until it is the Commission are content to leave it lie. The initiative currently rests with Member States, through the Council; there are no signs of any Member seeking to open the debate over engineers so far. This reflects the fact that there are currently no major barriers to free movement and practice for engineers throughout the Community. In the view of the Commission any future Directive for engineers is unlikely to resemble the current draft, the Commission's thinking having developed since 1969 as a result of their experience in dealing with the various other professions considered to date. The approach used in the case of architects is reckoned to provide a possible model for engineers.

134. In formulating and implementing Directives the Commission deals only with Member States via the Council of Ministers, and not with interested organisations or lobby groups, although these have access to the ears of the Commission. A Directive for engineers would be unlikely to require statutory registration of engineers in Member States, though in the cases of other professions States have delegated their domestic authority to various registration bodies. Further, in medicine and dentistry, the Directives have provided for the establishment of bodies to monitor the formation package in each country to ensure standards.

135. The Commission's duty under the Treaty of Rome to bring forward measures to remove hindrances to freedom of movement and practice involves them in ensuring that the systems of qualification in Member States do not obstruct these freedoms. On the other hand, there is no statutory basis for the mutual recognition of academic qualifications and awards for the purposes of Community interchange and harmonisation. Unless the Treaty is amended there is no prospect, for example, of Community Directives for the harmonisation of degree awards or the equivalence of diplomas. Thus the Commission's statutory interest is in removing barriers—negative integration—rather than in creating common European engineering qualifications—positive integration.

136. Nonetheless the Commission have taken some limited steps in the direction of positive integration and to this end have introduced various 'grass roots' measures, in which Member States can participate or not, as they wish. Several schemes and projects have been introduced to facilitate collaboration and interchange between educational institutions and Community funds are available for these. Engineering education has not been specifically singled out for support, but many British engineering schools have nonetheless become involved in Community schemes. The aim is to build up interchange between individual institutions so that lessons from one country might be transferred to others and with it greater recognition of the benefits of co-operation.

EINDHOVEN TECHNICAL UNIVERSITY

137. In our various visits overseas we looked at several engineering degree courses. In addition we made a special visit to Eindhoven in Holland to look in detail at the 'Ir' degree (equivalent to the German Dipl Ing) in mechanical engineering at the Technische Hogeschool (Technical University) Eindhoven. We considered the course in some depth and report here only the main features.

The overall structure

138. The course to the Ir degree takes a minimum of five years, but the University allows the student to go through the system in a relatively free way, selecting courses at an appropriate time according to the individual's progress. Most students take six or seven years, and the average time is 6·7 years. (Students with the Ing degree from a Higher Technical School can complete the Ir course in a further four years.) The five study years are made up of ten semesters, two each year. Each semester consists of 13 teaching weeks (exclusive of examination periods); each week involves 30 hours of instruction. However, there are additional 'study' weeks so that the total time spent by each student at the University is nearly 40 weeks per year. It is estimated that each lecture needs two hours further study; a three hour session of tutorial or practical work requires one extra hour of private study. The total maximum loading of the student during a year is thus estimated at 1,700 hours, if he takes all courses offered in that year.

236

The technical content

139. **The first three years** of the degree course are rigidly prescribed. There are five main 'streams'—mathematics, physics, design, production technology and social studies. In addition six weeks of industrial training are required at some time during the first three years.

The course has the following features:

(i) early emphasis on mathematics in the first year;

(ii) the physics stream includes much of the engineering science taught in UK university and polytechnic courses—continuum mechanics, thermodynamics, strength and properties of materials etc;

(iii) an early but limited introduction to production technology, with a major emphasis subsequently in the third year; over 40 per cent of time in the first three years is devoted to design and production;

(iv) The engineering design stream includes engineering drawing, machine elements, tribology, electronics and electrical machines, design exercises etc;

(v) strictly limited instruction in the so-called social studies or 'management' stream; economics and costs analysis appear in the production engineering stream.

140. **In the fourth year** the student makes a choice of the engineering 'chair' (or speciality) with which he is to be associated. Lectures are limited, the student choosing courses of relevance to his mainstream subject (eg, mechanism design, production engineering etc). For most students at this stage there is a developing emphasis on engineering practice (for example the design and manufacture of cams and gears) and on project work (but some students may choose a 'chair' which specialises in highly theoretical engineering science). A substantial further element of practical industrial training is required (10 weeks).

141. **In the fifth year** the student devotes all of his time to a major engineering project—for example the design, manufacture and costing of a remotely controlled mechanical handling device. Some final year students work in industry, supervised jointly by industrial engineers and members of the university staff. Others work in the university, mainly under the supervision of university staff but also with some instruction from visiting professors.

Survey of Engineering Departments in Universities, Polytechnics and other Colleges and of their Teaching Staff

Introduction

1. In the evidence submitted to us there was a good deal of comment concerning the alleged poor relationship between industry and academic institutions. To establish the facts in this respect we undertook a survey of engineering departments in universities, polytechnics and certain other colleges offering degree courses, aimed at providing details of the extent and nature of their links with industry. This survey took the form of a questionnaire sent to the senior member of staff in each department contacted. Besides asking for factual information on the department's links with industry, the questionnaire invited 'open ended' comments of a more subjective character regarding these links, for instance on what constraints, if any, faced the department in developing closer contacts with industry.

2. The questionnaire also asked for a list of names of the department's teaching staff. The names supplied were used as a sampling frame for the issue of a further questionnaire to individual teachers. The aim of this questionnaire was to elicit data on the industrial experience of individual teachers.

3. Taken together the results of the two questionnaires enabled us to build up a picture of the current industrial experience and contacts of engineering departments. This provided useful background on the extent to which the industrial orientation of engineering departments needs to be enhanced and on how this might be achieved. We would thank all those who co-operated in this survey. Many clearly took a great deal of trouble to respond to our questions.

Engineering departments

4. In all 178 engineering departments were contacted, 90 per cent of which responded. Of the university departments responding 44 per cent had one or more industrial professor or fellow attached to them, mainly on a part-time basis. In the polytechnics such appointments were rare.

5. Departments running sandwich courses almost always had close formal arrangements with industry in connection with the industrial placement of their students. Many academic staff, particularly those in the ex-CATs, polytechnics and technical colleges, saw employers as having a strong input to make to the curriculum and to examinations.

6. About half the university departments referred to collaboration with industry on research and consultancy. In many departments this was obviously on a massive scale, with a large financial input from industry. In other departments co-operation with industry was the result of SRC or other public support, rather than through a direct financial contribution from industry.

In polytechnics income from industrial research and consultancy side was less—but in some cases certainly not negligible.

7. Some departments stated that they had little or no industrial contact. Surprisingly this statement was sometimes made, when other departments in the same establishment had substantial contact with industry, suggesting that personal factors are important.

8. Respondents were invited to estimate the age of their main teaching and research equipment. Much of the equipment in the ex-CATs and in the new universities founded following Robbins is now over ten years old and in many of these establishments staff expressed concern about the lack of facilities for testing and developing new technologies. There were extremes as between establishments in the age of their equipment. For instance in one university all departments (other than Chemical Engineering) reported 70 per cent or more of their equipment to be greater than 10 years old, whereas the Electronics and Electrical Engineering Department at another university wrote 'there is no particular equipment we need to keep ahead of recent technological developments. In all modesty we reckon to be in the lead in those areas in which we specialise'. Comparing the universities and the polytechnics, the polytechnics generally have a higher proportion of new equipment than do the universities, but against this polytechnics in the London area appear to have a high proportion of aging equipment.

9. A recurring theme on the subject of collaboration, was the differing time-scales involved, with industry wanting quick answers to immediate problems and the university or polytechnic working to a longer time span, and being more concerned with the fundamental causes of a problem rather than its immediate solution. We were told that 'most of the problems inherent in university/industry collaboration stem from the differing objectives of the two sides'; that 'there are fundamental difficulties, that cannot be waived away with a wand, to achieving many forms of academic/industrial co-operation. These arise from the different tempos and pressures of the two functions'. While from many of our respondents there were reports of successful collaboration on the research front, there were also reports of failure: 'industrialists are extremely reluctant to co-operate or provide technical information on a co-operative basis'; 'industry is often an unwilling handmaiden; when we follow up a (possible) contract it too often appears they want a professional job done free'. A number of polytechnic departments were particularly critical of industry which suggests that bridge building is needed between polytechnics and industry just as much as, if not more than, between universities and industry.

10. In those departments where sandwich courses are undertaken, concern was frequently expressed about the problems of getting industrial placements for students. A typical claim was that 'many firms were only too willing to recruit those who graduated from sandwich courses, but were not willing to provide proper training places'. It appears that places are particularly difficult to find for some overseas students, as employing organisations are sometimes loath to take on students whose English may be wobbly and who, in the view of industry, are unlikely to benefit the organisation during the placement or to be available for employment after graduation.

239

11. When specifically asked what restraints there were to further collaboration with industry, the following were frequently mentioned: low staff/student ratios; the burden of administration; severe restraints on staff recruitment; and inadequate support staff (research assistants and technicians). Many respondents argued that it was quite wrong to apply similar staff/student ratios to engineering as to other departments, for example: 'our working conditions are so radically different from those in other departments that we *must* have preferential treatment in staffing resources—not for privilege—but to meet necessity—if we are to find time for the extra work entailed'.

12. Spontaneous comments were made about the relative salary levels in universities and polytechnics and those in industry. Concern was expressed about the difficulty (associated with salaries) of attracting those with industrial experience into teaching institutions, although the need for such people was recognised. 'Matters are made worse by the current lack of competitive edge in the universities' ability to attract good engineering staff for the salaries we offer . . . the principle of academic tenure of appointment is a disaster when salary scales make it difficult to recruit more than mediocrities'. 'It is extremely difficult to recruit new academic staff at any level because of the great disparity of salaries between chemical engineers in industry and those in academic life.' It was recognised that academics need to be familiar with the current practices and problems of industry so that their teaching and research activities are informed and relevant to industrial requirements.

Comment

13. While in many cases there was evidence of good collaboration between industry and academic establishments the survey highlighted the need for marked improvement in many areas. Clearly (and as might be expected) university and polytechnic departments see the need for a substantial injection of resources—and this at a time of retrenchment. Thus *if* collaboration depends only on this, the prospects for improvement are bleak.

Teaching staff

14. Questionnaires were sent to a structured stratified sample of those teaching in engineering departments in universities, polytechnics and other institutions offering degree courses in engineering. The response rate was 63·3 per cent.

15. The table opposite summarises the industrial experience of our respondents.

16. Nearly a quarter of the teaching staff in those universities which were not previously CATs have never worked in industry and well over half of all our respondents were ten years or more away from direct industrial experience. Thus, although a substantial proportion of all teachers had quite a lot of experience in industry (10 years or more), much of it was many years ago. It is noteworthy that in this survey, and in the PSI survey done for us, there was virtually no evidence of any movement from universities or polytechnics into industry.

240

Industrial Experience

	Time spent in Industry				Time since last worked full-time in Industry		
Years	Ex CATs	Other Universities	Polytechnics and Other Colleges	Years	Ex CATs	Other Universities	Polytechnics and Other Colleges
	%	%	%		%	%	%
None	6·0	22·4	7·1	Never			
1–3	19·7	18·0	13·2	worked	6·0	22·4	7·1
4–6	24·1	24·3	17·7	< 5 years			
7–9	17·5	11·3	16·8	ago	5·5	7·0	10·2
10 or				5–9	12·6	14·0	15·0
more	32·4	23·9	45·1	10–14	21·4	16·5	29·3
				15–19	23·6	18·0	21·1
				20–24	17·0	6·6	8·3
				25 or			
				more	13·7	15·4	9·0

17. On the academic qualifications of respondents, a number had no first degree, comprising 5 per cent of those working in universities; 13 per cent of those in polytechnics; and 16 per cent of those in other colleges. The distribution of higher degrees over our sample is shown in the following table:

Proportion of Teachers holding Higher Degrees

	PhD	MA/MSc	Advanced Diploma, etc
	%	%	%
Universities	63	26	17
Polytechnics	24	28	11
Others	18	24	8

Note: some respondents held two or three higher degrees or diplomas.

18. It is clear from the career histories that some of those now teaching in universities who left industry to read for a higher degree never returned to industry; they stayed on to do research and ultimately to become lecturers. There is also evidence of a small but regular flow of people from public service jobs into teaching establishments (and the PSI survey suggests virtually no movement the other way).

NOP Omnibus Survey

1. Space was bought in the NOP Omnibus Survey. The sampling frame was the Electoral Register from which a two-stage stratified random sample was drawn. Field work was carried out during the period 22 June–5 July 1978. 1,667 interviews took place with identified adults aged 18 or over. An additional 406 respondents were also questioned; these having been identified as having one or more children aged 11–19. There is no reason to suppose that the sample interviewed was not representative of the general public.

2. Respondents were asked to rate a number of jobs, including 'engineer', no attempt having been made to define the meaning of the work 'engineer'. The results are summarised in the following table.

Table 1: Answers to the question: 'How do you rate . . . . as a career for a young persons nowadays?'

	Very good career	Good career	Neither good or poor career	Poor career	Very poor career	Don't know
	%	%	%	%	%	%
Hairdresser	12	54	18	14	1	1
Policeman/woman	17	54	13	15	1	1
Secretary	19	61	13	6	–	1
Teacher	24	51	11	12	1	1
Welder	12	54	21	11	1	1
Accountant	57	37	4	2	–	1
Doctor	69	26	2	2	–	1
Draughtsman/woman	39	50	8	3	–	1
'Engineer'	38	53	6	3	–	1
Estate agent	30	46	16	7	–	1

Doctors were most highly rated as career prospects, followed by accountants, with 'engineers' and draughtsmen/women tying for third place—these four jobs being rated much more highly than the other careers. Respondents in households that included an engineer tended to mark 'engineering' as a career slightly less highly than did other respondents. Respondents classified by NOP as belonging to D/E social classes marked 'engineering' more highly than did those classified as belonging to higher social classes. 'Engineering' as a career was more highly thought of by women than by men. With the exception of welder, all the jobs shown in the above table (including 'engineer') were thought of as less good prospects by young people aged 18–24, than they were by people in older age groups.

3. Having attempted to illustrate to the respondent, the sort of person who would be called a professional engineer, further questions were asked which elicited the answers shown in Table 2.

Table 2: Answer to the question 'How would you rate professional engineering as a career for a young person?'

	For a Man	For a Woman
	%	%
Very good career	60	25
Good career	33	31
Neither good nor poor career	4	16
Poor career	1	20
Very poor career	—	5
Don't know	2	3

Professional engineering as a career was much more highly rated as a career for men than as a career for women: and, this response was almost identical from male and from female respondents. Those in social classes A/B rated professional engineering as a career for men less highly than did those in other social classes, but more highly as a career for women. Professional engineering as a career for men was less highly rated by the young than by those in older age groups; but as a career for women the reverse was true, perhaps reflecting past prejudices about women as engineers. Those respondents living in households that included an engineer rated professional engineering less highly than did those who had no engineer in their household, and, interestingly, there was no difference between the rating given if the engineer in the household was a manual worker and the rating given if that engineer was a professional engineer, ie no indication that professional engineering was looked upon by those with a manual engineer in the household, as being prestigious.

4. Attempts were made to establish why the respondents viewed professional engineering as a good or bad career with the following results:

(a) Most of those who thought professional engineering was a good career for a man, mentioned good prospects, good salaries and the availability of good jobs. Long training and the acquisition of particular skills were also mentioned.

(b) No particular reasons for their views were adduced from the 1 per cent of respondents who thought professional engineering was a poor career for men.

(c) Fifty-six per cent of respondents thought professional engineering would be a good career for women, and they specified very much the same reasons as those shown in (a) above relating to men. Many respondents spontaneously commented 'female professional engineers would be just as capable as male'. Even of those who thought professional engineering would be a good career for women, many expressed reservations about women being accepted.

(d) Twenty-five per cent of the respondents thought professional engineering would be a poor career choice for a woman, over half of this 25 per cent justifying their view with such comments as 'engineering is a man's career', 'women would not be suited', and over a quarter arguing that 'women would not be strong enough'. These prejudices were particularly marked among female respondents and amongst those of lower social class.

243

5. In order to assess the extent to which the sample of the general public who were interviewed could correctly identify the sort of work that might be done by an 'engineer' (ie someone the respondent identified as an engineer without any definition being given of the term) further questioning took place, resulting in the following:

Table 3: Type of work mentioned in response to the question: 'What kind of things do you think an "Engineer" might actually do?'

Type of Work	Proportion mentioning
	%
Manual level/making things/working with machinery	68
Professional level/design/planning/research	13
Vague answer/don't know	19

If no prompting is given, most people identify an 'engineer' as someone doing a manual level job. About a fifth of the respondents expressed ignorance when replying to this question.

6. Attempts were made to find out whether members of the general public could tell the difference between what an 'engineer' would do and what a professional 'engineer' would do, without having been prompted as to what a professional engineer does. The results follow:

(a) When asked about the difference in the work they do between an 'engineer' and a professional 'engineer', of the 68 per cent of our respondents who associated the word 'engineer' with someone doing a manual level job, (see Table 3) 14 per cent thought there was no difference; 38 per cent mentioned 'higher' manual jobs, eg 'foreman' or 'someone with more qualifications'; and 27 per cent mentioned jobs that could properly be classified as professional.

(b) Of the 13 per cent of our respondents who, when asked 'What kind of things do you think an "engineer" would do?', associated the word 'engineer' with someone doing a professional type job; 92 per cent thought there was no difference, ie confirmed that their idea of an 'engineer' was someone who did the sort of work they properly classed as professional; and 7 per cent incorrectly mentioned manual type jobs as being the likely work of the professional.

(c) The 19 per cent who, in response to the question 'What kind of things do you think an "engineer" would do?' said they did not know, produced some pretty wild responses when pushed to specify the difference between an 'engineer' and a professional 'engineer'—as would be expected.

7. While it would appear that the majority of the public identify the word 'engineer' with someone who does a manual level job, nevertheless about half the respondents recognised that a professional 'engineer' either did work that could properly be classified as professional, or that required higher qualifications than an 'engineer' or that carried some form of managerial responsibility.

8. Having been told about examples of various types of professional engineering work, respondents were asked to specify the exams and/or qualifications they thought were needed by the professional engineer to do the work described. The results follow:

(a) A minority of people thought that a degree was a necessary qualification for a professional engineer.

(b) A quarter and a third of those questioned thought that an apprenticeship was a necessary qualification for an electrical and for a mechanical engineer respectively.

(c) Eleven per cent of respondents answered 'Don't know'.

(d) Even if HNC/HND were accepted as an adequate qualification for a professional engineer, at least 38 per cent of our respondents thought a lower qualification was all that was needed.

These results bear out other evidence of the ignorance of most people about the qualifications needed by professional engineers. It is arguable that the population in general would be equally ignorant of the qualifications needed by other professionals, eg accountants or lawyers.

Examination of the detailed answers given to this question shows that:

(i) More women than men express a complete ignorance of the qualifications needed to become a professional engineer.

(ii) Those classified in the D/E social classes are more ignorant of the qualifications needed than are those in higher social classes.

(iii) Even those respondents living where there is an engineer in the house, appear to be no more knowledgeable about the qualifications needed, by a professional engineer, than are others.

(iv) A markedly higher proportion of men aged 25 and over think an HNC/HND is the required qualification of the professional engineer, than do women and younger men—maybe because this qualification in engineering is almost exclusively held by males, and by those over 24.

9. Respondents were invited to answer a question relating to pay, status and opportunities, and Table 4 (overleaf) summarises the results:

From Table 4 it will be noted that:

(a) In general, favourable opinions about professional engineers are supported.

(b) It is only on pay relative to responsibility that agreement and disagreement about match; pay relative to qualification is in general considered to be fairly good. (It is important to bear in mind the mental image respondents may have had implanted in their minds about the likely responsibilities of the professional engineer's job, from the 'prompt' statements made by the interviewer.)

245

Table 4: Impressions of Professional Engineers

	Strongly Agree	Agree	Neither Agree nor Disagree	Disagree	Strongly Disagree	Don't Know
	%	%	%	%	%	%
Professional engineers are well paid considering the qualifications they need to have	18	26	19	10	8	20
Professional engineering is a career where brains and hard work will get you to the top	44	24	11	7	4	9
Professional engineers do a lot to help the economy of this country	38	30	14	4	2	12
Professional engineers are well paid considering the responsibility they have to take	12	19	24	13	11	21
There are always plenty of good job opportunities for professional engineers	26	24	13	16	10	12
Professional engineers are hardly ever made redundant	22	21	24	11	5	18

Looking at the answers to the questions about pay, status and opportunities in more detail we find:

(i) A marked social class difference on the question of salary (but not on other questions). Those in classes A/B consider the professional engineer is neither well paid in relation to qualifications nor to responsibility; those in other classes (the majority) thought he was.

(ii) If there was an engineer living in the household the responses about the adequacy of pay relative to qualifications and relative to responsibility were less favourable than were those from other people—as might be expected.

(iii) Women tend to have a rosier picture of the pay of professional engineers then do men, and the young slightly more so than the old.

10. All those respondents who had one or more children aged between 11 and 19 were asked 'Do you think it would be a good idea for any of your children to try for a career as a professional engineer?' The results follow:

Table 5: Responses to the question 'Do you think it would be a good idea for any of your children to try for a career as a professional engineer?'

Reply	%
Yes	53
No	37
Don't know	10
	100

Thus a small majority of our respondents thought it a good idea for one or more of their children to try for a career as a professional engineer (and this question was asked towards the end of the interview after they had been told the sort of jobs a professional engineer might do). There is no indication that parents with children at the decision taking age have views that differ markedly from those of the general populus.

The Accreditation of Academic Formation in the United States

Background

1. 'Accreditation' is the process of validating programmes of education or training against specified standards. It is a relatively common procedure in the United States, where a wide range of academic courses are subject to accreditation. A National Commission on Accrediting supervises the general conduct of accreditation across all subject areas. The Commission recognises the Engineers' Council for Professional Development (ECPD) as the sole agency responsible for accrediting engineering degree courses. The Council was established in the 1930s by the various US professional engineering societies, the equivalent of the UK Institutions, at a time when there was concern in the States, especially within the profession but elsewhere too, over discrepancies in the standards of engineering courses. (Currently in most States in the USA an engineer wishing to register must have graduated from an engineering course accredited by the ECPD.)

2. We decided to look in detail at the ECPD's system because it is an extensive and well established system for accrediting engineering courses. As such it provides pointers for any accreditation system introduced in the UK.

3. The Council states the purpose of accreditation as 'to identify those institutions which offer professional programmes in engineering worthy of recognition as such ', with the following specific objectives:

' (i) To identify to the public, prospective students, educational institutions, State boards of examiners, the institutions and specific programmes that meet minimum criteria for accreditation.

(ii) To provide guidance for the improvement of existing educational programmes in engineering and for the development of future programmes.

(iii) To stimulate the improvement of engineering education in the United States.'

4. The ECPD see their role as to identify those engineering courses whose graduates are educationally qualified to practise as professional engineers and to apply standards which the profession itself has set as being the minimum required of the professional engineer. The Council is an autonomous body, acting as a federation of the professional Societies, and operates independently of Government and other agencies. Thus the ECPD system of accreditation is controlled by the profession itself. As such it differs from that proposed in our Report.

5. The statutory requirement in most States that registered engineers be graduates of accredited courses means that the process of accreditation has effective sanction since, whilst an engineer generally need not be registered in order to practice, registration is nonetheless sought by the majority of

engineers and *is* a requirement for certain areas and levels of practice. In consequence a course must usually be accredited if it is to attract students. Further courses offered by State colleges usually require accreditation in order to receive financial support from the relevant State authorities. The vast majority of engineering courses therefore seek and need to be accredited. The exceptions are the courses offered by some of the prestige engineering schools, such as MIT and California Institute of Technology, whose reputations are such that they can frequently attract students and support even to non-accredited courses.

6. We were told that accreditation, besides acting specifically as a check on the educational attainment of candidates for registration, also served to give the stamp of professional approval to college programmes, and thereby indicated to industry the courses deemed to provide a sound engineering education. Also, it was said to help parents, students and schoolteachers when it came to applying for admission to an engineering course.

Philosophy

7. A basic principle of the ECPD's approach is to accredit individual courses, rather than educational establishments as a whole, on the grounds that courses of varying standards are frequently found within the same establishment. (The accreditation of whole establishments is dealt with by separate machinery.) It is a rule that an establishment may not use the same title to identify both an accredited course and a non-accredited one. ECPD leave it to individual colleges to determine the degree designation of courses, that is, in effect, to decide whether a course is to be designated as a Bachelors or a Masters course. However, it is ECPD's decision whether to accredit at either 'basic' or 'advanced' level and different criteria are applied to each level.

8. Other ground rules include to prefer broadly based courses providing a range of employment opportunities, rather than those narrowly tied to specific careers; to refuse to accredit courses which, though containing elements of engineering, do not 'develop the basic abilities of the engineer'; not to accredit courses until they have produced graduates; and to encourage experimentation whilst ensuring that essential subjects are included.

Procedure

9. The accreditation procedure goes into considerable detail and involves the following principal elements:

(*a*) It is up to the educational establishment to apply to have its course, or courses, accredited; it is not approached by the ECPD;

(*b*) the college is sent a lengthy questionnaire to complete, containing a set of questions common to all engineering disciplines and a further set, or sets, of questions relating to specific disciplines drawn up by the relevant professional society;

(*c*) once the questionnaire has been returned to ECPD and considered, then a team of inspectors from ECPD visits the college for an on-site inspection usually lasting three days. The aim is for half the visiting team to be made up of academics and the other half of practising engineers, drawn from lists provided by the professional societies;

(d) the team of inspectors reports back to ECPD and, on the basis of all the evidence, the programme is accredited for two, four or, at the most, six years, or alternatively it is refused accreditation. There is provision for appeal by the college against the ECPD's decision but any appeals are considered by the ECPD, rather than by an independent arbiter;

(e) lists of accredited courses are publicly available but there is no list of courses which fail to be accredited.

10. The visit by the inspectors is a key part of the accreditation procedure. It is intended to assess the various qualitative factors associated with the course, such as the quality of the teaching staff and general atmosphere and environment; as well as more tangible factors such as staff-student ratios, accommodation and equipment, and admissions and examination procedures.

Criteria

11. The Council have formulated a set of general criteria which are applied to all courses under review. ECPD described these as follows:

'These criteria are intended to assure an adequate foundation in science, the humanities and the social sciences, engineering science, engineering methods as well as preparation in a higher engineering specialisation appropriate to the challenge presented by today's complex and difficult problems. They are intended to afford sufficient flexibility in science requirements so that programs requiring special backgrounds, such as in the life or earth sciences, can be accommodated. They are designed to be flexible enough to permit the expression of an institution's individual qualities and ideals. They are to be regarded as a statement of principles to be applied with judgement in each case rather than as rigid and arbitrary standards. Finally, they are intended to encourage and stimulate and not to restrain creative and imaginative programs. In any case in which the Engineering Education and Accreditation Committee is convinced that well-considered experimentation in engineering educational programs is under way, it shall give sympathetic consideration to departures from the criteria and shall make appropriate recommendations to ECPD.'

12. The criteria cover the following:

'1. The extent to which the program develops an ability to apply pertinent knowledge to the practice of engineering in an effective and professional manner. Included are the development of a capability to delineate and solve in a practical way the problems of society that are susceptible to engineering treatment, the development of a sensitivity to the socially related technical problems which confront the profession, and the development of an ability to maintain professional competency through continued self-study. These objectives are normally met by a curriculum in which there is a progression in the course work and in which the fundamental scientific and other training of the earlier years is given application in the later engineering courses.

2. The size and competence of the faculty: the standards and quality of instruction in the engineering departments and in the scientific and other operating departments in which engineering students receive instruction; and evidence of concern about improving the effectiveness of pedagogical techniques.

3. The admission, retention and scholastic worth of students and the records of graduates both in further academic study and in professional practice.

4. The attitude and policy of the administration of the engineering division towards teaching, research, and scholarly production; the quality of leadership at all levels of administration of the division.

5. The commitment of the institutions, both financially and philosophically, to the program in engineering. This commitment may be evidenced by the relationship of the engineering unit to the institution as a whole, by the fiscal policy toward and the financial resources available to the engineering unit, and by the suitability of facilities including laboratories, libraries, and computer facilities.'

13. Specific criteria are applied, in addition to these general ones, for the various branches of engineering. Further there are special criteria for 'co-op programs' (equivalent to sandwich courses) and for inter-disciplinary courses.

Organisation and cost

14. Around 1,600 different courses are currently accredited by ECPD. The accreditation process relies heavily upon volunteers, some 2,500 of them, particularly for the campus visits and also for ECPD's network of internal committees. Volunteers, who are drawn from the professional societies, are paid their travel and subsistence expenses but not for their time. ECPD maintains a full-time staff of around 50 for accreditation activities.

15. The Council estimate the total cost of accreditation for 1979–80 to be $355,000, not counting the internal costs of academic establishments in preparing documentation, staff time etc. Around 60 per cent of the cost is borne by the professional societies and the remaining 40 per cent by the colleges. They are charged at the rate of $630 per inspector. Thus the amount any one college pays depends largely upon the number of courses it submits for accreditation.

The system in operation

16. A member of the Committee of Inquiry went as an observer on an ECPD accrediting party to Georgia Institute of Technology (Georgia Tech) in November 1978 to see the system in action. Georgia Tech is a large State university with some 7,500 undergraduates, most of them in engineering.

17. The visiting team consisted of twelve accreditors, comprising eight senior academics and three senior engineers from industry, and three observers (the Chairman of the Georgia State Registration Board, a member of the

Council of ECPD—both industrialists—and our observer). The team was led by the Chairman of the ECPD Accreditation Committee, a professor of electrical engineering from Arizona State University.

18. The team inspected twelve courses in 11 departments (Civil, Mechanical, Electrical, Aeronautical, Chemical, Ceramics, Textiles, Engineering Science, Nuclear, Industrial, Metallurgy). Nearly all the courses were up for re-accreditation and most were at Bachelor level. The team inspected laboratory facilities, went through lecture notes, examples, projects and theses. They interviewed the Directors of Departments, Professors, teaching assistants and students. The whole process was intensive. The inspectors had previously read the documentation provided by the college and used this as a basis for 'grilling' staff and students.

19. At a final meeting the team presented verbal reports to Georgia Tech's President, Deans and Directors of Departments without informing them of their recommendations. These recommendations are presented to internal ECPD committees, a decision is then reached and communicated back to the college with a report inviting their comments.

Assessment

20. Our observer was impressed by the thoroughness of the approach, though he did not necessarily agree with all the decisions reached by the inspectors. A lot would seem to depend upon the calibre of individual inspectors. A general problem evidently is the difficulty of securing the services of senior engineers from industry. The colleges, for their part, take accreditation seriously and take a lot of trouble to present their case. They regard accreditation as an important stimulus to their activities. Further, a decision not to accredit is usually a major blow.

21. The ECPD system in practice would appear to have three principal weaknesses. First, there is an apparently low level of participation from industry. Secondly, and related to this, is a reliance upon academics inspecting one another. This produces a rather difficult situation where an inspector, say the Chairman of an engineering department, may be reluctant to turn down a colleague, a possible future inspector of his own department. Third, the profession—through the professional societies—sets its own standards and there are no arrangements for an organised employer input, save to the extent that employers are involved in these societies. There would thus seem to be a need for ensuring more of an outside check on the whole process.

22. We also have reservations regarding some of the criteria applied by ECPD—for instance the requirements that one-sixth of the course comprise humanities and social science and that the career records of graduates be examined. In spite of these points the ECPD approach provides a useful model for any system of accreditation introduced in the UK.

251

The Statutory Right to Study Leave in France

1. In 1971 France introduced a statutory right to study leave referred to in paragraph 4.111 of the main report. The details of this legal provision are set out below.

2. The national inter-occupational agreement on professional and occupational training of 9 July 1970, the additional clause of 9 July 1976, the Law of 16 July 1971 and the implementing legislation provided workers with the opportunity for study and improvement during working hours.

3. A distinction should be made between the case where a trainee is sent on a course by his firm and where the trainee asks for study leave to take a course.

4. When the firm decides to send an employee on a course, it pays the registration fees and also the trainee's wages. By agreement with the organisation providing training, it may charge these expenses against the compulsory contribution to training (a contribution of 1 per cent on wages to which all firms with more than 10 employees are subject, except for public and local authorities).

5. When the employee takes the initiative on a personal basis, he has to ask for study leave. Study leave is permission to be absent from work during normal working hours in order to take a full- or part-time training course. The right to paid leave is not affected and rights to social security and seniority are preserved. The maximum length of a training period is 1,200 hours in separate blocks and 1 year for complete blocks (except in the case of full-time professional training). A gap must be left between two training periods[1].

6. In order to apply for study leave, it is necessary:

—to have at least two years seniority in the firm[2]
—that the appropriate interval should have elapsed[2]
—that the percentage of employees absent from the firm at the same time should not be more than 2 per cent of the labour force[3].

---

[1] After a training period of 80 hrs, this is 6 months
  After a training period of 81–160 hrs, this is 1 year
  After a training period of 161–1,152 hrs, this is $\dfrac{T^*}{12}$ (T^* = length of training period in hrs; quotient in months)
  After a training period of > 1,152 hrs, this is 8 years.

[2] Unless the applicant was made redundant at his last job.

[3] Three per cent in the case of managerial staff and, in the metal-working industry, in the case of technicians, draughtsmen, clerical staff and skilled tradesmen. The 2 or 3 per cent only covers employees on study leave.

The application must be made to the management of the firm 60 days before the beginning of the training period if it is for 6 months or more and full-time in a single block and 30 days if it is to last less than 6 months or if it is a course in the form of separate blocks.

7. The management must reply within 15 days. It may postpone the application for reasons of work (for not more than 1 year) after consulting the enterprise committee or the staff representatives. In the event of disagreement, the labour inspector will arbitrate.

8. A distinction must be made between training periods of more than and less than 500 hours:

—Training periods of less than 500 hours: if the training period is approved by the competent professional committee, the trainee's wages are paid for the first 160 hours (or more if the committee so decides). In addition, a training allowance is paid to the trainee to cover registration fees etc. Up to 28 F per student/hour, this represents the actual costs. Beyond 28 F per student/hour, it represents 2/3 of the costs, with a maximum limit of 63·50 F per student/hour. It is paid for each hour of training which has to be paid for.

—Training periods of 500 hours or more: if the training period is approved by the competent professional committee, the employee's wages are paid for the first 500 hours or 600 hours in the case of an engineer or manager.

9. On the other hand, no allowance is provided to cover training costs. In addition, in order to be approved by the professional committee, the training period of 500 hours or more must include a test prior to admission and lead to an approved certificate or degree. The procedure of approval of 500 hour training periods by the national committee for a particular profession may be extended to other professions by the national inter-professional committee.

NB 0·50 per cent of the personnel of a firm may receive paid study leave at the same time.

10. There are also new provisions on training for employees threatened with redundancy or made redundant for economic reasons and on the role of the enterprise committee in the agreement of July 1976.

11. The law No 78–754 of 17 July 1978 on individual training, study leave and payment of trainees undergoing professional training supplemented the contractual provisions of the agreement of 16 July 1976 and extended them to all wage-earners.

INDEX OF ORGANISATIONS
(References in each case are to paragraph numbers)

255

MANUFACTURING ADVISORY SERVICE
see Department of Industry

MICROPROCESSOR APPLICATIONS PROJECT
see Department of Industry

MINISTRY OF DEFENCE
3.17

NATIONAL COUNCIL OF ENGINEERING EXAMINERS (USA)
5.11

NATIONAL ECONOMIC DEVELOPMENT COUNCIL
2.15, 2.29–2.32, 2.44(v), 3.31, 6.16, 6.18, 6.22

NATIONAL ECONOMIC DEVELOPMENT OFFICE
1.19, 2.32, 6.16

NATIONAL ENTERPRISE BOARD
2.17

NATIONAL OPINION POLLS
Random Omnibus Survey, Preface, Appendix G

NATIONAL RESEARCH DEVELOPMENT CORPORATION
2.17, 2.29

OFFICE OF POPULATION CENSUSES AND SURVEYS
3.5

ORGANISATION FOR ECONOMIC CO-OPERATION AND DEVELOP-
MENT
1.13

OVERSEAS TECHNICAL INFORMATION UNIT
see Department of Industry

POLICY STUDIES INSTITUTE
Survey of engineers, Preface, 3.35, 3.42, 4.109

ROYAL SOCIETY
5.64

ROYAL SWEDISH ACADEMY OF ENGINEERING SCIENCE
Preface, 5.65

Printed in England for Her Majesty's Stationery Office by Commercial Colour Press, London E7
Dd.626963 K40 1/80 CCP